With God on their Side

D0497135

'Sport' and 'religion' are cultural institutions with a global reach. Each is characterised by ritualised performance and by the ecstatic devotion of its followers, whether in the sports arena or the cathedral of worship. This fascinating collection is the first to examine, in detail, the relationship between these two cultural institutions from an international, religiously pluralistic perspective. It illuminates the role of sport and religion in the social formation of collective groups and explores how sport might operate in the service of a religious community.

The book offers a series of cutting-edge contemporary historical case-studies, wide-ranging in their geographical coverage and in their social and religious contexts. It presents important new work on the following topics:

- sport and Catholicism in Northern Ireland
- Shinto and sumo in Japan
- women, sport and American Jewish identity
- religion, race and rugby in South Africa
- sport and Islam in France and North Africa
- sport and Christian fundamentalism in the US
- Muhammad Ali and the Nation of Islam

With God on their Side is vital reading for all students of the history, sociology and culture of sport. It also presents important new research material that will be of interest to religious studies students, historians and anthropologists.

Tara Magdalinski is Senior Lecturer in Australian and Cultural Studies in the Faculty of Arts and Social Sciences at the University of the Sunshine Coast, Queensland, Australia.

Timothy J.L. Chandler is Associate Dean at the College of Fine and Professional Arts and Professor of Sport Studies in the School of Exercise, Leisure and Sport at Kent State University, USA.

30107 005 235 673

With God on their Side

Sport in the service of religion

Edited by Tara Magdalinski
and Timothy J.L. Chandler

Routledge
Taylor & Francis Group

LONDON AND NEW YORK

First published 2002
by Routledge
11 New Fetter Lane, London EC4P 4EE

Simultaneously published in the USA and Canada
by Routledge
29 West 35th Street, New York, NY 10001

Routledge is an imprint of the Taylor & Francis Group

© 2002 Selection and editorial matter, Tara Magdalinski and
Timothy J.L. Chandler; individual chapters, the contributors

Typeset in Garamond by Taylor & Francis Books Ltd
Printed and bound in Great Britain by The Cromwell Press,
Trowbridge, Wiltshire

All rights reserved. No part of this book may be reprinted or
reproduced or utilised in any form or by any electronic,
mechanical, or other means, now known or hereafter
invented, including photocopying and recording, or in any
information storage or retrieval system, without permission in
writing from the publishers.

British Library Cataloguing in Publication Data
A catalogue record for this book is available from the British Library

Library of Congress Cataloging in Publication Data
A catalog record for this book has been requested

ISBN 0–415–25960–6 (hbk)
ISBN 0–415–25961–4 (pbk)

BAR CODE No.	5235673	
CLASS No. 796.01		
BIB CHECK ✓	− 2 DEC 2005	PROC CHECK ✓
	FINAL ✓ 12/05	
OS	SYSTEM NO.	
LOAN CATEGORY	NL	

Contents

Notes on contributors

Becky Beal is Associate Professor in the Department of Sport Sciences at the University of the Pacific, Stockton, California, USA, where she teaches courses in the sociology of sport and the philosophy of sport. Her previously published work has focused on sport subcultures and gender relations. She has also served on the editorial board of the *Sociology of Sport Journal*.

Linda J. Borish is Associate Professor in the Department of History at Western Michigan University, Kalamazoo, Michigan, USA. She earned a PhD in American Studies and has written widely on American women's sport and health history with essays in the *Journal of Sport History*, *American Jewish History*, *International Sports Studies*, and contributions to *Sports and the American Jew*. She was a guest co-editor for *Rethinking History: The Journal of Theory and Practice*'s special issue on 'Labour, Leisure, and Sport' (2001). She has presented her research on Jewish women in American sport history internationally at conferences in Israel, Canada, Germany and the USA. She recently served as the International Ambassador, North American Society for Sport History, 2001–2002.

Timothy J.L. Chandler is Professor of Sport Studies in the School of Exercise, Leisure and Sport and Associate Dean for Graduate Studies in the College of Fine and Professional Arts at Kent State University, Kent, Ohio, USA. He has also taught at Syracuse University and has been a visiting lecturer in the School of Physical Education, Sport and Leisure at De Montfort University, Bedford, UK. He is co-editor (with John Nauright) of *Making Men: Rugby and Masculine Identity* (Frank Cass, 1996) and *Making the Rugby World: Race, Gender, Commerce* (Frank Cass, 1999), and is the author of a number of book chapters and articles on sport in the English public schools. His articles have appeared in the *International Journal of the History of Sport*, the *Canadian Journal of History of Sport* and *Youth and Society*. He currently serves on the editorial boards of *Sports History Review*, *Football Studies* and *International Sports Studies*.

Mike Cronin is Senior Research Fellow at the International Centre for Sports History and Culture at De Montfort University, Leicester, UK. He is the author of *Sport and Nationalism in Ireland* (Four Courts Press, 1999), *A History of Ireland* (Palgrave, 2001), with Timothy Chandler and Wray Vamplew, *Sport Studies and Physical Education: The Key Concepts* (Routledge, 2002) and with Daryl Adair, *The Wearing of the Green: A History of St Patrick's Day* (Routledge, 2002).

John Hughson is Principal Research Fellow in Cultural Studies at the University of Wolverhampton, UK. He is Reviews Editor for the journal *Ethnography* and co-author (with David Inglis) of the forthcoming book *Confronting Culture: Sociological Vistas* (Polity). He is also co-writing (with Marcus Free and David Inglis) a book on sport and cultural studies, *The Uses of Sport: A Critical Study*, for Routledge. He has published a number of papers on football supporter subcultures.

Louise Kinnaird lived and worked in Nagano and Yokohama in Japan before undertaking Japanese studies at Keio University. Upon her return to Australia in 1995, she completed a Master of Arts from the University of Melbourne, Australia. Her thesis topic was 'Sumo and women: the construction of tradition and ritual and the role of women in Japan's national sport' (1997). Whilst working with the Sumo tour to Melbourne in 1997, She gained further insight into the ritualistic world of sumo. Presently she works in the International Centre at the University of Melbourne, Australia. With a Japanese husband and two young children, her Japanese interests remain strong.

Richard Light lectures in physical education at The University of Melbourne, Australia. His research interests lie in the sociology of the body and the corporeal dimensions of learning as well as in the social and cultural dimensions of sport. He completed a PhD on the social dimensions of school rugby in Japan and Australia and publishes widely on culture, masculinity and sport in Japan. He spent six years coaching rugby in Japan, speaks Japanese and holds a fifth dan black belt in karate awarded by Shito Ryu master Hayashi Terou. He is one of the few Western researchers working on sport in Japan that can access local culture.

Tara Magdalinski is Senior Lecturer in Australian and Cultural Studies in the Faculty of Arts and Social Sciences at the University of the Sunshine Coast, Queensland, Australia. She has been widely published in the area of sports studies, focussing most recently on performance enhancement and bodily landscapes. Her articles have appeared in both sports history and mainstream journals, including *International Journal of the History of Sport*, *Media International Australia* and *AVANTE*. She serves on the editorial boards of *International Sports Studies* and *Sport History Review*, and is associate editor of *Sporting Traditions* and *Football Studies*. She is Vice-President of the Australian Society for Sports History.

John Nauright is Director of Research in the Division of Sport, Health and Leisure at the University of Abertay Dundee, Dundee, Scotland. He is the author or editor of nine books including *Sport, Cultures and Identities in South Africa* (Leicester University Press, 1997); *Rugby and the South African Nation* (Manchester University Press, 1998) (with David R. Black); *Making Men: Rugby and Masculine Identity* (Frank Cass, 1996) and *Making the Rugby World* (Frank Cass, 1999) (both with Timothy Chandler); *The Essence of Sport* (Odense University Press, 2002) (with Verner Møller) and *The Political Economy of Sport* (Palgrave, 2002) (with Kimberly Schimmel). He edits the journals *Football Studies* and *International Sports Studies* and is consulting editor of the *Journal of Physical Education and Sports Science*.

George D. Randels Jr is Associate Professor of Social Ethics in the Religious Studies Department of the University of the Pacific, Stockton, California, USA. He has also taught at Emory University and at New College (Florida). Randels has a PhD in religious ethics from the University of Virginia, and an MAR in social ethics from Yale University Divinity School. Besides gender and religion, his research interests include business ethics, biomedical ethics and information technology. Randels is currently working on a book about virtue theory and business ethics.

Paul A. Silverstein is Assistant Professor of Anthropology at Reed College, Portland, Oregon, USA. His work on sport, religion, immigration, and ethnic identity in North Africa and France has appeared in a number of academic journals, including *Social Text*, *Middle East Report* and *Migrations-Société*, as well as in a variety of edited volumes. He is currently completing a book manuscript entitled *Trans-Politics: Islam, Berberity, and the French Nation-State*.

Maureen Smith is Associate Professor in the Kinesiology and Health Science Department at California State University, Sacramento, USA. She received her BS and MS from Ithaca College and her MA and PhD at Ohio State University. Her research interests include race relations, sport fan behaviour and the history of African American athletes in US sport.

Acknowledgements

It's funny how projects come into being – during a break in a conference, through an email dialogue, or in our case, over bagels surrounded by the deafening throng of a Kent State University lunchtime. Neither of us quite remembers how we happened upon this topic, but we both recall being enthused with the prospect of examining sport and religion from a new angle. Although we were brimming with ideas, finding a publisher with a similar vision proved difficult, and it wasn't until a casual remark to an editor at Routledge that this collection garnered support. The speed and timing of the project from early 2001 through to its completion at the end of that same year is a testament to the dedication and commitment shown by the contributors published here. It is they who, despite relentless emails and pedantic queries from the editors, have produced a collection that reflects the approach we had conceived some years ago. And it is they who we would like to first acknowledge and thank for their support. A heartfelt thanks goes to our wonderful editor at Routledge, Simon Whitmore, who provided prompt and persuasive advice and ensured the collection appeared in a timely manner. Of course, all projects of this magnitude require support in many forms, institutional, administrative and emotional, and there are many who have provided these in abundance. We acknowledge the contributions made by our respective institutions, the University of the Sunshine Coast and Kent State University; by our friends and colleagues, particularly Dr Karen Brooks; and by our families. It is to them that we dedicate this book.

Tara Magdalinski, Sunshine Coast, QLD, Australia
Tim Chandler, Kent, OH, USA
December 2001

1 With God on their side

An introduction

*Tara Magdalinski and
Timothy J.L. Chandler*

Sport and religion, whilst possessing disparate philosophical foundations, appear to share a similar structure. Each offers its respective adherents a ritualistic tradition, a complement of suitable deities and a dedicated time and space for worship. Modern athletes acknowledge their respective gods in victory, and the invocation of a higher power on the playing field signals their respect for divine intervention in athletic outcomes. As such, the congregational acquiescence and hierarchical loyalties invoked in both cultural practices have prompted many to regard them as equivalent institutions.

When deciding whether sport can be rightfully regarded as a religion, many writers focus on structural similarities between religious engagement and sporting dedication, trying to explain the seemingly ecstatic devotion that supporters exhibit towards their team or the conformity of belief displayed by fans.[1] Some have even suggested that attending sporting events is akin to attending sacred prayers. The presence of religious icons, such as 'Touchdown Jesus' behind the endzone of the University of Notre Dame's gridiron, confirms for many that sports arenas function as substitute places of worship, as 'cathedrals',[2] with athletes replacing traditional deities and teams serving as surrogate denominations.

Yet the relationship between sport and religion extends beyond comparative frameworks, for athletes are not gods, regardless of media treatment, and sports stadia, for the most part, are not places of worship. This is not to say, however, that there are no meaningful links between religion and sport, nor do we contend that one cannot markedly impact the other. We do not deny the reverence shown by athletes for their faith, nor the group prayers, nor the zealous dedication to task. Yet neither do we wish to overstate the relationship or insinuate that there is some kind of 'natural' affinity between sport and religion, simply because the ritualistic character of one resembles that of the other. Indeed, as Robert Higgs suggests, sport and religion are in fact incompatible in many ways.[3] And contrary to those who argue that sport represents a kind of secular or civic faith,[4] we are more convinced by Joan Chandler who quite bluntly states that 'sport is not a religion'.[5]

We argue instead that the relationship between cultural institutions requires a nuanced approach, which explores more than cursory structural comparisons, and suggest that focussing merely on whether sport can be considered a religion obscures the complexities of this relationship. For this reason, we have conceived this volume to investigate the role of sport and religion in the social formation of collective groups, and we are specifically concerned with the means by which sport might operate in the service of a religious community and assist in the promulgation of its theology.

Whilst it may be useful to determine precisely what we mean when we speak of 'religion', securing a suitable definition has proven a complex task. Religious studies experts, sociologists and anthropologists of religion disagree on a singular definition of 'religion'. Having said that, most adhere to the notion that religion requires some sense of a supernatural being as well as a set of established rituals,[6] though even this broad definition presents problems. What one society regards as 'supernatural' may be regarded as part of the natural world elsewhere; and the nature of ritual has been at the centre of longstanding definitional debates.[7] Thus, a definition of religion may not be appropriate or indeed, in the context of this project, even necessary, as any narration of the concept must come from an essentialised, singular position. Indeed, the desire to define, categorise and delimit culturally variant concepts seems reminiscent of rationalist paradigms that suggest all aspects of culture can be scientifically labelled. Thus, for the purposes of this book, we focus more on religious communities, namely those communities that may or may not be geographically congruous, but nevertheless comprise groups of individuals who regard themselves as linked to others through both a faith of their choosing and shared cultural practices. We, therefore, consider it sufficient if the community defines its cultural practices, faith and rituals as a 'religion'. There are of course far more complex explanation, however, a treatise on the nature of religion serves little purpose here.

It is important to recognise that a 'religion' assumes additional social and cultural roles beyond the relaying of dogma. Indeed, far from being simply an organised structure based upon supernatural beings and rituals, religion can also be regarded as both 'individual and social behaviour' for it is 'both a collective, cultural configuration, and a personal assimilation of that configuration'.[8] For this reason, it is crucial that we do not regard religious behaviour as simply emblematic of an individual's own personal faith, nor as just an imposed power structure from an organised church. Instead, we need to recognise that religion intersects both personal devotion and social and cultural institutions and has a significant impact on the formation of both individual and group identities.

Linda Woodhead and Paul Heelas, in their annotation of an anthology of religion in modern times, differentiate religions based on their relationship to a transcendental god.[9] These 'religions of difference' tend to distinguish between divine and human entities, attributing 'authority first and foremost not to human beings nor to nature, but to the transcendent' so that members are 'saved by a God outside rather than a God within'.[10] Most of the religions dealt with in this collection fall into the category of 'religions of difference'. This classification serves an important purpose for this study, particularly as Woodhead and Heelas argue that the differentiation between a supernatural force and mere humans is reflected in the process of sharply distinguishing between those who belong to the religious community and those who do not. Indeed, religions of difference are 'actively involved in the maintenance of their difference from other religions and communities. Clear initiation rites, defined dogmas, prescribed moralities, authoritative teachings, texts and traditions, clear social structures, and organized authority structures all help in the maintenance of difference'.[11]

It is clear then that cultural activities, particularly those requiring ritualised performances, fulfil significant roles in the perpetuation of dominant social arrangements, and thus bear the responsibility for socialising citizens, teaching them the norms, values and expectations of defined groups or communities. Participating in social gatherings or ritualised activities, such as religious or sporting events, provides individual members with opportunities to achieve 'intimacy with real and imaginary others'.[12] Citizens find their place in social hierarchies through the participation in, and consumption of, events and discourses that reaffirm the unity of their community. But at the same time, as Woodhead and Heelas contend, religions of difference, through stringent maintenance of clear boundaries, 'are eminently well suited to the defence of threatened identities and the construction of communal ones'.[13] The production of boundaries between 'them' and 'us' is crucial to the formation of collective identities, for 'our identity depends on being able to locate ourselves in relation to others, preferably in some structure stable enough to be understandable'.[14] Communities function by establishing who they are *not*, as much as who they *are*. Religion and sport both provide sturdy frameworks suitable for a range of identificatory purposes, and as such the articulation between the two may reveal the ways that sport has contributed to the production of social identities within a religious context.

Over recent decades, researchers have become increasingly interested in identifying the mechanisms whereby collective social identities are formed through sporting practices.[15] This informed research differs considerably from the rather simplistic and often theoretically barren populist notion that argues sport's suitability for 'character-building'.[16] Given its fundamental competitive structure, which differentiates it from a range of other movement cultures, modern sport has proven a fruitful cultural device against which one group, such as a school, team or nation, can be contrasted with a rival. This deliberate juxtaposition of 'us' against 'them' delivers an effective public mechanism for communities seeking to explicitly distinguish themselves from others. For this reason, it is not surprising that modern sport, as a popular cultural practice, has served the imperatives of a range of ideologies. The international context of sporting events and competitions, for example, provides a site at which nationalist struggles can be performed in a kind of 'war without weapons', and the physical capital expressed on the playing field is respected as emblematic of economic and political strength. Citizens are taught to recognise athletic bodies as the embodied nation, and are reminded by the adornments, insignia and other physical markings that highlight and confirm the nationalistic enterprise. Individual bodies thus signify the greater imagined community and, as such, provide powerful, accessible symbols with which citizens are invited to identify.[17] At the same time, national interests are inscribed on the body, through costuming and symbols, whilst athletic performance is often explained by national stereotypes.[18] Whilst the role of sport in the construction of national identities has received considerable treatment, sporting teams or athletic individuals can, of course, represent a range of other communities, such as ethnic, gendered, racial, class, corporate and, indeed, religious communities.

If sport is an ideological practice, then it provides a lens through which we may determine the mechanisms by which citizens are socialised into their particular community. By emphasising the *processes* of socialisation, we emphasise that this collection is not designed to draw conclusions about the efficacy of the socialisation project. Rather, its purpose is to identify those structures that are put in place to assist in the construction of a cultural milieu conducive to socialising citizens into the ways of the religious community. If, as Steve Bruce contends, religious authorities rarely leave devotional instruction simply to families, then it is critical to determine precisely how religious ideology is communicated to their adherents.[19] Religious communities employ a range of cultural practices that assist them in the maintenance and reproduction of their faith and identity, and physical and other recreational activities have been incorporated into this process. This is not to say that sport represents the most effective means of socialising citizens, it simply highlights the differing socio-political roles that sport may play.

Despite the value of sport in some religious contexts, the relationship between organised religions and sport has not always been congenial. Within a Christian context, as Robert Malcolmson has noted, medieval preachers often denounced those festive gatherings and sporting contests that were invariably occasions for drunkenness and the cause of riot and bloodshed. Puritans were also much concerned about the tendency of sport and recreation to lure men from godly activities into an idle and undisciplined way of life.[20] And although the belief that Puritans were hostile to all sports in the Old and the New Worlds has been shown to be as much myth as reality,[21] criticism of the cruelty involved in many animal sports, of the idleness and drunkenness associated with many 'holy day' activities, and of the playing of sports on Sundays were important factors in the friction between sport and religion in the eighteenth century and the quest for respectability for sport in the nineteenth century.[22] The clash between sport and Sabbatarianism, highlighted in the film *Chariots of Fire* by Eric Liddell's refusal to run on a Sunday, is but one exemplar of the conflicted nature of this relationship even in the early twentieth century. An important form of accommodation in the search for sporting respectability and a less ascetic and effeminate religion was to be found in the mid-nineteenth century ideology of muscular Christianity widely adopted in the English public schools.[23] Here was a somewhat uneasy alliance of the sporting and the religious, of the promotion of the health and fitness of the body and mind with the quest for self-improvement and the moral elevation of the soul. Such an alliance also meant that 'for the better part of half a century YMCA leaders vigorously debated whether or not they should encourage "mere amusement", physical exercise, and competitive athletics'.[24] Was their mission to encourage young men to pray or to play?

A number of notable scholars have focussed on the production of identities through sport in a range of religious contexts,[25] and many have examined the formation and inculcation of British imperial identities in indigenous peoples through the work of Christian athletic missionaries and English Public Schools.[26] The development of a muscular Christian ethos in the mid- to late nineteenth century paved the way for the later developments of missionaries who would teach the way of the Christian god, embodied in British civilisation, to the indigenous communities they encountered wherever the British Empire landed. Cricket, in particular, came to be understood as a tool of British culture, spread by athletic missionaries.[27] Richard Cashman has shown how cricket was developed in the Indian subcontinent by the British in their efforts to build cultural bridges with local communities as well as entertain themselves when far from home.[28] Furthermore, through the efforts of muscular Christian missionaries such as Cecil Tyndale-Biscoe, the young were also taught to 'play the game' at their high-caste fee-paying schools.[29]

A major aim of these athletic missionaries was to co-opt indigenous peoples into British imperial civilisation, to produce 'acceptable' natives, and thus sport was employed in this context as a social integrator of sorts. Indeed, much has been written on the role of sport as a way of assimilating disparate communities. Cashman has argued that sporting activities in Australia were one way to break down boundaries between diverse ethnic groups,[30] whereas within the US context, a number of authors argue, as does Linda Borish in this collection, that organised sport acculturated immigrant communities into the American mainstream and yet at the same time helped maintain religio-ethnic identities.[31] Despite recognising sport's capacity to augment social divisions, much of this research is characterised by an insistence that sport does, at least on some level, offer an avenue for integration. What is lacking is an acknowledgment that sport can also function as a divisive mechanism, that it may be utilised by groups seeking to retain some kind of independent identity.

In order to redress these points, we originally formulated this collection to examine the way that minority religious communities, in a range of different national and cultural contexts, might use sport as an instrument to fortify their religious/cultural/ethnic identity against the overwhelming influences of a host community. We found, however, that many of the contributions went beyond this narrow construction, and so our focus broadened to consider the way that any religious community might employ physical activities to construct collective identities. Of course, the process of boundary maintenance is more pronounced in areas where the community is under a perceived threat from larger, more established groups. Woodhead and Heelas argue that religions of difference are often 'revitalized in the face of a serious threat from their socio-political or cultural environment'.[32] Similarly, Bruce contends that as groups of people migrate or are colonised by an external community, their religious identity may assume 'an additional purpose as defenders of the culture and identity of the people'.[33] This is particularly relevant as migrants are forced to abandon the social, cultural, political and economic foundations that supported their community. As such, religions may assist peoples 'to cope with the shift from one world to another', easing them into a new environment that provides some level of familiarity.[34] We contend that sport may operate effectively in the service of religion to ensure that communities can replicate their established social arrangements in new or rapidly changing circumstances.[35] Indeed, as Bruce states: 'Where identity is threatened in the course of major cultural transitions, religion may provide resources for negotiating such transitions'.[36] Whilst migration is one such cultural transition, there are many others. As such, this collection focuses on cultural transitions, be they temporal, geographic, social, political and/or economic. Many of our chapters reflect the problems confronted by migrant communities when faced with a hostile and culturally foreign host, whilst other examples, such as Richard Light and Louise Kinnaird's contribution, examine the maintenance of national boundaries around a culture that has felt under threat from without for centuries.

Regardless of which example we take, the production and maintenance of boundaries, particularly during times of social flux, remains central to the processes of establishing and ensuring the continuation of religious identity. Any exploration of identity formation and maintenance must take into consideration that social identities do not exist in isolation and require a carefully defined 'Other' against which a group may juxtapose its ideologies, behaviours and rituals. For this reason, Stuart Hall and others have suggested that identities are more a process of marking difference than of representing a homogenous unity; and of course, differentiating between groups requires the creation of boundaries to symbolise inclusion and exclusion.[37] This process establishes an oppositional relationship between self and Other, which necessarily, according to Laclau, generates 'a violent hierarchy' between the poles.[38] As such, the self can only be revealed in relation to the Other, thus identity must be understood as a cultural relationship, rather than a fixed or inherent ideology.[39] Meanings about 'us' are generated only through 'our' position in relation to 'them'.[40] In this sense, identities are constructed within strict boundaries that, whilst temporally and perhaps even geographically congruent, are policed nevertheless.[41]

Given that identities are 'more the product of the marking of difference and exclusion', it is important to identify precisely how these demarcations are invoked.[42] If a 'them' is critical to an understanding of 'us', then sport presents an ideal opportunity for groups to compare and contrast their relative value, and for this reason, athletic contests have become a crucial site for the construction of a range of identities. We will see this highlighted in many of the chapters that follow but it is particularly evident in the chapters by Chandler, Cronin and Randels and Beal, where the religious group constituting 'us' is part of the same broader cultural group (and could thus be easily confused as having the same identity) as those portrayed as 'them'. Maintaining identity through dedication to the group and through deliberate and careful distinctions between religious communities is one of the most important tasks of religious authorities.

Religious communities are faced with unique concerns when it comes to retaining their faithful, yet the initial step, namely generating membership, is, for many traditional religions, a process that occurs largely by default. Like other cultural identities, religious identity is 'socially acquired', and communicated initially from generation to generation.[43] Whilst many people develop their faith through the promotion of a specific religion by their parents and immediate community,[44] it is clear that religious identity must be reinforced through education and repetitive, and ritualistic, cultural practice.[45] Thus, as acquiring a religious identity is akin to acquiring any other social or mass identity, such as gender, class or nationality, the habits, meanings and orthodoxies are not intrinsic; they must be learned. Benjamin Beit-Hallahmi and Michael Argyle suggest that religious learning is fairly standard in most communities, relying on a combination of 'the study of sacred books, instruction in myths and theology, and taking part in rituals'.[46]

Where a religious community enjoys the status of being the dominant religion, there is little need for the 'formal training' of children into its doctrines.[47] For example, in a society underpinned by the fundamentals of Christianity, the practice of Christmas may not require explanation, whilst Hannukah, practised perhaps by only a minority, requires the dedicated transmission of its history, significance and meaning. In this case, a Jewish community may take every opportunity, not just religious occasions, to teach its young about the practices, customs and rituals specific to their faith, including special schools, clubs, social and charitable organisations, and recreational activities. In such instances, the rearing of the child into a particular religious community is not a task left solely to the discretion of the parents; it is a process orchestrated carefully by those who oversee the promulgation of the faith.[48]

Simply learning appropriate social behaviours, however, is not generally sufficient for sustaining a community. Members of any social group must rehearse and perform their identity. For this reason, Hall indicates that identity is best understood as a process, rather than a product. As it is 'constantly in the process of change and transformation',[49] we can view identity as 'becoming' rather than 'being'. If we accept this conceptualisation, then we should seek out those aspects of rehearsal that contribute to the rearticulation of the desired identity. Within religious communities, commitment is demonstrated actively in prayer meetings, during worship, through social engagement and through the conspicuous display of devotion. Clifford Geertz, for example, argues that religion 'persists on the basis of a constant rehearsal of its complicated dramas, woven as they are into the whole rhythm of social and cultural life'.[50]

When we consider the efficacy of any religious community in communicating their identity outcomes to their members, it must be remembered that individual interpretation is subject to human agency. Ideologies cannot simply be transmitted without question to receptive minds, ready to absorb and act upon the imparted wisdom. If noviciates are to 'buy in' and make the ideology their own, they must do this of their own free will. Indeed, many religious communities encourage the doctrine of free will and stress the significance of human agency, yet 'all make sure to create structures which lead to only particular outcomes, namely religious commitment'.[51] We argue that the process of social learning is far more extensive than simply formal education, and thus religious communities often seek to provide 'total' environments for their members. Cultural activities, social occasions and sporting events coupled with formal devotional meetings provide a range of sites where members can rehearse and perform personal commitment. Church groups, the Young Men's Christian Association and Young Women's Christian Association, and the Young Men's Hebrew Association and Young Women's Hebrew Association, of which Borish writes, all employed sport as a mechanism through which to influence commitment and loyalty as well as religious and moral discipline. Joe Willis and Richard Wettan suggest that by the 1920s in the USA, 'sport was not only accepted ... but enthusiastically supported as a modality for teaching moral behaviour as well as a means whereby potential converts could be attracted to the church'.[52] The philosophy of sport was thought to parallel religious morality whilst providing a secular activity that could generate interest in the more formal religious structures.

In order to curb the influence of competing doctrines in pluralistic societies, religious authorities may try to limit access to conflicting traditions and alternative belief systems, through the control of communications or social segregation. Geographically and philosophically isolated religious communities, such as the Amish in the USA or the Hare Krishnas in Australia, have agitated for the right to establish their own schools in order to restrict exposure of their young to opposing ideologies. Beit-Hallahmi and Argyle suggest that minority groups that are 'more distant culturally' impose greater limitations on younger members. Indeed, '[r]estricting social interaction with non-members by creating clubs and summer camps means keeping children and adolescents busy in activities with other members only'.[53] They further argue that minority religious communities are more likely to establish and police social boundaries and keep 'close control' of teenagers and children. Yet it is a mistake to focus too closely on the younger members of a community. All members of a group must continually learn and perform their role in the group, thus 'extra-curricular' activities are provided for all.

Yet maintaining religious exclusivity requires more than simply filling in leisure time with doctrine. Boundary maintenance requires a vigilant surveillance of the members, to quickly reject those who stray from the central tenets. Bruce argues that it is relatively simple to discount the actions and faith of those not included within one's own religious community, yet greater struggles and a more concerted policing occurs when challenges arise from within, from members of the community who have rejected the central ideologies.[54] These members are quickly expelled, but their relationship to members of the community remains a threat. In the US, Promise Keepers participate actively in the surveillance of the boundaries between themselves and their antagonists, believing in particular that their group must struggle against members of their own faith whom they feel have turned away from the fundamental religious principles. In Northern Ireland, as Cronin demonstrates in his chapter, Catholic soccer players who played for Protestant clubs have often been sanctioned more violently by members of their own community than by their religious opponents.

In the chapters that follow we investigate the cultural practice of sport within the social formation and maintenance of collective religious groups. Dealing with issues such as gender, nation and ethnicity, the chapters reveal mechanisms by which religious communities seek to establish and preserve an exclusive identity for their members. At the same time, some communities have adopted religious rhetoric, as a way of furthering their sporting agenda. Beginning with Northern Ireland, Mike Cronin emphasises that sport in Ireland cannot be divorced from religious concerns. For Cronin it is the importance of religious identity that has led to the development of exclusively Catholic sport and the relative failure of 'inclusive' sport at all levels in the state. He argues forcefully that, despite the 'hopeful' view of sport as an agent of integration, it is as an agent of division, which has fostered the sectarian nature of Northern Ireland, that we can better make sense of the place of sport in that society. Sport has served as an instrument of religious difference, which has dissociated itself from its integrative possibilities, and thereby has ultimately become another religious battleground.

The reasons for this dislocation are evident at the highest levels where organisational confusion abounds. As there is no uniform administration of sport, some sporting organisations govern the entire island, whilst others are split at the border. For Cronin, these organisational differences lead readily to contested identities since sporting bodies appear to 'reinforce and legitimise' the division of communities in Northern Ireland. Additionally, the role of the Gaelic Athletic Association (GAA) in the promotion of Catholic and Irish identity has highlighted the desire by Catholics to undermine Protestant influence in the North. The GAA has become synonymous with Republicanism and republican terrorism. This is unlikely to change unless and until the GAA 'removes its apparently sectarian message from its sporting agenda'. By the same token, soccer has failed to be inclusive of Catholics in Northern Ireland despite its global nature. The game is predominantly Protestant and has acted as another forum in which to promote and reinforce religious division and separation, as evidenced by the fact that there are now only two Catholic professional clubs remaining in the Northern Irish League. For Cronin, in terms of both the GAA and senior level soccer, sport has failed as an agent of religious inclusion in Northern Ireland.

The relative failure of sport as a mode of integration is also an important theme for Paul Silverstein. In France and North Africa, where sports programmes have been designed by the state to combat sectarianism, subnational groups have appropriated and used sport as a means of building ethnic and religious subjectivities and identities. By comparing and contrasting mosques and stadia as sites for contesting and producing such subjectivities and identities, Silverstein highlights the significance of bodily practices in this process. He focuses specifically on the role of 'stadium politics' in the articulation of anti-national forms of ethnic, religious, class and racial belonging, both in the French urban periphery and the North African hinterland. In particular, he investigates the centrality of the *Jeunesse Sportive de Kabylie* (JSK) soccer club in the growth of a transnational Berber/Amazigh cultural movement, with the team serving as a symbol of cultural pride and their matches as arenas of protest. In addition he discusses how soccer clubs have served as spaces of Amazigh politics in France, competing on terrains that are themselves already subject to low-intensity racialised class warfare between groups reified as 'French' and 'Immigrant'/'Muslim'.

In discussing the role of these sites in the negotiation of the public character of Islam in France, Silverstein notes the growing links between labour and religious concerns, and the beginnings of reverse-colonisation. Other post-colonial societies are facing similar concerns. In Britain the effects of such a 'reverse-colonisation' are being felt in the sports industry, particularly within cricket and soccer. The threat of a loss of control over immigrant bodies in Britain and of political Islam in France has led, in the French case at least, to attempts by the state to 're-master immigrant bodily practices' through sport at the youth level. As Silverstein notes, however, these efforts have fostered as much cultural innovation as they have integration. Public spaces have been privatised by young residents and, as such, sports facilities have become both sites and objects of struggle. Despite the role of sport in the service of religion and the nation, the limits of the nation as an analytic category for understanding and explaining social belonging are highlighted by both Cronin and Silverstein.

John Hughson similarly explores the contribution of both sport and the church to the construction of a 'sub-national' Croatian identity within second generation migrants in Australia. For many recent arrivals, a range of social, cultural and religious networks eased the transition from the homeland into the new national culture. In particular, soccer clubs became a focal point, which assisted in the maintenance of migrant cultural traditions during the post-World War II era of mass migration to Australia from Southern and Eastern Europe. Similarly, for many within the Croatian community, soccer became a means of providing a 'Croatian-friendly' recreational environment for immigrants and their descendants, as well as an outlet for the performance of Croatian identity. Hughson argues that soccer clubs allowed the expression of Croatian identity, in order to both retain a sense of their cultural heritage and distinguish themselves from other former Yugoslavian identities, particularly Serbian. In addition to soccer, Catholicism served as a significant marker of difference between Croatian and Serbian descendants, for example, yet Hughson does not suggest that the organised religion was a motivator behind Croatian soccer in Australia. What he does reveal is that religious, social, political and sporting spaces each contribute markedly to the construction of a modern Australian Croatian identity.

By focussing on the Bad Blue Boys (BBB), a group of devoted Sydney United (formerly Sydney Croatia) fans, Hughson explores the assertion of cultural and religious difference within the sportscape of the soccer terraces. He examines the use of religious chants, national colours and team emblems to communicate a dedication not simply to the team, but to a shared ethnic background. By drawing on French sociologist Michel Maffesoli, Hughson suggests that the BBB might reasonably be described as a 'neo-tribe', a group that emerges as a result of a shared ethnicity and their embrace of the traditions and customs of their ancestral heritage. The soccer stadium, like other private/public places such as the church, provides this neo-tribe with a central space to express their cultural collective identity both within the grouping as well as publicly to their own community, rival spectators or the nation as a whole. As such, sport is a critical site through which Croatianness, as imagined, understood and replicated by descendants of immigrants, can be projected into the wider Australian community.

Whilst Hughson focuses on an ethnic minority that embraces sport as a means of resisting assimilation through the preservation of their cultural heritage, Linda Borish discusses the way that sport in Jewish Women's Settlement Houses was designed to provide a range of Jewish cultural experiences, whilst simultaneously offering a seamless transition to mainstream American culture. Borish stresses that the history of sport for Jewish women has been neglected and seeks to remedy this academic oversight. She notes that it was not just white middle-class women who were afforded or grasped opportunities for participation, but also working-class women who, through the efforts of a variety of Jewish organisations, were able to preserve Jewish

life and identity whilst participating in Americanising sporting activities
and gaining access to American cultural traditions.

Borish highlights the contributions made by Jewish American women –
both athletes and administrators – that resulted in increasing athletic opportunities for women in the late nineteenth and early twentieth centuries. As
part of the Americanisation of lower-class female immigrants, middle-class
reformers designed programmes to promote physical health through
sporting participation, whilst at the same time preserving Jewish traditions.
The tension between maintaining Jewish ethnic and religious practices and
becoming familiar with, and socialised into, new American traditions was an
inherent part of the experience for many of these women when participating
in sport. Settlement houses for immigrants provided one of the earliest sites
for the promotion of spiritual and bodily well-being.

Drawing on some of his previous work on rugby and masculinity,
Timothy Chandler investigates the role of the sport in the making of
Catholic men at public schools in twentieth-century Britain. Whilst public
schools are often regarded as a homogenous group, Chandler maintains that
important differences exist between Protestant and Catholic schools, as well
as within these broader religious categories. He suggests that in addition to
class, religion has played a pivotal role in not simply the intellectual education of boys in public schools, but also their physical development, such that
a Protestant or Catholic 'way of playing' sport may be identified. He argues
that theological differences are expressed not simply through faith and
prayer, but through the corporeal expression on the playing field. In order to
demonstrate the way that sport can operate in the service of religion,
Chandler identifies the mechanisms by which a 'Catholic' style of playing is
engendered in the pupils at Downside School in England, and how this
image of a 'fearless' and 'fearsome' athleticism is communicated to their
long-standing rivals through traditions, meditations and monks, as well as
through the physical and cultural landscape of their school.

Chandler suggests that such philosophical or religious differences are
embodied in the role of the institution as, on the one (Protestant) hand, a
corporate body and, on the (Catholic) other, an extended family. As public
schools, muscular Christianity remains key to both of these institutions; yet,
at a theological level, a significant difference lies in the contrasting
approaches to the disciplining of the male body. Chandler summarises these
differences by suggesting that the Protestant schools disciplined the male
body to 'stand in' for religion, whilst the Catholic view was that the disciplined male body would 'stand up' for religion. There is a sense in which the
bodily discipline required of the monks as a sign of their devotion to and
standing up for God is, in important ways, mirrored in the bodily disciplining of their charges in their devotion to sport.

The theme of bodily discipline as an expression of the relationship
between sport and religion is also explored in John Nauright and Tara
Magdalinski's examination of rugby within the 'Coloured' community in

Cape Town, South Africa. This chapter traces the development of two independent 'Coloured' rugby unions in Cape Town in the late nineteenth and early twentieth centuries. Whilst the Western Province Coloured Rugby Football Union (WPCRFU) was dominated by Muslim clubs, their rival, the City and Suburban Rugby Union (CSRU), was decidedly non-Muslim, imposing a ban on Muslim players in their competition. The rivalries between the two organisations were certainly more complex than simple religious differences, and the differences between the urban, Muslim working class and the more affluent, suburban Christian communities led to friction between the two unions culminating in bloody battles on the field.

Within the Muslim community, teachers and community leaders alike regarded rugby as an important mechanism for the development of tough, disciplined bodies, characteristics that were deemed necessary for survival in the cramped working-class areas of District Six and the Bo-Kaap. Whilst both unions played unrelenting football, the Muslim community came to be associated specifically with both on- and off-field violence, their reputation furthered by their visible associations with protection rackets and gangs. Yet, despite the significance of the game to Cape Town's Muslims, rugby was not a site for religious evangelism, but rather provided a leisure activity that was 'Muslim-friendly', which, in other words, allowed Muslims to recreate within the confines of their faith.

The following two chapters on sumo and the US-based Promise Keeper movement provide examples of the way that sporting or religious rhetoric may be used in the service of the other. Despite the fact that modern sport is a relatively recent invention, a number of physical activities profess to centuries of traditions. Sumo, for example, suggests it draws on over a millennium of history, yet, as Richard Light and Louise Kinnaird suggest, sumo in its current form is clearly a modern phenomenon. They argue that many of the alleged 'traditions' of sumo were politically expedient inventions designed by promoters looking to secure the sport's position in Japanese culture. The manner in which sumo and the Japanese religion, Shinto, have been grafted together to provide an important set of social and cultural meanings highlights the significant part that sport can play in the development of religious identity. Light and Kinnaird argue that it has been sumo's links with Shinto as well as its political appropriation that have enabled it to become the consummate Japanese cultural icon. In fact, by binding sumo to Shinto, the Japanese have provided not only a model of religious identity through sport but also a symbol of national identity and social cohesion. Furthermore, through this association they have been able to increase the respectability of sumo.

Whilst Light and Kinnaird identify the way that sumo organisers appropriated a religious rhetoric in the promotion of their recreational activity, George Randels and Becky Beal highlight the processes by which the Promise Keepers employ sporting rhetoric in the dissemination of their religious ideology. In particular, their study of the US Protestant evangelical group addresses issues of negotiating masculine identity in present-day America and examines 'what makes a man' within Promise Keepers literature. They indicate that the rhetoric of sport plays a significant role in both 'the formulation and maintenance of religious identity for Promise Keepers' but also stress that such an identity is neither a modern version of muscular Christianity nor an unambiguous model of 'traditional' manliness. Rather, they argue that the religious identity of the Promise Keepers is deeply contested and that sport contributes to its ambiguity. Significantly, there is little insistence on the playing of sport within the movement, but rather the group's leaders, particularly their founder, a former college football coach, adopt the language and symbolism of mainstream American male-dominated sport.

One way in which the identity espoused by the Promise Keepers is contradictory is in terms of the movement's gender ideology. Randels and Beal note that Promise Keepers employs the traditional masculine model of manhood by invoking sports as a metaphor for promise-keeping. Yet, at the same time, the organisation encourages a cooperative and 'softer masculinity' that emphasises 'caring, emotion and self-disclosure', factors typically at odds with hegemonic masculinity. In order that this revised masculinity is not misunderstood, Promise Keeper meetings are held in sports stadia, which provide a traditionally masculine and sexually unambiguous site in which expressions of emotion and male physical intimacy cannot be confused with homosexuality. As such, the quintessentially masculine stadium is contrasted with the culturally feminine space of the church, which, for the Promise Keepers, has failed men.

By contrast, not all religious communities have willingly embraced sport as a mechanism for communal integrity.[55] As Maureen Smith highlights, the Nation of Islam was initially reticent about supporting a practice that was so clearly implicated in the continuing oppression of African Americans. At the same time, the success of a number of high-profile Islamic athletes in the USA, and the public conversion of others, meant that sport presented both an expedient avenue to highlight the continued oppression of Black Americans as well as an opportunity to advance the cause of the Nation. This religious community focussed on Muhammad Ali as representative of both Black oppression and progress and used his success, reputation and charisma to confirm their position in the USA and to enhance their civil rights struggle. As a black Muslim, Ali was the victim of white Christian persecution, whilst as world champion, he became a hero for those promoting black pride, and for those protesting the Vietnam War. As long as he was not a threat to the Nation of Islam and its leadership, and his sporting success did not openly conflict with its religious teachings, Ali was embraced. When Ali became bigger than the Nation of Islam, however, he was marginalised and sport returned to being what it had once been in the Nation's thinking – a Christian activity, responsible for all manner of wickedness in the USA. Through her analysis of the Nation of Islam's newspaper, *Muhammad Speaks*, Smith provides a valuable insight into the juncture between sport, religion and political action, demonstrating that the appropriation of a cultural activity can begin to dismantle the hegemonic control by the dominant group.

The chapters in this collection provide an initial glimpse into the differing roles that sport plays in a range of religious communities. Whilst membership in a particular club might denote one's religious identity, in other instances, actually playing sport is regarded as less important than the rhetoric, symbolism and imagery that sport proffers. In some cases, it is clear that sport constitutes a practice, and not strictly a theology, such as in the case of Jewish women's participation in sport; yet in the case of the Promise Keepers, sport clearly represents a theology rather than simply a practice. One notion that deserves further examination is that, in some examples, nationality and religion are not coterminous, such as in the case of Jewish sport, whereas in Cronin's case study, one's religion is essentially used to mark one's national allegiance, even where the two may not correlate.

These points suggest that religion needs to be viewed as an important unit of analysis in a broader understanding of sport. As such, a consideration of religion should accompany analyses of other cultural variables. We do not assert that religion is never addressed (indeed, there are some notable studies in this regard), yet we do maintain that religion needs to be foregrounded alongside the tripartite of class, race and gender. Indeed, the chapters in this collection offer a finely grained analysis that takes account of the interactions within and amongst a broader range of variables, such that religion, gender, ethnicity, race and nation combine to reveal the processes of identity formation and community maintenance.

Whilst all of these chapters reveal that sport as a cultural practice has to some degree been incorporated into a range of religious communities and has adopted important roles in communicating ideology, each reveals that sport, far from being a major avenue, is but one of a range of techniques that authorities may invoke. Thus, the significance of this collection, for us, is that it clearly addresses the differential roles of sport for religious groups, without overemphasising its importance. As such, we suggest that further evidence should be collected to demonstrate how sport, in conjunction with a range of other cultural practices, contributes to the perpetuation of social ideologies, be they religious, gendered, racial, national or ethnic.

In any collection there will be gaps. Some may wish to see additional geographical or national examples, others would prefer a greater range of religions. Of course there are a plethora of world religions as well as all manner of regional variations, and a book of this size is not able to cover every one of them. Because it was impossible to be representative of all of them, we selected chapters that we felt best communicated the issues of boundary maintenance, identity formation and community, and the role of sport within those enterprises. In putting together this collection we faced the additional problem of wanting to examine a range of sports, as well as national and religious contexts. In doing this we wished to acknowledge the diversity of sporting cultures that have penetrated religious communities, as well as the diversity of religious cultures that have penetrated sporting practices, in varied geographical locations.

If this collection achieves nothing more than to bring religion to bear as an important variable in future examinations of sport and sporting cultures around the world, we will have realised one of our major aims. Beyond this, we have been at pains to emphasise the significance of both sport and religion as arenas through which citizens can participate to reaffirm the unity of their communities. We have suggested that physical culture can and does contribute to the learning and performance of religious identity and have gone further, highlighting the inter-relationships between the two arenas as tools in boundary maintenance. If we have been at all persuasive in these efforts we will be delighted. If such a collection can help promote further, more detailed social and cultural analyses of sport in the service of religion, we will feel blessed by sporting such success!

Notes

1   M. Novak, *The Joy of Sports. End Zones, Bases, Baskets, Balls, and the Consecration of the American Spirit*, New York, Basic Books, 1976.
2   R. Cashman, *Paradise of Sport. The Rise of Organised Sport in Australia*, Melbourne, Oxford University Press, 1995; M. Novak, *The Joy of Sports. End Zones, Bases, Baskets, Balls, and the Consecration of the American Spirit*, New York, Basic Books, 1976.
3   R. Higgs, *God in the Stadium. Sports and Religion in America*, Lexington, University of Kentucky Press, 1995.
4   M. Novak, *The Joy of Sports. End Zones, Bases, Baskets, Balls, and the Consecration of the American Spirit*, New York, Basic Books, 1976. See also J.A. Mathisen, 'From civil religion to folk religion: the case of American sport', in S.J. Hoffman (ed.), *Sport and Religion*, Champaign, Human Kinetics, 1992, pp. 17–33.
5   J. Chandler, 'Sport is not a religion', in S.J. Hoffman (ed.), *Sport and Religion*, Champaign, Human Kinetics, 1992, pp. 55–61.
6   B. Beit-Hallahmi and M. Argyle, *The Psychology of Religious Behaviour. Belief and Experience*, London, Routledge, 1997.
7   V. Turner, *The Ritual Process. Structure and Anti-Structure*, London, Routledge & Keegan Paul, 1969; R. Firth, *Symbols. Public and Private*, London, Allen & Unwin, 1973; R. Bocock, *Ritual in Industrial Society. A Sociological Analysis of Ritualism in Modern England*, London, Allen & Unwin, 1974; C. Lane, *The Rites of Rulers: Ritual in Industrial Society – the Soviet Case*, Cambridge: Cambridge University Press, 1981; P. Connerton, *How Societies Remember*, New York, Cambridge University Press, 1989; R.A. Rappaport (ed.), *Ritual and Religion in the Making of Humanity*, Cambridge, Cambridge University Press, 1999.
8   B. Beit-Hallahmi and M. Argyle, *The Psychology of Religious Behaviour. Belief and Experience*, London, Routledge, 1997, p. 8.
9   L. Woodhead and P. Heelas (eds), *Religion in Modern Times. An Interpretative Anthology*, Oxford, Blackwell, 2000.
10 Ibid., p. 27.
11 Ibid., p. 264.
12 B. Beit-Hallahmi and M. Argyle, *The Psychology of Religious Behaviour. Belief and Experience*, London, Routledge, 1997, p. 25.

13 L. Woodhead and P. Heelas (eds), *Religion in Modern Times. An Interpretative Anthology*, Oxford, Blackwell, 2000, p. 265.

14 S. Bruce, *Religion in the Modern World. From Cathedrals to Cults*, Oxford, Oxford University Press, 1996, p. 109.

15 M. Cronin and D. Mayall (eds), *Sporting Nationalisms. Identity, Ethnicity, Immigration and Assimilation*, London, Frank Cass, 1998; T. Magdalinski, 'Organized remembering: the construction of sporting traditions in the GDR', *European Review of Sports History*, vol. 1, 1998, pp. 144–63; T. Magdalinski, 'Reinventing Australia for the Sydney 2000 Olympic Games', *International Journal for the History of Sport*, vol. 17, no. 2/3, 2000, pp. 305–22; J. Nauright and T.J.L. Chandler (eds), *Making Men. Rugby and Masculine Identity*, London, Frank Cass, 1996.

16 D.L. Shields and B.J. Bredemeier, *Character Development and Physical Activity*, Champaign, Human Kinetics, 1995.

17 J. Hargreaves, *Sport, Power and Culture. A Social and Historical Analysis of Popular Sports in Britain*, Cambridge, Polity Press, 1986.

18 J. Garland, and M. Rowe, 'War minus the shooting? Jingoism, the English press, and Euro 96', *Journal of Sport and Social Issues*, vol. 23, no. 1, 1999, pp. 80–95.

19 S. Bruce, *Religion in the Modern World. From Cathedrals to Cults,* Oxford, Oxford University Press, 1996.

20 R. Malcolmson, *Popular Recreations in English Society 1700–1850*, Cambridge, Cambridge University Press, 1973.

21 J. Ruhl, 'Religion and amusements in sixteenth and seventeenth century England', *British Journal of Sports History*, vol. 1, no. 2, 1984, pp. 125–65.

22 R. Holt, *Sport and the British*, Oxford, Clarendon, 1989.

23 D.E. Hall (ed.), *Muscular Christianity: Embodying the Victorian Age*, Cambridge, Cambridge University Press, 1994.

24 W. Baker, 'To pray or to play? The YMCA question in the United Kingdom and the United States, 1850–1900', *International Journal of the History of Sport*, vol. 11, no. 1, 1994, p. 42.

25 See for example D. Cavallo, *Muscles and Morals: Organized Playgrounds and Urban Reform, 1880–1920*, Philadelphia, University of Pennsylvania Press, 1981; M. Oriard, *Sporting with the Gods: The Rhetoric and Play and Games in American Culture*, New York, Cambridge University Press, 1993; C. Prebish, *Religion and Sport: The Meeting of Sacred and Profane*, Westport, Greenwood, 1993.

26 J.A. Mangan, 'Christ and the imperial games fields: evangelical athletes of the Empire', *British Journal of Sports History*, vol. 1, no. 2, 1984, pp. 184–201; A. Odendaal, 'South Africa's black Victorians: sport and society in South Africa in the nineteenth century', in J.A. Mangan (ed.), *Pleasure, Profit, Proselytism. British Culture and Sport at Home and Abroad 1700–1914*, London, Frank Cass, 1988, pp. 193–214.

27 C.L.R. James, *Beyond a Boundary*, London, Hutchinson, 1963; J.A. Mangan, 'Christ and the imperial games fields: evangelical athletes of the Empire', *British Journal of Sports History*, vol. 1, no. 2, 1984; J.A. Mangan, (ed.), *The Cultural Bond. Sport Empire, Society*, London, Frank Cass, 1992.

28 R. Cashman, 'The Phenomenon of Indian Cricket', in R. Cashman and M. McKernan (eds), *Sport in History. The Making of Modern Sporting History*, St Lucia, University of Queensland Press, 1979, pp. 180–204.

29 J.A. Mangan, 'Christ and the imperial games fields: evangelical athletes of the Empire', *British Journal of Sports History*, vol. 1, no. 2, 1984.

30 R. Cashman, *Paradise of Sport. The Rise of Organised Sport in Australia*, Melbourne, Oxford University Press, 1995, p. 168.

31 G. Gems, 'The Prep Bowl: football and religious acculturation in Chicago, 1927–1963', *Journal of Sport History*, vol. 23, no. 3, 1996, pp. 284–302; G.R. Mormino, 'The playing fields of St. Louis: Italian immigrants and sports, 1925–1941', *Journal of Sport History*, vol. 9, no. 2, 1982, pp. 5–19; S. Regalado, 'Sport and community in California's Japanese

American "Yamato Colony", 1930–1945', *Journal of Sport History*, vol. 19, no. 2, 1992, pp. 130–43; S.A. Riess, *City Games. The Evolution of American Urban Society and the Rise of Sports*, Urbana, University of Illinois Press, 1989.

32 L. Woodhead and P. Heelas (eds), *Religion in Modern Times. An Interpretative Anthology*, Oxford, Blackwell, 2000, p. 29.

33 S. Bruce, *Religion in the Modern World. From Cathedrals to Cults*, Oxford, Oxford University Press, 1996, p. 99.

34 Ibid., p. 96.

35 G. Gems, 'The Prep Bowl: football and religious acculturation in Chicago, 1927–1963', *Journal of Sport History*, vol. 23, no. 3, 1996; S. Regalado, 'Sport and community in California's Japanese American "Yamato Colony", 1930–1945', *Journal of Sport History*, vol. 19, no. 2, 1992; S.A. Riess, *City Games. The Evolution of American Urban Society and the Rise of Sports*, Urbana, University of Illinois Press, 1989.

36 S. Bruce, *Religion in the Modern World. From Cathedrals to Cults*, Oxford, Oxford University Press, 1996, p. 108.

37 S. Hall, 'Introduction: who needs "identity" ', in S. Hall and P. du Gay (eds), *Questions of Cultural Identity*, London, Sage, 1996, pp. 1–17; D. Sibley, *Geographies of Exclusion. Society and Difference in the West*, London, Routledge, 1995; M. Sarup, *Identity, Culture and the Postmodern World*, Edinburgh, Edinburgh University Press, 1996.

38 Cited in S. Hall, 'Introduction: who needs "identity" ', in S. Hall and P. du Gay (eds), *Questions of Cultural Identity*, London, Sage, 1996, p. 5.

39 K. Robins, 'Interrupting identities: Turkey/Europe', in S. Hall and P. du Gay (eds), *Questions of Cultural Identity*, London, Sage, 1996, pp. 61–86.

40 S. Bruce, *Religion in the Modern World. From Cathedrals to Cults*, Oxford, Oxford University Press, 1996; G. Revill, 'Reading *Rosehill*. Community, identity and inner-city Derby', in M. Keith and S. Pile (eds), *Place and the Politics of Identity*, London, Routledge, 1993, pp. 117–40; K. Robins, 'Interrupting identities: Turkey/Europe', in S. Hall and P. du Gay (eds), *Questions of Cultural Identity*, London, Sage, 1996; D. Sibley, *Geographies of Exclusion. Society and Difference in the West*, London, Routledge, 1995; M. Sarup, *Identity, Culture and the Postmodern World*, Edinburgh, Edinburgh University Press, 1996.

41 D. Sibley, *Geographies of Exclusion. Society and Difference in the West*, London, Routledge, 1995.

42 S. Hall, 'Introduction: who needs "identity" ', in S. Hall and P. du Gay (eds), *Questions of Cultural Identity*, London, Sage, 1996, p. 4.

43 B. Beit-Hallahmi and M. Argyle, *The Psychology of Religious Behaviour. Belief and Experience*, London, Routledge, 1997, p. 24.

44 S. Bruce, *Religion in the Modern World. From Cathedrals to Cults*, Oxford, Oxford University Press, 1996, p. 107.

45 P. Connerton, *How Societies Remember*, New York, Cambridge University Press, 1989.

46 B. Beit-Hallahmi and M. Argyle, *The Psychology of Religious Behaviour. Belief and Experience*, London, Routledge, 1997, p. 109.

47 Ibid., p. 98.

48 Ibid., p. 109.

49 S. Hall, 'Introduction: who needs "identity" ', in S. Hall and P. du Gay (eds), *Questions of Cultural Identity*, London, Sage, 1996, p. 4.

50 Cited in B. Beit-Hallahmi and M. Argyle, *The Psychology of Religious Behaviour. Belief and Experience*, London, Routledge, 1997, p. 98.

51 B. Beit-Hallahmi and M. Argyle, *The Psychology of Religious Behaviour. Belief and Experience*, London, Routledge, 1997, p. 109.

52 J.D. Willis and R.G. Wettan, 'Religion and sport in America: the case for the Sports Bay in the Cathedral Church of Saint John the Divine', *Journal of Sport History*, vol. 4, no. 2, 1977, p. 193.

53 B. Beit-Hallahmi and M. Argyle, *The Psychology of Religious Behaviour. Belief and Experience*, London, Routledge, 1997, p. 112.

54 S. Bruce, *Religion in the Modern World. From Cathedrals to Cults*, Oxford, Oxford University Press, 1996, p. 46.

55 Whilst football in the American South is a popular and important social ritual, it was once actively rejected by Southern Baptist evangelicals. See A. Doyle, 'Foolish and useless sport: the Southern Evangelical crusade against intercollegiate football', *Journal of Sport History*, vol. 24, no. 3, 1997, pp. 317–40.

2 Catholics and sport in Northern Ireland

Exclusiveness or inclusiveness?

Mike Cronin

Of all the trouble spots in the world in the post-1945 period, the Northern Ireland problem has been one of the most enduring, yet the resulting loss of life, over 3,000 killed since 1968, is by no means the highest when compared to other more violent clashes, such as those in the former Yugoslavian states. What distinguishes the conflict in Northern Ireland is that it is fought out under the jurisdiction of one of the world's most stable liberal democracies, that of Britain. The religious identities involved, namely those of Catholicism (represented by the forces of nationalism) and of Protestantism (represented by unionism), are not fundamentalist, misunderstood or demonised in the way that Islam, for example, has been by politicians in the West. The struggle mirrors the religious identities found across the Western world, and this familiarity with the competing religions in the context of Northern Ireland makes the conflict all the more difficult to understand.[1]

On 19 October 1996, an Irish League match in Northern Ireland between Portadown and Cliftonville was abandoned after Cliftonville supporters and their buses were attacked by a stone-throwing mob before kick-off. The fans did not make it into the ground, and once the team had been made aware of the incident, Cliftonville refused to play the second half. In response to the violence, one supporter, Gary Arthurs, vowed never to watch his beloved Cliftonville again. He said: 'It's only a matter of time before somebody is killed and no football match is worth that.'[2] The problem for Arthurs and his fellow Cliftonville supporters is that they are identified by their Protestant/unionist opponents as Catholics and nationalists. Whilst it might be argued that the negative connotations of such identification, which stem from broad perceptions of religious belief, have been tempered by the ongoing paramilitary ceasefires in Northern Ireland, it is clear that religious identity remains a key issue.

This chapter assesses how the Catholic population of Northern Ireland has sought to stress its own identity through practices such as sport in a state that, although democratic, is divided clearly along sectarian lines and is constantly overshadowed by either the threat, or the reality, of violence. By examining the two major spectator and participation sports, 'Gaelic

Games' and soccer, it is possible to demonstrate that the feelings of alienation felt by the Catholic community have resulted in the development of exclusively Catholic sport and the relative failure of inclusive sport. Like much of the rest of the community, sport in Northern Ireland seems divided along religious lines. Gaelic Games are regarded as sports that support the Catholic population through its maintenance of religious exclusivity, that stress political aspirations that champion the cause of an Irish Republic, and that deliberately and actively exclude the broad Protestant/unionist population. By contrast, soccer is a global game and has enjoyed a widespread following amongst both sections of Northern Irish society. Yet, since 1968, it has failed to include the Catholic community. This has meant that Catholic clubs have either been forced out of existence or have had to transfer their allegiance to the Southern Football Association of Ireland (FAI), leaving the Northern Irish Football Association (IFA) to run a league with only one team that can be said to represent the Catholic community. The chapter concludes that despite the usual 'hopeful' view of sport as having an integrative capacity that should bring about a commonality of experience and togetherness, in Northern Ireland sport has been an active force of division that underpins, rather than counteracts, the bitterness of a sectarian society.

Historical background

Any discussion of sport in Northern Ireland requires some understanding of the extremes of the contemporary situation. In the quotations given below, random samples were selected from recent press reports, though they are certainly representative of the years of the modern troubles. They reveal the extent to which sport, an activity that is popularly regarded as 'apolitical', and its relationship with religious identity may endanger individuals in Northern Ireland. The selection is indicative of how, when taken to its violent extremes, religious belief dislocates normal sporting behaviour and those connected with it.

> At 15 he [Donal Gray] had signed for last season's Irish League winners Portadown and joined Partick Thistle as a professional at 17, but moved back to the Northern Irish team Glenavon to be with his family after his Mother died ... as an Irish Catholic he dreamt of representing Celtic or Liverpool and had got as far as trials for the Scottish club and was planning a move across the water when the masked men came. ... They ran up to the door shouting: 'Open up, IRA'. 'One of them put a gun to my head and they dragged me out into the yard. I didn't think I would die but thought I'd never play football again. They were beating me with iron bars and wooden clubs. I just felt myself go dizzy and I just lay there, half dead, so they went.' The attack left Gary with a broken leg, a fractured knee, puncture wounds where he had been beaten with nail

studded wooden clubs and head, chest and arm injuries ... he had done nothing to provoke the attack ... a message from the terrorists has been filtered down through the community to tell him as much.[3]

The North of Ireland Cricket and Football Club is on the brink of the most important decision of its 138-year history – to forsake its lovingly tended pitches in South Belfast's lower Ormeau Road and move to the mainly Protestant east of the city. Last month the club's pavilion was burned down. ... The changing demographics of Belfast have left the club increasingly isolated in a zone of working class nationalism. Last month's arson attack was the third in as many years.[4]

His comments as he dismounted from the Grand National winner were echoed by the vast majority of Irishmen disgusted by the IRA. Tony Dobbin, a Catholic Ulsterman, said he was ashamed to say he was from 'over there' after terrorists forced the postponement of the world's most famous horse race with a bomb hoax. Patricia Perry, Dobbin's elder sister, has been subjected to a campaign of intimidation from alleged Republican paramilitaries in the jockey's home town of Downpatrick, Co. Down. She has been threatened by masked men armed with baseball bats on four occasions this month, and she also claims that one of her assailants had a gun. ... They suspect that the encounters are linked to Dobbin's post-race comments.[5]

These extracts confirm how important religious labels are in Northern Ireland and further demonstrate how sport has become another site for religious conflict. In the Province, sport is used to reinforce, rather than break down, sectarian identities, resulting in incidents where a Catholic man is beaten by paramilitaries fighting for a unified Catholic Ireland, even though his religious identity locates him on 'their side'; where a cricket club is forced to move because it is a Protestant club playing an 'English' game in a Catholic neighbourhood; and where the family of a Catholic jockey who dared to condemn the tactics of the IRA is intimidated. This is the modern reality of sport and its links to the politico-religious battle plaguing Northern Ireland, yet it is crucial to bear in mind that this conflict has long-standing historical roots.

Northern Ireland came into existence in 1920 as a result of the Government of Ireland Act, a partition of Ireland that was underpinned further by the establishment of the independent Irish Free State in 1921. After the bitterness of the Irish Home Rule campaign and the War of Independence, politicians in London, Dublin and Belfast hoped that Ireland had found a way towards peaceful co-existence that would avoid in the future the bitterness of the Home Rule campaign. This was not to be the case. Whilst the Free State became the Irish Republic in 1948 and functioned as a stable and peaceful democracy, Northern Ireland has been dogged since its foundation by a range of social, economic and political problems, all of which have been reinforced and underpinned by sectarianism. Whilst the Irish Republic has been predominantly Catholic and has largely been able to satisfy its people's nationalist demands, the Northern Irish state has been divided between a Catholic and Protestant population. The Protestants have always been in the majority and chose from 1920 to marginalise the other community. Catholics were denied access to fair voting, jobs and housing, and levels of intercommunal violence have always been high. In the late 1960s, the problems came to a head when the Protestant-dominated Stormont Parliament could not respond quickly enough to the demands of the predominately Catholic Northern Ireland Campaign for Civil Rights. With the introduction of British troops, the rise of paramilitary bodies on both sides of the sectarian divide, and flashpoints such as the use of internment and the events of 'Bloody Sunday', Northern Ireland descended into a cycle of violence from which it has struggled to escape.[6] Despite legislation that has tried to remove discrimination on religious grounds in the areas of employment and housing, legal efforts to outlaw paramilitary organisations and the recent and continuing attempts at a peace process, Northern Ireland remains a bitterly divided society. The Catholic and Protestant communities live in separate housing estates, vote differently, are schooled separately, attend separate churches and largely play different games. Thus, the conflict continues to affect all spheres of life in the Province, including sport.

The division in sport has manifested itself in a number of ways, some historically determined, whilst others have developed in response to the contemporary situation. Following Ireland's partition in the early 1920s, several sporting bodies, such as that of soccer, divided along the lines of the border. The IFA controlled the game north of the border, whilst the FAI controlled the south.[7] Both organisations ran, and continue to run, separate professional leagues and both were recognised by the international governing body, FIFA, and the European body, UEFA. Some sports, such as boxing, however, did not alter their jurisdiction after the foundation of the republic, and continue to run their affairs on an All-Ireland basis. This differential organisation of sport across the Irish divide has led to confusion for athletes competing at the international level, particularly at the Olympics, where international federations determine the 'nationality' of individual competitors based on which national organisations are affiliated with them. In boxing, this confusion has created a number of difficulties for Protestants from Northern Ireland. Despite being British citizens, if they wish to participate at the Olympics, they can only compete as part of Ireland's team. They are not recognised as hailing from a province of the UK, whereas a show-jumper or track and field athlete from Northern Ireland would compete for Britain. The problem that such confusion provokes is evidenced by the experience of Wayne McCullough, a Protestant from the fiercely loyalist Shankill Road in Belfast. He fought for Ireland at the 1988 and 1992 Olympic Games, winning a silver medal in Barcelona.

The celebration of his success in Northern Ireland was muted as it was won under a foreign flag, which led to his relatives being intimidated and beaten by Loyalist paramilitaries.[8] Other sports, despite initially accepting the border, have since split within Northern Ireland into two bodies, and in the case of cycling formed the Northern Ireland Cycling Federation (NICF) and the Ulster Cycling Federation (UCF). Although both bodies state that they are non-sectarian, it does appear that the NICF is predominantly Protestant whilst the UCF is largely Catholic.[9] Sport is thus divided historically along religious and ideological lines. The domestic official bodies have no general consensus as to whether or not they recognise partition, and the international sporting bodies do nothing to enforce a common norm from above.

The official divisions in sport that stem from the 1920s are replicated in the symbols of identity used by different sporting organisations. Some, such as the Gaelic Games, which organises on an All-Ireland basis, fly the Irish tricolour at Gaelic Athletic Association (GAA) grounds, and its sportspeople stand for the anthem of the Irish Republic, 'A Soldier's Song'. Soccer in Northern Ireland uses the Red Hand of Ulster as its flag, yet the national team stands for the British anthem, 'God Save the Queen'. At the Olympics the Irish Amateur Boxing Association will use the Irish Tricolour and stand for 'A Soldier's Song' whereas at the Commonwealth Games the Northern Irish representatives will fly the Red Hand of Ulster and sing 'The Londonderry Air'.[10] Within all this official confusion as to which territory a particular team or individual represents, it is hardly surprising that sport often acts as a force of division in Northern Ireland. Michael Billig wrote that he:

> read the sporting pages, turning to them more quickly than is appropriate, given the news of suffering on other pages. Regularly I answer the invitation to celebrate national sporting triumphs. If a citizen from the homeland runs quicker or jumps higher than foreigners I feel pleasure. Why, I do not know. I want the national team to beat the teams of other countries, scoring more goals, runs or whatever.[11]

Billig was writing from the perspective of an Englishman who also accepts and celebrates the fact that he is part of a wider Britain. For him there is a clear sense of who his team is – England in soccer and cricket, Britain at the Olympics or Commonwealth Games. Catholics in Northern Ireland (and to a lesser extent Protestants) cannot embrace national and international competition in the same way as Billig as there is no agreed notion, either domestically or internationally, of what the nation is. There is no single anthem nor flag, no single sporting body, and no congruence between the Ireland that Catholics want to see on the sports field and the geographical reality.[12] Once this historical and organisational confusion, with the concomitant contest over national identity, is coupled with the modern religious conflict, the rationale for the development of exclusive Catholic sports, and the relative failure of inclusive sports, emerges.

Whilst there is much confusion within the sporting arena, it remains apparent that sporting bodies reflect, reinforce and often legitimate divisions between communities in Northern Ireland. In this, is sport in Northern Ireland any different from debates about policing, the religious divides evident in education, and the complexities of identity that plague housing provision?

Gaelic Games and the choice of exclusiveness

Michael Cusack founded the GAA in Thurles in 1884. It formed part of the wider revival of Gaelic culture and identified political nationalism as one of the cornerstones of its belief. Cusack argued that Irish pastimes and sports had been destroyed by the English influence and believed that if the late nineteenth century trend for Irish people to play so-called 'garrison games', namely soccer and cricket, continued, then indigenous Irish culture would not survive. Without a specifically Irish sporting culture, which could form links in the popular imagination between athletic endeavour, the Irish language, the Catholic religion and the ancient spirit of the Gael, then there could never be a successful Irish national reawakening. In organising the first meeting Cusack demanded that there was a need 'for Irish people to take the management of their games in[to] their own hands'.[13] In the context of religion and sport Cusack's choice of patrons for the new body is revealing: Charles Stewart Parnell (Leader of the Irish Parliamentary Party), Michael Davitt (Founder and leading member of the Land League) and Archbishop Croke of Cashel. As W.F. Mandle notes, Cusack's choices 'demonstrated accurate recognition of the three most important streams feeding Irish nationalism of the time'.[14] Croke represented the Catholic Church, one of the central forces underpinning the Gaelic revival as well as the late-nineteenth-century resurgence in nationalism. In accepting the invitation to become patron of the GAA, Croke offered the clearest statement of how sport, religion and politics were to be linked in Ireland:

> One of the most painful, let me assure you, and at the same time, one of the most frequently recurring, reflections that, as an Irishman, I am compelled to make in connection with the present aspect of things in this country, is derived from the ugly and irritating fact, that we are daily importing from England, not only her manufactured goods, but together with her fashions, her accents, her vicious literature, her music, her dances, and her manifold mannerisms, her games also, and her pastimes, to the utter discredit of our own grand national sports, and to the sore humiliation of every genuine son and daughter of the old land. ... Indeed if we continue travelling for the next score years in the same direction that we have been going in for some time past, condemning the sports that were practised by our forefathers, effacing our national features as though we were ashamed of them, and putting on, with

England's stuffs and broadcloths, her masher habits and such other effeminate follies as she may recommend, we had better at once, and publicly, abjure nationality, clap hands for joy at the sight of the Union Jack, and place 'England's bloody red' exultantly above the green.[15]

The appointment of Croke linked the GAA with Catholicism from the outset, and it is a relationship that has not waned with the passing years. Of the twelve patrons that the GAA had during its first century, seven of them, two Cardinals and five Archbishops, have come from the hierarchy of the Catholic Church.

The centrality of the GAA within Irish life was underpinned by the events of the revolutionary period from the 1890s until the foundation of the Irish Free State in 1921. As a movement, albeit a primarily sporting one, the GAA championed the cause of a thirty-two-county Irish Republic, attracting the interest of the radical Irish Republican Brotherhood (IRB), members of which gradually infiltrated the GAA. As a result, the sporting body became intensely political and operated as a front for the promotion of radical nationalism. The clerics involved in the GAA in the late nineteenth and early twentieth century opposed the IRB involvement, as the IRB was a secret organisation. The Church opposed all such secret societies fearing that they may divert their members away from the true faith. The Church battled the IRB for control of the GAA, but was ultimately defeated. Yet, despite clerical opposition to its role within the Association, the IRB was committed to the creation of a Catholic Ireland.[16] Such a commitment did much to assure members of the clergy that the GAA was still an important vehicle in the promotion of Catholic values. Thus, even in division, as the GAA has often been through its history, the Catholic identity of the movement has always been central.

The GAA entered the twentieth century as part of a nationalist coalition determined to expel the British from Ireland, and ultimately played a key role in this struggle. Members of the GAA were involved in the events of the 1916 Easter Rising and, although such participation was not officially sanctioned by the Association, countless others were arrested by the British in the aftermath of 1916 as the British regarded the GAA as a subversive national organisation. It is clear from the literature surrounding the Easter Rising how important the imagery and ideology of Catholicism was to those who took part.[17] In 1920, during the War of Independence, the GAA was the target of a reprisal attack after Michael Collins and his IRA operatives had killed members of British intelligence. Thirteen people, including one player, died when the Auxiliaries of the British Army drove into Croke Park in Dublin and fired into the crowd. Whilst this event was depicted poorly by Neil Jordan in his 1996 film, *Michael Collins*, the inclusion of the incident highlights the centrality of the GAA in the mythology of Catholic and nationalist struggles for independence. As Marcus de Burca has commented, 'the GAA was justly proud of the recognition by the British, implicit in the selection of the target for the reprisal, of the Association's identity with what one of the shrewdest observers called, "the underground nation" '.[18] With the foundation of the Irish Free State, the GAA became the third pillar underpinning the nation after state and church. As John Sugden and Alan Bairner have argued, the GAA's

> pre-political function [was] more or less inverted from a traditional position of antagonism to the state to that of outward supporter; whereas the GAA had been formed in the 1880s as part of a campaign of resistance against British hegemony, by the late 1920s it had become a vital part of the institutional infrastructure of the fledgling Irish Free State.[19]

Since 1922 the GAA has performed an important but politically low-key role in Southern Ireland. As an all-Ireland body with a clear nationalist, and thus tendentially religious agenda, however, it was bound to play a more controversial role in Northern Ireland with the onset of the modern troubles.

In the North, the GAA has assumed a role similar to the one it believes it played in the South until 1922. It has effectively positioned itself as one of the few legally functioning national bodies in the North[20] and from there has assumed a central role in defining nationalist identity. The GAA has consistently stressed a separate Catholic and Irish identity, whilst pursuing the cause of Irish unity and the concomitant destruction of the Northern State. To achieve this end, the GAA has relied substantially on its history to promote its standing amongst the nationalist community. It refers constantly to the nationalist heroes of the past and uses the language of romantic Catholicism and nationalism by stressing the fourth green field ideal.[21] Yet, the correlation between the Irish revolution of 1912–22 and the Northern situation is problematic: in the revolutionary period Catholics in Ireland were in a majority whereas in Northern Ireland they are in a minority. The GAA has pursued in its rhetoric ideals that belong alongside the language of physical force Republicanism, akin to the politics of Sinn Féin and the IRA, rather than the more realistic constitutional nationalism of the SDLP. A common revisionist critique of the IRA and Sinn Féin is that their history has been distorted in the pursuit of a contemporary political agenda. The same is true of the GAA, though not only in the thrust of its own beliefs, but probably more importantly in view of the dynamics of the North, in the way the Association's aims have been perceived by their opponents, who consider the Association as a front organisation for the IRA. John McGarry and Brendan O'Leary have summed up the GAA's position by stating:

> the GAA has been the most successful cultural nationalist organisation in Ireland, and has undoubtedly revived and strengthened traditional native sports – and on a wholly amateur basis. However, its success has been at a price. Ulster Protestants and the security forces have viewed

the GAA with suspicion, as a nursery school for republicans – Padraig Pearse was one of its most famous graduates, and numerous convicted IRA prisoners have followed in his footsteps. It is not therefore surprising that GAA games and members have been subject to harassment.[22]

The GAA's position as a Catholic and nationalist flagbearer has been transferred to the North, not only in its own mind, but also and problematically, in the minds of its opponents. This position has resulted in the GAA taking a central role in the politics of the North whilst 'operating a very narrow definition of politics'.[23]

Under the GAA's Rule 21, members of the Royal Ulster Constabulary and the British Army are excluded from membership. As evidenced by Bloody Sunday and the attack on Croke Park, the security forces and loyalist community largely identify GAA clubs with Catholicism and nationalism, with clubs targeted for violence and arson. In October 1991, the Ulster Defence Association added the GAA to its lists of legitimate targets because of its 'continual sectarianism and support for the republican movement'.[24] This was reinforced by a further press release that declared targets are 'those associated with the republican war machine ... and identified at least a dozen members of the Gaelic Athletic Association as being involved'.[25] Such threats have resulted in the deaths of a number of people associated with, or merely present at, GAA owned premises as well as attacks on GAA clubhouses. In 1992 a man was shot dead whilst at the Sean Martin GAA club in east Belfast, and the landmark 3,000th victim of the troubles was killed whilst outside the Lámh Dhearg GAA club in Hannahstown West Belfast. The attitude of the British Army has added to the feeling of besiegement amongst members of the GAA. As Gaelic games were organised on a thirty-two county all-Ireland basis there has always been constant traffic of officials, players and supporters across the border, many of whom have been stopped and searched by the army. In 1988 Aiden McAnespie was shot by the army at a checkpoint whilst travelling to play Gaelic football in the South. The Army has also been criticised for its occupation of Belfast's Casement Park in the early 1970s, and its use of the Crossmaglen Rangers' ground in South Armagh as a helicopter base. The place of the GAA at the centre of the Catholic and nationalist community whilst existing primarily as a sporting organisation has thus led to heightened levels of animosity towards it.

The British government has funded the GAA's capital works programmes and the promotion of its activities through the Sports Council and the Department of Education. At the same time the GAA maintains its ban on British Army and RUC personnel, despite the fact that Unionist politicians object to what they perceive as a front organisation for terrorism receiving funding. In this there is a clear dichotomy. Whilst on the one hand the British state funds the GAA, on the other its elected officials in the Unionist parties, the army and the RUC remain deeply suspicious.[26] Such distrust has led at times to increased surveillance of the GAA by British security forces and a heightened sense of animosity from the Protestant community generally, and Loyalist paramilitaries specifically, who view the GAA, its clubs and its members as inseparable from the cause of Republican terrorism. This cycle of mutual suspicion and conflicting political ideologies cannot be broken until the GAA removes its sectarian philosophy from its sporting agenda, a notion that was unthinkable until the initiation of the peace process.[27]

In the North during the troubles the GAA has been a central focus for the Catholic and nationalist community under its cover as a sporting association. It has espoused the broad republican and nationalist cause and in so doing has cemented its support amongst the Catholic and nationalist community whilst bringing about the wrath of Unionist politicians, Loyalist Paramilitaries, the RUC and the British Army. Institutionally and socially the GAA has backed the creation of a thirty-two county Ireland in direct contradiction to the wishes of Ulster's other traditions and resolutely fails to recruit Protestants to its ranks; indeed, they are actively excluded by the rules of the Association.[28] In contrast to Gaelic Games, soccer is dominated at the professional, semi-professional and organisational level by one tradition in Northern Ireland, Protestantism, and as such it has neglected to include members of both religions. The historic and contemporary experience of Catholic soccer clubs demonstrates how destructive the troubles and the accompanying sectarianism can be.

Soccer and the failure of inclusiveness

After partition, two separate bodies emerged to govern football: in the Irish Free State the FAI assumed control, whilst in Northern Ireland the IFA prevailed. In the North, teams such as Linfield and Belfast Celtic continued to dominate the soccer scene in the Province's first city, and in 1929 Derry City was founded. Soccer was extremely popular and competition was intense. Not only were Linfield, Belfast Celtic and Derry City the three leading teams from the two most important urban centres, but the rivalry was fuelled by the sectarian divide in the rest of Ulster. Linfield was identified as Protestant and unionist, whilst Belfast Celtic and Derry City were deemed Catholic and thus nationalist. Violence off, and sometimes on, the pitch was part and parcel of matches between these teams. Although this violence may have been based simply on sporting rivalries, it was always played out against the backdrop of sectarian hatred and remains a problem endemic in Northern Irish society. As Dominic Murray notes:

> the more obvious manifestations of cultural life in Northern Ireland are inextricably built into the separated communities. The normal avenues of communication and contact between people which would provide a tendency towards the creation of a single shared culture are closed.[29]

Within this framework we can recognise the root of soccer's problems. Although it can be a leisure pursuit, a common language and an experience that unites elements within a society, in Northern Ireland this has not been, and perhaps cannot be, the case. As John Sugden and Scott Harvie conclude: 'the vast majority of clubs currently operating at senior level are associated to a greater or lesser degree with the Protestant community and are, by and large, administered and supported by people from such backgrounds'.[30] Despite the fact that soccer remains a game that provides a common language for all in Northern Ireland, as evidenced by the high interest in the English and Scottish Leagues within both Protestant and Catholic communities as well as participation at the grassroots level, the actual operation of senior soccer in the Province has not reflected this common interest. As the game is predominantly Protestant, and thus can be regarded as tendentially unionist, individuals on the terraces, in the boardrooms and on the pitch, have always brought their own preconceived notions of what they, and their opponents, represent into the soccer arena.[31] It was almost immaterial that Derry City, for example, had always pursued an open recruitment policy, both in terms of players and administration, and traditionally had been supported by fans from both the Catholic Bogside and the Protestant Waterside. What mattered most was that the followers of teams such as Linfield, the representatives of Protestantism and unionism, perceived Derry City and other Catholic clubs as bastions of Catholicism and nationalism. This is a key point. Soccer, as indeed most cultural practices in Northern Ireland, acts not as an arena in which competing traditions within the community may be unified, but instead functions as yet another forum in which division, mutual suspicion and sectarian hatred are reinforced.[32]

In order to contextualise the experiences of Derry City in the period after 1968, it is worth exploring the events surrounding the demise of Belfast Celtic in the late 1940s. Such a discussion demonstrates that soccer in Northern Ireland, even prior to the modern troubles, was rife with sectarian tensions that ultimately led to the dissolution of Derry City some twenty years later.

Belfast Celtic was founded in 1891. It was based in Catholic West Belfast and took the inspiration for its name from the famous Glasgow Celtic. As a junior team Belfast Celtic had defeated Linfield 1–0, heralding the arrival of a great rivalry. After their admittance to the senior league in 1896, Belfast Celtic and Linfield became locked in a constant struggle for footballing dominance, with the league championship and the cup regularly shuttling across the city between the two. As a result of the intense competition, as well as the religious and political nature of their respective support bases and because of the huge political upheavals in Ireland by the mid-1920s, Belfast Celtic withdrew from the league in 1915–18 and again in 1920–4, largely in response to club fears over the safety of their staff and supporters. The last game of the 1919–20 season reveals the legitimacy of these concerns. At a Belfast Celtic–Glentoran game, violence between sections of

LANCASHIRE LIBRARY

the crowd led to the match being abandoned, which prompted an individual in the Belfast Celtic section to fire a revolver at the Glentoran crowd.[33] It was clearly difficult for sporting normality to exist in such a climate.

Belfast Celtic rejoined the league in the 1924–5 season, though their games against traditional enemies such as Linfield and Glentoran continued to be marred by violence. By 1948, the death-knell had sounded for the club. On Boxing Day Belfast Celtic played Linfield at the latter's Windsor Park ground. The game ended in a 1–1 draw, whilst the final whistle provoked a riot in which Linfield supporters attacked Belfast Celtic players. Most of the team and many officials received serious injuries, the worst being Belfast Celtic striker Jimmy Jones, who suffered a broken leg, and, as a result of his injuries, never played again. The irony of this sectarian brawl was that Jones, though identified as Catholic through his affiliation with Belfast Celtic, was actually Protestant.[34] The response of the Belfast Celtic board to the events of Boxing Day was swift and absolute. They announced that at the end of the season they would withdraw from senior football, as they could no longer play soccer under such conditions. Despite their inter-war record of fourteen league championships and their undoubted pedigree as one of the finest and best supported teams in Northern Irish football, Belfast Celtic left the league and never returned.

Derry City is one of the most famous casualties of the sectarian divide in football.[35] Derry City's ground was, from its earliest days, the Brandywell in the heart of Derry's Catholic Bogside. During the late 1960s, the first explosive years of the modern troubles, the Brandywell was at the heart of the battleground between the forces of radical nationalism, most notably the Northern Ireland Civil Rights Association and the fledgling Provisional IRA, and the massed ranks of the Stormont Parliament security machine, including the B Specials, the RUC and eventually the British Army.[36] In such a climate it was impossible for Derry City to play their league and cup matches at the Brandywell, and they were forced to play their 'home' matches some twenty miles away at Coleraine. Derry City did their utmost to stay in the league, but the IFA declined to give them any real backing or encouragement, preferring instead to believe that the situation was provoked by security forces as well as the decision of other IFA clubs to stay away from Derry. As a result, Derry City withdrew from the league in 1972. Whilst the political and security situation in Derry made the weekly hosting of games difficult, the failure of a Protestant-dominated IFA Council and the refusal of mostly Protestant soccer clubs to play at the Brandywell were the under-lying reasons for their departure. Derry City eventually reformed and joined the Southern-based League of Ireland in 1985, indicating that sectarian forces had made its continued participation in the Northern league untenable, for Catholic teams were clearly unwanted by both the IFA and the majority of its constituent clubs.

It is clear from the experiences of Belfast Celtic and Derry City that soccer in Northern Ireland cannot be divorced from sectarianism. Since the

departure of Derry City, only two clubs in the league have been clearly identified with Catholic and nationalist traditions: Cliftonville and Donegal
Celtic. There are numerous examples of Cliftonville matches ending in
violence, but here I use Donegal Celtic to demonstrate that the divisions
that effected the demise of Derry City are still extant in Northern Irish
soccer.

In 1990 Donegal Celtic, an Intermediate League team from the fiercely
nationalist Andersonstown area, had been drawn at home in the Cup to play
Linfield. The RUC, as they had done with Derry City, advised the IFA that
the game could not be staged safely at the Donegal ground, and recommended it be moved to Linfield's Windsor Park. Despite seeking a High
Court judgement to overrule this move, Donegal were forced to play at
Linfield. Despite the RUC's concerns about playing at Andersonstown, the
game nevertheless ended in a riot, where plastic bullets were fired and over
fifty people were injured. The nationalist press attacked both the RUC and
the IFA for failing to ensure crowd safety and cast doubts on the political
and sectarian neutrality of the IFA in making such decisions; namely,
suggesting that the IFA, based at Windsor Park, would always favour
Protestant and unionist teams over Catholic and nationalist ones.[37] These
incidents confirm that the problems of the early 1970s, and the manner in
which they were viewed by members of the Catholic and nationalist tradition, had not been resolved some twenty years later.

I suggested earlier that soccer in Northern Ireland is dominated by one
tradition, namely the Protestant, though I do not argue that soccer is solely
a Protestant and unionist concern in the way that Gaelic Games are the
preserve of the Catholic, nationalist tradition. Instead, I assert that the
senior levels of soccer, in terms of team loyalty and administration, are
dominated by Protestantism. Indeed, the actions of FIFA and the FAI reinforce their power. The case of Donegal Celtic again proves instructive. In
1991, another Irish Cup game, against Ards, was again relocated by the
RUC, which cited concerns over public order as its principal motivation. In
response, Donegal Celtic withdrew from the competition and applied to the
FAI to join the Southern League, as Derry City had done some years earlier.
Both the FAI and FIFA rejected the proposed move, despite the Derry City
precedent, and the similarity of Donegal's plight. Just as Derry City could
no longer operate in Northern Irish soccer because of the prejudices and
ensuing violence, in 1991, Donegal Celtic faced similar circumstances as the
safe conduct of soccer matches in Andersonstown could not be guaranteed.
The FAI and FIFA rejected the proposed change in league as a result of
Donegal Celtic's geographical location: no one could ensure the safety of
Southern teams travelling across the border into the heart of Belfast.[38]

Northern Irish soccer has reached a position where it cannot, and some
would say will not, deal with teams coming from predominantly Catholic
and nationalist areas. By seeing the Derry City situation as an isolated case,
which it certainly is not, the FAI and FIFA wash their hands of any responsi-

bility to teams from Northern Ireland's margins. The result, as Sugden and Bairner conclude, is that 'the integrative potential of football is increasingly difficult to realise'.[39] In a similar vein Arthur Aughey, in his submission to the Forum for Peace and Reconciliation, points out that 'In Northern Ireland association football has emerged during the troubles to become the symbol of Ulster Loyalist identity'.[40] Finally, Bairner argues that 'the impression created is of a Protestant community seeking to maintain control over a sport in a manner which could be said to reflect Unionist political efforts to maintain the Union in the face of growing encroachment by Irish Nationalists'.[41] In this I see few signs of hope for Northern Irish soccer. Even if the current peace process is an ongoing success, the question remains whether sectarianism and its accompanying violence can be removed from soccer. In fact, perhaps with the removal of terrorist violence from the political scene, other sites, such as football grounds, will become locations where sectarian divisions can be expressed. As such, sport cannot represent an arena for religious inclusion in Northern Ireland and remains a cultural practice that reinforces differences.

When Derry City joined the League of Ireland in 1985, the club looked forward to welcoming both Catholic and Protestant supporters back to the Brandywell. They were going to play soccer in a League devoid of Linfield matches, security forces and all the related problems. In 1985 a Protestant from the Waterside told a local reporter that he would not, despite being a lifelong supporter, be returning to the Brandywell. 'Look at the game against Shamrock Rovers last year. The majority of the crowd were only intent on annoying those people who were not of their own religious persuasion. They seem to me to have found a vehicle for their bigotry that they have searched for years to get. I want no part of that scene'.[42] In 1995, veteran Derry sports writer Frank Curran maintained that Protestants from the Waterside still would not attend the Brandywell.[43] In a similar vein Sugden and Bairner suggest: 'Most of them [Protestants] express their feelings simply by staying away from the Brandywell. The hooligans amongst them, however, lie in wait ready to throw missiles at busloads of Derry City supporters as they return from games in the Irish Republic.'[44] This perhaps best summarises the experience of Derry City as well as the context within which soccer exists in Northern Ireland. After being forced out of the Northern Irish competition and having to reinvent itself in a foreign league, Derry City was still unable to escape sectarianism. The Protestant and unionist supporters chose either to stay away or to attack the club as a symbol of Catholicism and nationalism, now overemphasised by their move to the Southern League.

Derry City, Belfast Celtic and Donegal Celtic were all victims of violence. Despite deserving credit for reforming, Derry City's return was an isolated incident and offers little to clubs facing similar issues. Yet despite their inclusion in the southern league, Derry City remained subject to the same sectarian forces they had faced in the 1970s, though the intensity of the situation had certainly abated. These examples clearly demonstrate that sport in Northern Ireland cannot be removed from its political and social context, that the divisions in soccer, for example, will continue as long as religious alienation characterises the broader society.

In Northern Ireland symbols of allegiance are central to everyday life. The selection of a soccer team or even the decision over which game you choose to play defines in many respects your identity. This is, of course, not simply a contemporary issue and pre-dates the emergence of the modern troubles. Rather than being a common unifying theme in a conflicted environment, sport in Northern Ireland provides yet another arena in which division and antagonism can thrive. This is certainly not to suggest that sport is solely an instrument of division between the religious communities in Northern Ireland; undoubtedly it has the potential to bridge gaps. Even during the ongoing peace process, sport, like other cultural practices in Northern Ireland, remains deeply divided and a source of nationalistic and religious identifications.

Notes

1 For a discussion of many of the themes here see M. Cronin, *Sport and Nationalism in Ireland: Gaelic Games, Soccer and Identity since 1884*, Dublin, Four Courts, 1999.
2 *Irish Times*, 26 October 1996.
3 J. Turner, 'Irish pain that does not cease', *The Guardian*, 21 July 1997, p. 8.
4 D. Sharrock, 'Goodbye to all that, as the Belfast sporting club where W.G. Grace swung his bat uproots for Protestant sanctuary', *The Guardian*, 13 August 1997, p. 6.
5 H. McDonald and A. Alderson, 'IRA terror for family of jockey who spoke out', *The Sunday Times*, 27 July 1997, p. 6.
6 For details of the origins of the modern troubles, see S. Wichert, *Northern Ireland Since 1945*, London, Longman, 1991; C. Kennedy-Pipe, *The Origins of the Present Troubles in Northern Ireland*, Harlow, Longman, 1997.
7 For details see H.F. Moorhouse, 'One state, several countries: soccer and nationality in a United Kingdom', in J.A. Mangan (ed.), *Tribal Identities. Nationalism, Europe, Sport*, London, Frank Cass, 1996, pp. 55–74.
8 To understand the complexities of the McCullough case see M. Cronin, 'Which nation, which flag? Boxing and national identities in Ireland', *International Review for the Sociology of Sport*, vol. 32, no. 2, 1997, pp. 131–46.
9 See J. Sugden and S. Harvie, *Sport and Community Relations in Northern Ireland*, Coleraine, Centre for the Study of Conflict, 1995, pp. 118–26.
10 For the confused and contradictory use of anthems and flags by different sports see ibid., pp. 38–42.
11 M. Billig, *Banal Nationalism*, London, Sage, 1995, p. 125.
12 Rugby union is one of the few sports which operates on an agreed and widely accepted All-Ireland basis that is accepted by both Catholics and Protestants; however, the majority of Catholics involved at the top level are from the South, especially from Leinster and Munster. As a result of this clear zoning of Rugby support we cannot speak of a game that operates across the divide in Northern Ireland, as rugby union in the Province is still the preserve of Protestants.
13 *United Ireland*, 11 October 1884.
14 W.F. Mandle, *The Gaelic Athletic Association and Irish Nationalist Politics, 1884–1924*, London, Croom Helm, 1987, p. 99.

15 Cumann Lúthchleas Gael, *A Century of Service, 1884–1984*, Dublin, Cumann Lúthchleas Gael, 1984, p. 18.

16 For an excellent and detailed coverage of the IRB and GAA relationship see W.F. Mandle, *The Gaelic Athletic Association and Irish Nationalist Politics, 1884–1924*, London, Croom Helm, 1987.

17 For details see F.X. Martin, '1916 – myth, fact, mystery', *Studica Hibernica*, vol. 7, 1967, pp. 1–129.

18 M. de Burca, *The GAA: A History of the Gaelic Athletic Association*, Naas, Cumann Lúthchleas Gael, 1980, p. 150.

19 J. Sugden and A. Bairner, *Sport, Sectarianism and Society in a Divided Ireland*, Leicester, Leicester University Press, 1993, p. 33.

20 After the Catholic Church, the GAA is the second largest organisation across the thirty-two counties in terms of membership. It operates successfully and legally on both sides of the border. Political parties have, with the exception of Sinn Féin, operated strictly on one side of the border only.

21 The four provinces of Ireland, Munster, Connaught, Leinster and Ulster are referred to as the four green fields. The aim of nationalists is to reunite the fourth field, namely Ulster, with the others as part of an independent and unified Ireland.

22 J. McGarry and B. O'Leary, *Explaining Northern Ireland*, Oxford, Blackwell, 1995, p. 224.

23 J. Sugden and A. Bairner, *Sport, Sectarianism and Society in a Divided Ireland*, Leicester, Leicester University Press, 1993, p. 35.

24 *The Independent*, 9 October 1991.

25 *The Guardian*, 16 November 1991.

26 See J. Sugden and A. Bairner, *Sport, Sectarianism and Society in a Divided Ireland*, Leicester, Leicester University Press, 1993, pp. 35–6.

27 In 1998 the political parties in Northern Ireland signed the Good Friday Agreement, which paved the way for a peaceful settlement of the troubles. It was ratified by a huge vote in referenda held on both sides of the Irish border. Despite such promising signs the GAA refused, at a Special Congress held to debate the issue, to delete Rule 21. At the time of writing the Rule had been suspended with a view to further debate at an unspecified future date.

28 According to one survey the membership of the GAA is 100 per cent Catholic. For details see J. Sugden and S. Harvie, *Sport and Community Relations in Northern Ireland*, Coleraine, Centre for the Study of Conflict, 1995, p. 30.

29 D. Murray, 'Culture, religion and violence in Northern Ireland', in S. Dunn (ed.), *Facets of the Conflict in Northern Ireland*, London, Macmillan, 1995, p. 228.

30 J. Sugden and S. Harvie, *Sport and Community Relations in Northern Ireland*, Coleraine, Centre for the Study of Conflict, 1995, p. 95.

31 For a recent analysis of soccer in Northern Ireland, especially from the mid-1990s, see A. Bairner and P. Shirlow, 'The territorial politics of soccer in Northern Ireland', in G. Armstrong and R. Giulianotti (eds), *Football Cultures and Identities*, Basingstoke, Macmillan, 1999.

32 For useful coverage of some of the themes dealt with here see J. Sugden and A. Bairner, 'Sectarianism and soccer hooliganism in Northern Ireland', in T. Reilly, A. Lees, K. Davids and W.J. Murphy (eds), *Science and Football*, London, Spon, 1988, pp. 572–8; J. Sugden and A. Bairner, 'Observe the sons of Ulster: football and politics in Northern Ireland', in A. Tomlinson and G. Whannel (eds), *Off the Ball. The Football World Cup*, London, Pluto, 1986, pp. 146–57.

33 See J. Sugden and A. Bairner, *Sport, Sectarianism and Society in a Divided Ireland*, Leicester, Leicester University Press, 1993, p. 82.

34 For full details of the match see J. Kennedy, *Belfast Celtic*, Belfast, Blackstaff, 1989, pp. 91–102.

35 See V. Duke and L. Crolley, *Football, Nationality and the State*, Harlow, Longman, 1996, pp. 70–5.

36 For a good description of political events in Derry, see E. McCann, *War and an Irish Town*, third edition, London, Macmillan, 1993.

37 See J. Sugden and A. Bairner, *Sport, Sectarianism and Society in a Divided Ireland*, Leicester, Leicester University Press, 1993, pp. 87–9.

38 Ibid., p. 89.

39 Ibid., p. 89.

40 *Building Trust in Ireland. Studies Commissioned by the Forum for Peace and Reconciliation*, Dublin, Mercier Press, 1996, p. 41.

41 A. Bairner, 'The arts and sport', in A. Aughey and D. Morrow (eds), *Northern Ireland Politics*, Harlow, Longman, 1996, p. 172.

42 *The Sentinel*, 24 July 1985.

43 Frank Curran, interviewed by Mike Cronin, Derry, November 1997.

44 J. Sugden and A. Bairner, *Sport, Sectarianism and Society in a Divided Ireland*, Leicester, Leicester University Press, 1993, p. 87.

3 Stadium politics

Sport, Islam and Amazigh consciousness in France and North Africa

Paul A. Silverstein

Introduction

This chapter examines the construction of ethnic and religious subjectivities in post-colonial France and North Africa. It situates this production in the dynamics and dialectics of competition and collusion between various institutional actors (from the nation-state to local ethnic and religious organisations) for the control of the bodily practice and social reproduction of the region's citizen-subjects. In an ambivalent desire to 'integrate' the subject's racialised body into the unmarked national body politic, these institutions have largely engaged in a problematic metonymical operation by which the 'body' is understood to stand in for the transcendental individual subject, and the subject for the society as a whole. In particular, as this chapter argues, these efforts at national integration have been part of a double dialectic that positions two sets of social practice as mutually exclusive yet ultimately co-dependent: the first, religious – communal prayer and bodily adornment; the second, athletic – primarily soccer.

Moreover, the discourses and practices of national integration in France and North Africa have resulted in the creation of two sites – mosques and stadia – which carry opposite moral valences but which both exist as contested spaces for the production of particular infra-national subjectivities. Indeed, I argue that the desire and efforts to construct binary oppositions between Mosque and State have been ambivalent and have led to unintended consequences. This chapter demonstrates that, rather than being erased in the social reproduction of the French and North African nations, alternate categories of ethnic and religious belonging are continually mobilised by a variety of groups for the engendering of social totalities and hierarchies constituted largely through bodily practice. This chapter concludes by focusing on how these dynamics are played out in the construction of a transnational Berber (Amazigh) polity across the Mediterranean.

Islam and public life in France

The relationship between Mosque and State has not been static over time. Whilst alarmist writers today insistently point to an essential clash of civilisations that has opposed Western and Islamic belief systems (with the Mediterranean serving as an imminently porous boundary), Mosque and State have in fact not always been at odds in France. There are several sites in which to examine the transformation in the public life of Islam and its contribution to the production of colonial and post-colonial subjectivities. One such area is the construction of mosques in metropolitan France. The history of the construction of the Grand Mosquée de Paris contrasts greatly with that of more recent ventures. Already in 1849, a colonial institution based in Algiers and consisting of both representatives from the French government as well as indigenous leaders from Algeria, Morocco, and Tunisia, the Algerian Colonial Oriental Society (*Société orientale algérienne et coloniale*), had recommended the construction of a mosque in Paris as a symbol of the Empire's commitment to its Muslim subjects.[1] The project was delayed repeatedly by bureaucratic considerations, intra-governmental dissension, the 1896 Armenian massacres and World War I, until it was finally approved by the municipal council in 1921. The final approval was viewed simultaneously as compensation to the 26,000 Algerian Muslims who had given their lives in the recent war and as an assurance of future loyalty of the southern colonies. In the words of councilman Barthélemy Rocalglia voting on the decision:

> Paris is not only the capital of metropolitan France *(la France métropolitaine)*, but also the capital of overseas France *(la France d'outre-mer)*, the capital of Greater France *(la plus grande France)*! ... It is by such means [of establishing a Muslim mosque in the centre of the Capital] that France can secure the love of all its indigenous subjects who, one day, will not hesitate to sacrifice their lives for the defense of such a beautiful fatherland *(une si belle patrie)*.[2]

Conforming to the 1905 law that formally separated Church from State in France, the mosque, which still stands today in the intellectual fifth arrondissement within a short walk of the Sorbonne and the Senate, has played primarily a diplomatic (as a meeting place for dignitaries from Muslim countries, complete with conference rooms, a library, a restaurant, a Turkish bath and overnight accommodation) rather than a religious role.[3]

The history of the mosque on rue Tanger in the popular Stalingrad neighbourhood in the nineteenth arrondissement of northeastern Paris stands in stark contrast. In 1969, the first Islamic association in France, the Islamic Cultural Association (*Association culturelle islamique*), garnered official recognition from the municipality and began to gather funds to build a permanent place of worship in northeast Paris.[4] These plans were repeatedly forestalled by financial problems and the withdrawal of local support. In the meantime, temporary mosques were established within a condemned building on rue de Belleville (1969–76), in the crypt of a local church, Notre-Dame-de-la-Croix de Ménilmontant (1976–81), and finally in a reno-vated garment warehouse on rue Tanger, a few blocks from the Stalingrad subway stop and market (1981–97). In 1985, the warehouse was condemned to demolition, at which point the association leaders once again initiated plans to build a large 'Pakistani-style' mosque in its place.[5] The expropria-tion decision, however, was forestalled indefinitely after a public demonstration against the decision in Lyon in December 1985, the interven-tion of the Mosquée de Paris, and the support of the socialist minority in the local assembly. In the years that followed, the warehouse Ad-Da'wa Mosque became one of the prime places of worship in Paris, attracting up to 5,000 visitors a day during the holy month of Ramadan. In 1994, having finally gathered sufficient funds, the association applied to the mayor's office for a construction permit for a 2,200 square foot building including prayer rooms with 3,600 seats and a set of administrative offices. The permit was origi-nally refused for the official reason that either 'it did not correspond to security norms'[6] or because its 'insertion into the urban tissue would cause severe traffic problems'.[7] In either case, the association responded to these concerns by revising the plan, and submitted a new application in 1995 including a reduction of the size of the prayer room (down to 1,500 seats) and a parking lot. Once again, the project was refused. A revised application was once again prepared and submitted, but no decision was forthcoming.

In the meantime, however, the plans had elicited national attention. The extreme-right National Front (FN) political party of Jean-Marie Le Pen had utilised the project as a rallying point to redirect its anti-immigrant plat-form against Islam, holding a series of public demonstrations against the project in both March and May of 1996. Approximately three hundred FN protesters rallied behind banners as varied as the xenophobic 'France for the French!' and the economistic 'Housing, not mosques!' In particular, they appealed to residents of the quarter to stand up against the project which would 'make the installation of immigrant populations definitive' and lead to the 'Islamisation' and 'Lebanonisation' of the racially and religiously diverse neighbourhood.[8] In fact, the FN utilised these demonstrations to simultaneously present its opposition to a parallel project by the Loubavitcher Youth movement to build an orthodox Jewish high school in the near vicinity. In their speeches, FN officials Jean-Yves Le Gallou and Martine Lehedieux expressed the need to 'defend French identity [as a] higher principle than freedom of religion'.[9]

In other words, the opposition to the mosque's construction revolved primarily around the legitimacy of public expressions of Islam in France and the effects such practices would have on the unity of French society. In the 1985 debates surrounding the decision to close down the Ad-Da'wa Mosque, the exchanges between conservative and socialist aldermen demon-strate how the official policy of state secularism (the separation between

Church and State that underlines the official tolerance of religion) in France remains openly contested and multiply interpreted even at the local level. Having just indicated that plans to renovate the quarter failed to recognise the demographic importance of the warehouse mosque and account for its replacement, the socialist alderman, M. Hubert, was rebuked by the conservative adjunct president of the municipal council, M. Chérioux, with: 'Thank God, the socialist group is far from secularist, and I rejoice in this interest for religion!' Hubert responded: 'On the contrary, that is an example of secularism (*laïcité*)'.[10] On the ground as well, these questions regarding the public stature of religion divided participants. The FN demonstrations elicited a wide range of opposition not only from Muslim, Catholic and anti-racist associations, but also from mainstream political parties (the Socialist and Green parties) and even from certain member delegates of the FN itself who maintained that religion belongs to the realm of 'individual conscience' and therefore should not be constrained.[11] Despite such demonstrations of support, concerns for security and the radicalisation of Muslim residents of the quarter continued to haunt the project. Although the Islamic Cultural Association eschewed all direct political affiliation and preached an overt doctrine of tolerance and integration, its rector, Larbit Kechat, was at the time of the demonstrations living under a year-long house arrest for his reputed ties to outlawed Algerian Islamist political groups.

Likewise, the Mosquée d'Ivry stands out largely in terms of the various, conflicting responses it invoked. Built in the 1980s through personal contributions from the large Muslim community of this '*ville nouvelle*' ('new city') outside of Paris, the mosque drew the ire of the local Catholic community, which lacked a similar place of worship. In the name of religious equality, they appealed to the government for financial support for a project to build a neo-gothic cathedral. Whilst the 1905 law forbade such overt government support, the government, under the aegis of socialist minister Jack Lang, finally agreed to finance the project as a museum of sacred art. In this sense, French state secularism, rather than simply assuring the individual freedom of religious expression, has taken an active role in mediating the plurality of religious communities.[12] This has implied both the support for and the obstruction of religious structures as proves necessary to maintain national unity and underwrite particular notions of French identity.[13] More importantly, these recent cases point to how, by the 1990s, mosques in France were no longer primarily a means utilised by the State to produce imperial unity, but had come to operate (and be perceived as operating) as a potentially independent and dividing force within its metropolitan populations.

Islam and immigrant labour

A second site for the negotiation of the public character of Islam in France has been suburban factories. In the 1950s, the Renault and Citroën automobile companies, with overt support from the Gaullist government, established prayer rooms in a number of their factories for their North African Muslim employees. The companies viewed this as a means to maintain the divide between immigrant workers and labour unions.[14] As was also evidenced in the construction of the Mosquée de Paris, the state's implicit support of Islam generally amounted to a paternalistic strategy to gain subject loyalty and defuse potential proletarian revolt.

By the 1970s, however, the scene had changed entirely. With the independence of Algeria in 1962, followed quickly by the liberation of France's other African possessions, the Empire had collapsed. Transient migrant workers responded to changes in immigration policy by transferring their domestic units to France and, correspondingly, by adopting a more active role in the determination of the exigencies of their daily lives, protesting insalubrious living and working conditions and demanding religious facilities. These struggles, originally localised to a single housing project or factory,[15] soon took on a larger breadth of engagement. The Arab Workers' Movement (*Mouvement des travailleurs arabes*), founded in Marseilles in 1970, had by the mid-1970s gained support amongst the North African workers in Paris who, despite continued mutual mistrust, were also joining the mainstream Marxist labour unions, the General Confederation of Labor (*Confédération général du travail*) and the Confederation of Free Unions (*Confédération des syndicats libres*) in greater numbers.

Two instances of protest demonstrate the overlap between labour and religious concerns. Beginning in December 1975 and continuing sporadically for the next four years, the mostly Algerian residents of several hundred dormitories run by the National Company for the Construction of Lodging for Algerians (SONACOTRA)[16] staged a series of sit-ins in the Paris area, protesting a threatened hike in rent and demanding the construction of additional prayer rooms in the buildings. During this same period, factory workers in the Renault, Citroën, and Talbot automobile plants in the northern industrial suburbs of Paris (Billaincourt, Aulnay-sous-Bois, Poissy) circulated petitions and held strikes for increased wages and the re-establishment of worship areas on the factory floor. Whilst by no means supported by every resident or factory worker of Muslim beliefs, the protests nonetheless had the effect of appropriating secular private and public spaces for religious performance. Islam proved to be no longer a tool wielded by the State to hold subaltern labourers in check, but rather a rallying point around which immigrant workers of different national and ethnic backgrounds could organise themselves.[17] For many French observers, this amounted to an unforeseen and unwanted imposition – a reverse colonisation in effect.

Suburbs of Jihad

More than the increase in metropolitan mosques or prayer rooms, it was the connection of such overt religious institutions with the younger generation growing up in the *banlieues* on which most alarmist journalists and officials

focussed. The election of Mitterrand and his legalisation of immigrant associations paved the way for the development of a diverse and thriving
Islamic civil society in France. The number of Islamic associations in
France increased from 150 in 1981 to over 600 by 1985.[18] Varying greatly
in size, adherents' nationality, and purpose, these groups – often poorly-
organised, short-lived, and sometimes marginalised even within the local
Muslim communities – attracted little attention from the French media or
government.

By the 1990s, however, these groups had become the target of generalised
fears over the cultural break-up of France, with politicians and media sources
conflating Islam and terrorism. In large part, this 'Islamalgam', as the
conflation was termed, derived from French reactions to the bloody Algerian
civil war, which has claimed more than 100,000 lives since the outlawing of
Islamic opposition parties and the declaration of martial law in 1992. French
newspapers and television, relying almost entirely on local media sources
which, in turn, rely primarily on official government reports, have tended to
focus more on spectacular instances of violence, such as car bombings and
village massacres, supposedly perpetrated by Islamist forces, than on daily
military operations by Algerian government forces. The result has been that
Islamist resistance forces and their supporters have been consistently
branded as 'terrorists' by the national press.

In the process, suburban Muslim associations came to be seen as a potential Fifth Column of such an Islamic terrorist organisation. Often filling the
institutional vacuum left by the secular Beur Movement of the early 1980s,
in the early 1990s these organisations became the main sites for local organisation and grassroots development, offering unemployed men and women
jobs working in mosques or selling wares in local markets, and even
arranging summer camps in the provinces for suburban youth. They also
gained a higher stature within Algerian neighbourhoods by becoming, along
with nascent Berber associations, one of the prime means by which news
from Algeria was circulated to and from France. The numbers of young men
and women who have joined these groups are unclear and certainly vary
from one housing development to another. Nonetheless, for researchers,
journalists and security officials investigating this phenomenon, 'Islamism',
as the religious social movement was often called, appeared to offer itself as
the main viable alternative to drugs, delinquency and prison for these
'excluded' (male) youth.[19] In the most extreme version of such alarmism,
reports portrayed young Franco-Algerian 'delinquents' as being recruited
through Islamic associations, indoctrinated in 'Islamist summer camps' and
then shipped off to Bosnia or Afghanistan or Algeria proper to fulfil their
destiny of '*jihad*'.[20]

One of the constants of the alarmist accounts has been the portrayal of
Islam as a mass movement through the repeated use of certain kinds of
images of demonstrations and group prayers. Whether in the form of gatherings to hear the Friday sermon with banners flying and Qu'rans held high[21]

or street scenes of multiple people simultaneously kneeling in prayer,[22] these pictures focus on the uniform and public character of Islam, rather than on its internal diversity and its emphasis on a personal, and private, relationship with Allah. Lurking behind this portrayal is the potentiality of these collective, uniform practices (of prayer as a repeated bodily practice) to erupt into a mass uprising or civil violence. In this way, the media discursive structures have largely contributed to the production of a reified image of Muslim religious difference that is inassimilable to French secular standards.

In totalising Islam into a single, fundamentalist frame, the alarmist discourse ignores the fact that the neo-orthodox religious movement – with a radical political and conservative social agenda – is decidedly modern. Whilst employing 'traditional' Islamic critical practices of moral advice (*nasiha*) and proselytisation (*ad-da'wa*) in an attempt to unite the North African immigrant community, Muslim leaders have utilised the French state's legal system, industrial tactics (unions, strikes) and tentative multicultural policies (embodied in FAS funding for immigrant associations) to assert their right to live in a 'culturally distinct manner' with their own religious institutions, such as mosques, butcher shops and schools, and everyday practices, such as communal prayer.[23]

Moreover, the discourse of these groups is likewise modern, borrowing directly from the same tropes of universalism and particularism as the French state. Their contemporary rise is predicated on the ambivalence of difference within France, on the colonial and post-colonial states' reification of the very categories of ethnic and racial difference they have sought explicitly to eliminate. Given the French state's repeated attempts to appropriate Islam to unite colonial subjects under the aegis of a paternalistic Empire and to disunite proletarian workers in other times of internal class conflict, it is of little wonder that such a category of religious difference should provide an effective script to express and protest on-going socio-economic hierarchies and inequalities. As such religious identities, in the context of an exacerbated Algerian civil war, come to be politicised, they threaten to outline independent corporate bodies that call into question 'the inevitability of the absolute nation-state – of its demands to exclusive loyalty and its totalizing cultural projects'.[24] As in governmental and media discourse, these newly-politicised religious groups likewise rely on a metonymic operation by which the body (as mobilised in prayer) stands in for the transcendental subject (the Muslim citizen) which itself comes to represent the potential for a new social order (a Muslim France?). As such, the two groups, French state and political Islam, find themselves in direct competition on the same discursive playing field.

Sports against religion

In response to this threat over the loss of control of immigrant bodies and subjectivities, the French state has attempted to re-master immigrant bodily practice through the medium of sports.[25] In the early 1990s, the French government began to take pro-active measures to halt the perceived rise of radical Islam in France. On the one hand, as occurred just prior to the 1998 World Cup, the government proceeded to militarise the *banlieues* in question and re-assert direct bodily control over its Muslim citizens, conducting round-ups of suspected terrorists, breaking into prayer rooms and association locales. On the other hand, the state established a set of redevelopment schemes, sometimes termed 'Marshall Plans', to revitalise the neighbourhoods in which Muslim associations were attracting membership. One of the consistent features of such revitalisation projects has been the construction of social centres and sports facilities. Housing projects designed by chief architect Roland Castro under the 'Banlieues 89' plan have included central areas featuring soccer fields and basketball courts, as well as indoor gymnasiums replete with boxing rings.[26] Moreover, sports figured highly in the twenty measures proposed by Prime Minister Michel Rocard in 1990 in response to the youth riots in the working-class suburbs of Vaulx-en-Velin and Mantes-la-Jolie. In September 1992, the Ministry of Urbanisation, headed by entrepreneur and then owner of the Olympique-Marseille soccer club, Bernard Tapie, launched a 'Youth and Sports' (*J-Sports*) programme which invested 40 million francs over the next several years in the construction of 1,000 sports installations and 100 fields in 120 different municipalities.

One 'Youth and Sports' activity was the 'Summer Prevention' operation, originally experimented with in 1982, which in 1992 alone sponsored over 1,500 *banlieue* youth to go on weekend excursions and summer camps.[27] The camps were intended not only to 'prevent' violence, delinquency and drug abuse, but also to defuse the 'communitarianism' supposedly created in the parallel summer camps organised by Muslim associations, camps that would become popularised in the media as training bases for armed struggle. The plans' emphasis on sports as a 'privileged remedy for contemporary social dysfunction'[28] hence derives from its vaunted capacities to re-train Muslim bodies away from religious practices, to re-constitute these young *banlieusards* into the docile, moral subjects – as defined by secular attitudes, a sense of fair play, and a strong work ethic – that their fathers, as factory workers, had been.

Street sports

These top-down sports development models seeking to re-impose state national structures onto seemingly uncontrollable immigrant neighbourhoods have not, however, produced the envisioned integrative results. Instrumentalist theories of sports and play have often failed to explain how games, rather than reproducing *habitus*, can actually become sites for cultural innovation.[29] Moreover, whilst often promulgated by French sociologists and government officials as a means for defusing potential asystemic violence, sports can also serve as a rallying point for class conflict and anti-national sentiment and violence. Residents of the *banlieues* are painfully aware of the intimate connection between sports development programmes and state surveillance procedures. Violent struggles with security forces have often destroyed sports facilities along with schools and police commissariats. Whilst the newspapers, following police reports, have classed these 'riots' (*émeutes*) within the category of juvenile delinquency, the conflicts have in fact been relatively well-organised displays of resistance targeting the particular state structures imposed upon the neighbourhoods. In Vaulx-en-Velin in 1991 and again in Bron in 1994, residents destroyed the gymnasia and climbing walls that had been recently unveiled through one of the government's sports programmes.

Nonetheless, the *banlieue* sports scene does not reduce to violent resistance. Young residents regularly utilise the facilities for daily sports practice, and, compared to twenty years earlier, participation in organised sports has increased dramatically. This should not, however, imply an equivalence between the soccer or basketball practised in a housing project courtyard and the games played in the professional or international leagues. Rather, young residents have appropriated these public spaces for their own games based on their own revised sets of rules; they have in effect privatised them and created what critics of government sports projects have bemoaned as 'ghetto-sports'.[30] A single playing field may be the scene of multiple games occurring simultaneously, with bookbags and jackets used to demarcate goals and boundary lines. Player rotations and consequentially offside rulings, a fundamental aspect of official soccer which largely contributes to the low scoring in matches, will vary with the number of participants, and opposing players will often ignore certain formal penalties. Far from constituting an unruly chaos, such practices reveal an internal organisation and permissive creativity which, whilst flexible to the field and player constraints, allow for self-organised challenge matches and tournaments.[31]

Spatial contention

More importantly, the appropriation – or privatisation – of public sports spaces involves the demarcation of categories of belonging and local identity. Whilst Pascal Chantelat *et al.*, in their ethnographic study of suburban Lyon street soccer and basketball, found little evidence of the spatial appropriation of terrains by local residents, my own anthropological fieldwork in the Parisian *banlieues* indicates that municipal sports structures often serve as spaces of contestation between residents and deemed 'others'.[32] During my nine-month residence in Pantin, an inner northeastern suburb of Paris of mixed class and ethno-racial character, I pursued my daily exercise routine in a municipal weight room. The gym was normally located squarely in the petit bourgeois, pavilion-dominated neighbourhood of Le Petit Pantin, in the Charles Auray stadium, and drew its clientele primarily from either the immediate area or from the surrounding pavilion communes of Les Lilas and

Romainville. In the autumn of 1995, however, the Communist municipality[33] decided to renovate the stadium and temporarily move the weight room to a new location on the edge of Quatre Chemins, a neighbourhood dominated by public housing projects. The building in question was a former health centre which had itself been moved next door to a more modern facility; AIDS and hepatitis awareness posters dotted the walls between hastily attached pictures of Arnold Schwarzenegger and diagrams of various exercises, haunting the gym's healthy workout ethic. No effort was made to remove these health posters or the old biological warning signs, or even to repair the broken window and cracked walls, as the city had informed the gym's management that the stadium's renovation would be finished within a few months. Given this avowed short-term duration, and despite the squalor and deficiencies, such as a lack of changing facilities or drinking fountains, former members chose to continue attending the gym instead of joining one of the other similarly-priced weightlifting facilities offered in the neighbouring suburbs.

As such, for the first month, the facility operated very much as it had previously, if in a slightly more improvised way. The managers set a workout schedule, but, in recompense for the shabby conditions, allowed members to use the gym whenever they chose; the front door was secured solely with a digicode lock and members were each entrusted with the combination. Yet, as the months passed and the stadium's repairs lingered – due in large part to a series of strikes from November 1995 to February 1996 by French public workers (*functionnaires*) – the demography and practices of the gym altered. The old health centre was not only located on the border of Quatre-Chemins, but had also been built on the grounds of a public housing estate, and its former patients had been primarily the residents of the complex. As such, local youth, mostly of North African and Antillean descent, soon discovered the gym and began using it regularly as a complement to their kick-boxing and basketball interests. Initially, beginning in February 1996, the volunteer manager (*responsable*) of the gym, Philippe, a city employee and trade unionist, welcomed these young members even though officially one could only join the gym at the beginning of the academic year (October–November), either pro-rating or eschewing their membership fees.[34] For Philippe, this decision resulted from a willingness to maintain good social relations with the community in light of the temporary nature of the gym's location. As he told me later, 'Most others would have simply refused, but, as long as they seemed mature (*sérieux*), I didn't see any reason why not'.

This attitude would change. As the gym became better known in the area, more and more local young men began using its equipment outside opening hours, having learned the code from friends (or friends of friends) who had been officially enrolled. On several occasions, Philippe 'opened' the gym to find weights scattered across the floor and the benches in a general state of disarray, when he knew that everything had been neatly arranged when he had 'closed' the previous evening. In response, he installed a key lock in the front door and informed those younger members from the housing estate that they were responsible for cleaning up after themselves, and that their use of the gym 'was a privilege, not a right'. Unfortunately, these measures proved ineffective, as non-members (as well as members disgruntled by the new policies) continued to enter after hours through a partially boarded-up window (one friend demonstrated to me how this could be easily accomplished). Several weights and bars were discovered to be missing, and a portable radio belonging to the gym was broken. Philippe grew increasingly impatient, placing the blame squarely on those younger 'Blacks' and 'Arabs' whom he had recently admitted.

One Saturday morning in June he arrived at the gym in order to lock the doors. Noticing that the weights had not yet been properly arranged and that a group of local youths were still there, he flew into a fit of rage and began hurling weights and benches in their direction, yelling: 'This is how you clean up after yourselves?! I can play that game too!' After calming down, he fumed to me, 'They treat this place like it's their house (*chez eux*). Maybe that's OK where they come from, but not here. I'm not a racist, but those youth (*jeunes*), those Blacks (*noirs*) and North Africans (*maghrébins*), always mess things up for us. They force me to act like this'. In the following days I had a chance to talk to several of the 'offenders' who, in point of fact, were amongst the most regular, competent and 'serious' members of the gym, much more so than Philippe himself who of late had only visited the gym to lock up or to sit in the back room and drink whisky. Ahmed (a Beur of Kabyle origin) interpreted the incident to me as follows: 'I don't know what came over him. He went crazy! We have been good about putting away the weights we use. Why doesn't he yell at others? He's completely racist. We have as much right to be here as he does. We live here [in the neighbourhood]'. Within two months, the weightlifting gym had moved back to the stadium, and Ahmed and his friends began to use a different municipal gym, on the Quatre-Chemins side of the canal.

This incident indicates less the irreconcilability of ethno-racial difference in contemporary France than the production of and resistance to physical and imaginary borders through the use of municipal structures. In designating these spatial divisions and underwriting their separation, the (unequal) distribution of municipal services, viewed by the state as a primary element of social justice and integration, has contributed to the reification of social categories of belonging as seen from below. The dispute was over who was really 'at home' (*chez soi*) in a liminal space of sports represented by the state but over which two differently imagined groups had equal claim: one, through temporal means, as long-standing gym members; the other, through spatial means, as proximate residents. In the end, both groups successfully asserted their claims, for Ahmed and his friends proved they could not be evicted from a space that they occupied as their own, but in which they could never be allowed to feel 'at home'. As such, local residents create bonds of solidarity not only through their domestic proximity to each other, but also through their access to and symbolic appropriation of particular sports facilities and clubs.[35] In many cases, these alternate categories of social belonging derive from the very structural demarcations embedded in the revitalisation plans and resultant sports facilities which are imbued with the identity of a distant and oppositional state structure.

Sports and religion

Moreover, residents not only utilise government sports programmes in the construction of localised intra-national identities, but they also manipulate them in the service of the very ethnic and religious practices that the French state has hoped to curtail (or at least privatise). In fact, even from at a relatively young age, children will group themselves into teams according to background and challenge co-residents of different origins to matches on these bases.[36] Berber and Islamic associations have followed in this practice and incorporated soccer and judo teams into their activities, in part to attract younger members, in part to foster loyalty to a political or religious cause via the medium of sports.[37] Some Islamic associations have gone as far as investing in local sports facilities in order to recruit membership, taking over financially in many cases where government programmes leave off.[38] Likewise, in a process that interestingly mirrors contentious political lines in Algeria, the main Paris-based Algerian Berber cultural association, Berber Cultural Association (ACB), founded a club soccer team, FC Berbère, in its ongoing attempt to counter the perceived ascendancy of Islamism in France by attracting young Franco-Algerian children to Berber identity politics through sports and music. At the end of a match against a rival club in Drancy in February 1995, a supporter of the club, a young boy of Algerian origin, was shot and killed. For the next year, the ACB set up a memorial to him on the premises of its locale, placing his picture alongside those of Tahar Djaout, Cheb Hasni and other Algerian/Kabyle artists and journalists killed by Islamists during the ongoing civil war in Algeria.

As such, the conflict between sports and ethno-religious practice implicit in much of the French state's discourse on integration fails to correspond to everyday sports practices amongst France's marginal, immigrant populations. French Muslim youth, initiated to sporting activity in French grammar schools, remain enamoured by heroic images of North African Muslim athletes on the international scene – from the world champion Algerian distance runners Nourredine Morceli and Hassiba Boulmerka, to Beur (Franco-Maghrebi) soccer stars such as Sabri Lamouchi (forward for Auxerre's professional club), Mustapha Hajji (star striker of Morocco's national side) and Zinedine Zidane (centre-midfielder in the victorious French World Cup team) – without denying their ethnic or religious identities. The measures adopted by government programmes to control the re-production of immigrant (and national) subjectivity through the control of masculinised bodily practices thus find themselves co-opted by individuals and associations for the production of potentially transgressive categories of belonging. Whilst certainly not producing the *intifada* imagined by alarmist discourse, such transformations have nonetheless facilitated an identity politics in which sports facilities themselves, as icons of particular categories of belonging, become objects of struggle.

Stadia and political struggle in Algeria

It is important to note that stadia and mosques are not merely contested spaces within a larger identity politics – they themselves can also be sites for political struggle. In Algeria, where a single-party government held power from independence in 1962 until a military coup (and de facto beginning of the civil war) in 1992, public assemblies, and the public spaces in which such assemblies were conducted, held both nationalistic and transgressive potentialities. As in all totalitarian political systems, organised demonstrations, marches and sporting rituals functioned as dramatic enactments of national unity that indexed to both rulers and ruled the regime's legitimacy. Such techniques, however, proved open to poaching by a growing number of oppositional social movements beginning in the late 1970s. The rise of the revolutionary Islamist front, and its utilisation of the Friday public prayer sessions and sermons of Ali Belhadj at the Great Mosque of Algiers to transmit its agenda and garner popular support throughout the 1980s, has been well documented.[39] Less well-known is the Berber Cultural Movement's simultaneous transformation of soccer stadia into sites for the transmission and enactment of its own secularist, multicultural agenda.

'Je Suis Kabyle!'

As much a tool of national integration within the metropole, sports practice was instrumentalised as part of a larger 'civilising mission' (*mission civilisatrice*) within the French colonial periphery. Whilst sports education constituted a central aspect of the colonial administration system, however, following extant policies of spatial and institutional apartheid of French and Muslim populations in the colony,[40] amateur and professional indigenous Algerian sports clubs competed in separate divisions that were less-well financed than their French counterparts. Under these conditions, a group of young Muslim athletes from the eastern Berberophone region of Kabylia formed the Sporting Youth of Kabylia (*Jeunesse Sportive de Kabylie* or JSK) soccer team in the provincial capital of Tizi-Ouzou in 1946. After suspending its activities during the Algerian War (1954–62), the JSK returned to compete in Algeria's newly-constituted national league, acceding to the first division by the 1968–9 season. Since then, the JSK has been one of the premiere clubs within Algerian, and indeed African, soccer, winning eleven national club championships, four Algerian Cups, two

Africa Club Champions Cups, one Africa Cup Winners' Cup and one Africa Super Cup. Moreover, in the last few years, the JSK has spawned a number of other male and female sports sections, including highly successful judo and swimming clubs.[41]

The success of the JSK has made it not only a mainstay of the Algerian sporting heritage, but also a readily consumed sports team within the Algerian community abroad (via satellite television). And yet, rather than becoming a source of Algerian patriotism, the JSK has proved to be a thorn in its nationalist side. Since the early days of the nationalist movement, expressions of regional or ethnic identity had been actively suppressed in favour of a monolithic Arab and Islamic national personality.[42] Following independence, the ruling National Liberation Front (FLN) pursued a policy of Arabisation, making Arabic the sole official and national language of the country, and gradually translating colonial toponyms and institutional titles into Arabic. In 1972, the national Director of Sports, Si Mohamed Baghdadi, followed suit by imposing a name change on the JSK, turning them into the *Jam'iyya Sari' al-Kawakib* ('The Star Runners'), thus eliminating the regional identification whilst retaining the acronym.

In spite of such an imposition, however, the JSK continued to serve as a locus of ethnic pride and a rallying point for a nascent ethno-nationalist cultural movement. With each victory and international success, the initials 'J-S-K' reinvigorated in the minds of its supporters that *'Je Suis Kabyle'* ('I am Kabyle'). On 19 June 1977, in the midst of the nationally televised championship match of the Algerian Cup between the JSK and the Nasr de Hussein-Dey club, JSK fans present in the 1st of November Stadium (Stade du 1er Novembre) in Tizi-Ouzou shouted a series of culturalist and oppositional chants, including 'Long live the Berber language!', 'Down with the dictatorship!' and 'Long live democracy!', at President Houari Boumedienne who was present for the game. In response to this event, the national sports governing body integrated the JSK into the National Electrical Company (Sonelec) and changed its name to *Jam'iyya Electronic Tizi-Ouzou* (JET).[43] Not to be put down, Kabyle (Amazigh) activists responded by deforming the new acronym into *'Jugurthe Existe Toujours'* (Jugurtha Still Lives), making reference to the Carthaginian leader of the Punic Wars who has since become part of the pantheon of Amazigh cultural heroes.

As the Berber Cultural Movement increased in strength, so too did the role of the JSK and its stadium as symbolic sites. After the April 1980 Berber Spring (*Tafsut Imazighen*), a series of student demonstrations, general strikes and military repression in Kabylia following the government's cancelling of a lecture on Ancient Berber Poetry, the Tizi-Ouzou stadium was closed by authorities in order to avoid further demonstrations. JSK/JET supporters, however, religiously followed the team's peregrinations, unfurling banners written in Berber script (Tifinagh) and calling for the release of imprisoned Berber activists. The stadium, subsequently re-opened, is the site for yearly commemorations of the Berber Spring, with Kabyle activist-folksingers such as Lounès Matoub, Ferhat M'henni, and Lounis Aït-Menguellat. The latter likewise composed praise songs throughout the 1980s in honour of the JSK, succeeding in transmitting Amazigh slogans at a time when more explicitly culturalist songs were banned from Algerian airwaves.

In more recent years, JSK matches and paraphernalia have continued to serve as sites and symbolic registers of Amazigh activism. After the June 1998 assassination of Lounès Matoub, presumably by Islamist 'terrorists', nearly every JSK match for the next two seasons – and most notably the 1 December 2000 finals of the Africa Club Champions Cup against the Egyptian club, Ismaïlia – became the occasion for cries of 'Pouvoir assassin' ('Government, assassins') and other anti-regime manifestations.[44] Similarly, yellow JSK jerseys became the de facto uniform of the hundreds of thousands of young Kabyle men and women who took to the streets in Algeria and France in a series of demonstrations and marches throughout the summer of 2001 to protest the marginalisation and successive police killings of Kabyle youth. Stadium politics in Algeria have thus assumed a direct political, if not violent, character.

Finally, the JSK's moral valence as an icon of Amazigh politics has transcended the Algerian borders. Not only have Kabyle youth in France, under the aegis of various Berber cultural associations, established supporters networks and parallel soccer clubs such as the FC Berbère discussed earlier, but the JSK's prominence has become a source of ethnic pride throughout Berberophone North Africa. For instance, in the town of Goulmima, in the southeastern sub-Atlas region of Morocco where I have pursued ethnographic research for the last several years, JSK support has become a local phenomenon. Part of the historical periphery or *bled es-siba* ('land of chaos') that has been, according to local townspeople, in continual revolt against the central power since time immemorial, Goulmima has been since the 1980s, if not earlier, a regional centre of Amazigh activism and opposition to the monarchy. On more than one occasion, most recently in 1994, state police have arrested and imprisoned local leaders for their support of regionalist platforms or linguistic sectarianism. Such repression has merely reinforced the sense of local political solidarity, with cultural associations multiplying and Tifinagh graffiti plastering much of the public wall space. Much of the graffiti refers to the JSK, which in the case of Goulmima refers not only to the Kabyle soccer club, but also to the local team, the *Jeunesse Sportive* du Ksar, named in honour of the casbah that occupies the historical centre of the town. In December 2000, the Goulmima JSK won the local Ramadan tournament, a month-long competition against neighbouring communes. In the stands of the championship match Amazigh flags flew high, and after the victory the yellow-jerseyed team was serenaded with an all-night celebration featuring Berber folksinging and poetry recital. In this way, whether one actively follows the JSK virtually through its Fan de JSK website, or participates in one of its filial clubs throughout the Berberophone world, rooting for the JSK has become the *sine qua non* marker of a transnational Amazigh consciousness.

Conclusion

Stadium politics thus indexes a double dialectic of sports and religion: on the one hand, a process of national integration and communitarian recrudescence in which Mosque and Stadium represent potentially opposed yet ultimately convergent categories; on the other hand, a bipolar set of sites of contestation that, whilst ideologically opposed, both constitute salient challenges to unitary narratives of national identity. In both France and North Africa, religion and sports – Islam and soccer – have become terrains of conflict in which state regimes exert domination and subaltern populations defy hegemony. The recent transnationalisation of the JSK as an icon of Amazigh consciousness points, in the final analysis, to the limits of the nation as an analytic category for the mapping of social belonging. Indeed, whilst sports may continue to be in the service of religion, its service to the nation may be in severe jeopardy.

Notes

1 This society was later reformed as the Islamic Property and Holy Sites Society (*Société des Habous et Lieux saints de l'Islam*) in 1917.

2 R. Weiss, *Réception à l'hôtel de ville de S.M. Moulay Youssef, sultan du Maroc. Inauguration de l'Institut musulman et de la mosquée*, Paris, public record, 1927, p. 27, cited in G. Kepel, *Les banlieues de l'Islam*, Paris, Seuil, 1991, pp. 69–70.

3 Rather than creating a rift between Church and State, the 1905 law actually occasionally brought these two institutions closer together. For one, it put all extant religious buildings into the hands of the government, which, in the name of the preservation of France's historical and cultural heritage, has maintained responsibility for their upkeep to this day. Given its cultural and diplomatic role, the Mosquée de Paris was grandfathered into this category. In 1982, however, its funding and control were handed over to the Algerian government. See G. Kepel, *Les banlieues de l'Islam*, Paris, Seuil, 1991, pp. 64–70.

4 This recognition involved a subtle contortion of the 1939 anti-fascist law which prohibited immigrant associations in France. The association's president, a French citizen of Algerian origin, was an employee of the Ministry of Interior and was able to use his connections to bypass the law.

5 See G. Kepel, *Les banlieues de l'Islam*, Paris, Seuil, 1991, pp. 94–105.

6 *Le Monde*, 1 June 1996, p. 9.

7 *Libération*, 18 March 1996, p. 16.

8 Ibid.

9 *Le Monde*, 1 June 1996, p. 9.

10 *Bulletin municipal officiel de la ville de Paris. Débats du Conseil de Paris*, vol. 5, no. 7, 7 September 1985, cited in G. Kepel, *Les banlieues de l'Islam*, Paris, Seuil, 1991, p. 102.

11 *Le Monde*, 1 June 1996, p. 9.

12 D. Hervieu-Léger, 'La laïcité', lecture given in the Maison Française, Columbia University, 5 February 1999.

13 For a similar set of dynamics and debates in mosque building in Marseille, see J. Cesari, *Être musulman en France. Associations, militants et mosquées*, Paris, Karthala/IREMAM, 1994.

14 Labour unions already opposed immigrant labour, for they saw in it a means for capital to hold wages at a subsistence level. As I have discussed elsewhere, the workers in question

largely saw themselves and were believed to be a temporary, although structurally integral, labour force; their presence in metropolitan France was limited by the duration of their employment contracts, and their dependants remained abroad. See P. Silverstein, 'Les politiques migratoires et les politiques d'intégration dans une perspective européenne: l'état des connaissances', *Migrations Société*, vol. 8, no. 43, 1996, pp. 7–28; L. Talha, *Le salariat immigré devant la crise*, Paris, Editions du CNRS, 1989.

15 The non-generalisation of this movement is understandable given the recent history of the Algerian War. On 16 October 1961, an FLN-organised demonstration in Paris to protest against selective curfew laws imposed on the immigrant population was brutally repressed by Parisian police, resulting in the deaths of several hundred protesters.

16 SONACOTRA managed 275 dormitories throughout France, housing over 70,000 persons, nearly seventy per cent of whom were of Algerian origin. See G. Kepel, *Les banlieues de l'Islam*, Paris, Seuil, 1991, p. 127.

17 The nationalist movement in Algeria was constituted along similar lines. From the Ouléma Movement of the late 1940s to the formal adoption by the FLN of a discourse of 'Arab Algeria' (*Algérie arabe*) at the 1959 Soumam Conference, Islam became the primary lens through which Algerian identity could be officially articulated. The organisers of the 1970s strikes came of political age during the nationalist struggle and were deeply marked by it. In addition, one cannot overlook the organising role played by the Friendship Society of Algerians in France (*Amicale des algériens en France*), the independent Algerian government's (i.e., the FLN's) wing in France, within the immigrant community. Algerians in France remained dependent on this organisation for their official papers, birth registrations, travel and the shipping of relatives' corpses back to Algeria.

18 These figures, compiled from G. Kepel, *Les banlieues de l'Islam*, Paris, Seuil, 1991, pp. 229–42, are necessarily inaccurate, as they only correspond to the official creation of these associations (as recorded in the *Journal officiel de la République française*) and do not in any way indicate their duration or membership. Immigrant associations, in my experience, have a half-life of about three years at best. Usually resulting from financial difficulties or internal schisms, associations frequently disband only to be re-established several years later under different guises.

19 C. Guéant, 'Des responsables extrémistes cherchent à utiliser certains jeunes délinquants', *Le Monde*, 12 September 1995, p. 11.

20 D. Pujadas and A. Salam, *La tentation du Jihad*, Paris, J.C. Lattès, 1995, pp. 107–37.

21 See R. Boudjedra, *FIS de la haine*, Paris, Denoël, 1992.

22 See *Libération*, 29 June 1995, p. x; *Le Figaro*, 16 August 1995, p. 7.

23 T. Asad, *Genealogies of Religion: Discpline and Reasons of Power in Christianity and Islam*, Boston, Johns Hopkins University Press, 1993, p. 272.

24 Ibid., p. 266.

25 The historical relationship of sports discipline to French discourses of national moral strength has been well studied. See P. Arnaud and G. Andrieu, *Les Athlètes de la République: gymnastique, sport et idéologie républicaine, 1870–1914*, Toulouse, Editions Privat, 1987; P. Chambat, 'Les fêtes de la discipline gymnastique et politique en France (1879–1914)', in P. Arnaud and J. Coupy (eds), *La naissance du Mouvement Sportif Associatif en France*, Lyon, Presses Universitaires du Lyon, 1986, pp. 85–96.

26 Castro would later be one of the prime celebrants of the victorious World Cup soccer team as the symbol of a new 'World France' (*la France Mondiale*) and a new 'hybrid Republic' (*une République métisse*). R. Castro, 'Allez la France Mondiale!', *Libération*, 10 July 1998.

27 Z. Daoud, 'Brève histoire de la politique de la ville', *Panoramiques*, vol. 2, no. 12, 1993, p. 141; F. Sakhoui, 'L'insertion par le sport des jeunes d'origine maghrébine des banlieues en difficulté', *Migrations Société*, vol. 8, no. 45, 1996, pp. 82–3.

28 F. Sakhoui, 'L'insertion par le sport des jeunes d'origine maghrébine des banlieues en difficulté', *Migrations Société*, vol. 8, no. 45, 1996, p. 81.

29 See E. Dunning and C. Rojek (eds), *Sport and Leisure in the Civilizing Process*, Toronto, University of Toronto Press, 1992; J. Hargreaves, 'Sex, Gender and the Body in Sport and Leisure: Has There Been a Civilizing Process?', in E. Dunning and C. Rojek (eds), *Sport and Leisure in the Civilizing Process*, Toronto, University of Toronto Press, 1992, pp. 161–82; J. Hoberman, *Sport and Political Ideology*, Austin, University of Texas Press, 1984; J. MacClancy (ed.), *Sport, Identity and Ethnicity*, London, Berg, 1996.

30 See F. Sakhoui, 'L'insertion par le sport des jeunes d'origine maghrébine des banlieues en difficulté', *Migrations Société*, vol. 8, no. 45, 1996, pp. 92–5.

31 For a discussion of the differences between street sports and club sports and the flexible usage of the housing project terrains, see P. Chantelat, M. Fodimbi and J. Camy, *Sports de la cité. Anthropologie de la jeunesse sportive*, Paris, Harmattan, 1996.

32 Ibid.

33 Pantin has historically been part of the *banlieue rouge*, the primary constituency of the French Communist Party (PCF). This continued link of the PCF to the Parisian northern suburbs is today symbolised by its holding of its annual 'Humanity Festival' (*Fête de l'Humanité*) in the five square-mile park at La Courneuve.

34 The municipality charged 400 francs (approximately 80 USD) for the year and only required a doctor's certification of fitness. Membership in a private club with similar facilities in the Paris area generally cost 400 francs *per month*, and required purchase of an insurance policy at the price of 1000 francs (200 USD) per annum.

35 Pascal Duret has examined how older residents (known colloquially as 'big brothers' (*grands frères*) have utilised participation in sports clubs to foster a sense of community spirit (often glossed in the language of kinship) and local citizenship amongst younger *banlieue* youth. Such a process of appropriation can engender spatially-based rivalries and conflicts of the sort illustrated in the Pantin weight room. In the Parisian *banlieue* of Mantes-la-Jolie, for instance, occasional conflicts have arisen between young residents of the neighbouring Val-Fourré and La Noé housing projects over the use of the former's skating rink. See P. Duret, *Anthropologie de la fraternité dans les cités*, Paris, Presses Universitaires de France, 1996, pp. 149–73.

36 *Banlieue* youth generally employ race and ethnicity primarily as symbolic markers. Informal groups and organised teams will often adopt ethnonyms that derive from historical associations, but which bear little relation to the actual composition of the group in question. Françoise Gaspard (personal communication) has described contentious relations in Dreux between residents of neighbouring public housing towers known colloquially as 'Moroccans' and 'Harkis' (Algerian Muslims in the employ of the French during the Algerian War), names that supposedly corresponded to the buildings' original, but not their current, residents. For a discussion of the ethnic dimension (or lack thereof) of Lyonnais street soccer and basketball teams, see P. Chantelat, M. Fodimbi and J. Camy, *Sports de la cité. Anthropologie de la jeunesse sportive*, Paris, Harmattan, 1996, pp. 51–2.

37 An amusing portrayal of this appropriation of sports by religious groups occurs in Mahmoud Zemmouri's 1998 film *100% Arabica*, when a Muslim association in France decides to reconfigure itself as a martial arts club in order to counter the attraction of raï music on the younger residents of the largely immigrant urban quarter.

38 Séverine Labat, interview in *Le Monde*, 13 October 1995.

39 See S. Labat, *Les islamistes algériens: entre les urnes et le maquis*, Paris, Seuil, 1995; W. Quandt, *Between Ballots and Bullets: Algeria's Transition from Authoritarianism*, Washington, Brookings Institute Press, 1998; M. Willis, *The Islamist Challenge in Algeria*, Berkshire, Ithaca Press, 1996.

40 Citizenship laws in Algeria required the disavowal of Islam as a prerequisite for the granting of full citizenship rights, something that the vast majority of Algeria's indigenous population was loathe to do. As a result, Muslim populations, as colonial subjects (*sujets*), were under a different political and legal system from Algeria's Christian and Jewish inhabitants. For questions of spatial apartheid in colonial North African cities, see

J. Abu-Lughod, *Rabat: Urban Apartheid in Morocco*, Princeton, Princeton University Press, 1980; Z. Çelik, *Urban Forms and Colonial Confrontations: Algiers Under French Rule*, Berkeley, University of California Press, 1997.

41 For a complete history of the JSK, see the JSK fan club website, *Fan de JSK*, retrieved 27 September 2001 from the World Wide Web http://www.multimania.com/fandejsk. See particularly the introductory article, M. Haouchine, 'Voici la JSK', *Fan de JSK*, retrieved 27 September 2001 from the World Wide Web http://www.multimania.com/fandejsk /voicilajsk.htm.

42 This entailed the repeated marginalisation (if not physical elimination) of Berberophone leaders and intellectuals who identified too closely with their native region. For a further discussion of the place of Berber culture in the national movement, see S. Chaker, *Imazighen ass-a (Berbères dans le Maghreb contemporain)*, Algiers, Editions Bouchene, 1990; P. Silverstein, 'Franco-Algerian war and remembrance: discourse, nationalism, and post-coloniality', in K. Salhi (ed.), *Francophone Studies: Discourse and Identity*, Exeter, Elm Bank Publications, 2000.

43 The change to JET was part of a general reform of allying independent sports clubs to the nationalised industries locally present. Other teams were similarly tied to the petroleum (Algiers – Sonatrach) and machinery (Belcourt – Sonacome). After denationalisation, the team name was changed again, this time to JST, 'Jeunesse Sportive de Tizi-Ouzou'/'Jam'iyya Sari' Tizi-Ouzou'. Finally, the original JSK name, as well as the original names of other local teams, has been restored.

44 J. Garçon, 'Un procès embarassant pour le pouvoir algérien', *Libération*, 13 December 2000.

4 'We are red, white and blue, we are Catholic, why aren't you?'
Religion and soccer subculture symbolism[1]

John Hughson

The Bad Blue Boys (BBB), a group of young Australian-born men of Croatian parentage, use soccer support as a means of displaying nationalistic allegiance to their ancestral homeland, though the performance of ethnicity occurs across a range of different cultural, social and religious sites. This display and expression of Croatianness is indicative of a unique collective social identity constructed by the young men within the BBB subculture, which is promulgated in their reverence for, and devotion to, soccer. This chapter examines a particular aspect of that subcultural expression – religion – and explores how the BBB incorporate their 'devotion' to Roman Catholicism into football support. Whilst religious commitment is not strictly central to soccer fandom, the role of the Roman Catholic Church in providing a means by which the BBB can distinguish themselves from their athletic rivals is important. At the same time, religious spaces, as well as sporting locales, are critical learning sites where Croatian ethnicity is rehearsed, performed and, in the case of the BBB, aggressively communicated to rival fans typically from differing ethnic backgrounds. Theoretically, the chapter draws on the French sociologist Michel Maffesoli's idea of the neo-tribe, in order to explain the BBB in terms of a postmodern grouping, exhibiting an affectual commitment to subcultural life.[2] As such their approach to religion cannot be considered in traditional terms, and, indeed, it can be seen that their particular expression of religion is indicative of the happy confusion between the sacred and profane that typifies postmodern life.

Soccer, ethnicity and community in Australia

To followers of soccer in Britain the association of the colours red, white and blue with Roman Catholicism will no doubt seem strange. In relation to the major site of the religious rivalry in British soccer, red, white and blue are the combination of colours seen on the strip of the Protestant Glasgow Rangers, and Roman Catholicism remains very closely associated with the green and white of Glasgow Celtic. For the BBB, however, there is no contradiction, as their team, Sydney United, carry the colours of their parental homeland and the national religion of Croatia is Roman Catholicism. Within Australia, the relationship between soccer clubs and religious denominations has not been particularly apparent, yet that is not to say that there have been few links. By contrast, particularly since World War II, there have been visible links between ethnicity and soccer clubs. Contrary to the typical model of sports organisation in Australia, which favours spatial relationships between a club and its suburb, for example, soccer clubs have often been organised and maintained by ethnic communities as a way of preserving their national traditions, including language, religion, customs and habits. Sydney Croatia was founded in 1958 and quickly became a means by which new Croatian immigrants could ease themselves into Australian life, without abandoning their cultural heritage. The club was renamed Sydney United in the early 1990s following an edict by the Australian Soccer Federation (ASF), banning the allegiance by name of soccer teams in the national league to ethnic communities.[3]

The ASF ruling struck at the heart of soccer support for many of those from non-English-speaking ethnic backgrounds. Since the post-war years the history of Australian soccer has traced the history of immigration.[4] Ethnic communities, particularly those from Southern Europe, developed soccer clubs and teams that soon became prominent at the premier level of the sport. Their success on the field was accompanied by a growth in organisational power and the respective clubs gained a strong voice in how soccer was administered. This situation was not without rancour as the traditional Anglo-Australian elements within the sport wrestled to maintain organisational control. A constant key site of contestation, as indicated, was the on-field representation of ethnicity in the very names of teams such as Sydney Croatia, Pan Hellenic, Preston Macedonia and Sydney Hakoah. Over the years the opponents of this relationship advanced a number of initiatives to sever the explicit linkages between ethnicity and soccer. This culminated in the Bradley Report, which was tabled with the ASF in 1990.[5] Compiled by an academic in accounting, the report was commissioned by the ASF to investigate a viable commercial and organisational future for premier-level soccer. One of its major findings was that soccer needed to relinquish its association with ethnic communities and establish other types of support bases, determined principally on geographical locations, such as districts and cities. The Bradley Report gave the opponents of ethnic affiliation an economic imprimatur – soccer needed to establish alternative support arrangements if it was to compete commercially with the dominant football codes in other states, namely rugby league and Australian rules. Whilst the report was never properly implemented by the ASF, it certainly provided the air of legitimacy needed for the 1993 decision to remove 'ethnic' team names from the premier league.

To say that this was a slap in the face to the tradition established by particular ethnic communities in the post-war years would be an understatement, particularly as soccer clubs fulfilled functions beyond simply providing recreational opportunities. They were central to the community and acted as support networks for a number of ethnic groups. Indeed, the centrality of soccer to the Australian migrant experience was recognised in the exemplary work of the Australian sociologist Jean Martin and in other related studies.[6] For example, Rachel Unikoski claims that 'outside the sphere of economic development ... [soccer] is probably the largest single contribution by migrants to Australian life'.[7] Of course, soccer clubs were one amongst a number of avenues through which community or ethnic identity was cultivated, that also included social and religious organisations.

The relationship between soccer, religion and ethnic communities may be explored utilising Australian sociological analyses of community. Whilst most of this work, with the notable exclusion of Martin, does not address soccer *per se*, it does provide a means for explaining the significance of the sport within the overall ethnic community realm. For the most part, the sociology of community studies within Australia has followed a Weberian interpretation of community as being based in shared non-coercive experience. In effect, this shifts an emphasis from the notion of community, as traditionally understood in fairly restrictive terms, to the concept of the communion or the communal. Accordingly, Ronald Wild offers the following terminological distinction: a community is a 'social order developed on the basis of natural interdependence through traditional relationships';[8] a communion is based on shared concerns, feelings or sentiment. Communities are given – they simply exist, whereas the communion is experienced. Wild argues that people might remain unaware of belonging to a community but that they have a 'conscious recognition' of belonging to a communion.[9] As suggested, this typology offers an interesting means for reflecting on the nature and workings of ethnic communities and groups in Australia. What emerges when we look at the relationship of a group such as the BBB to their parent culture is a complicated picture, one that embraces dimensions of both community and communion.

Important to this picture is the pattern of institutional networking, which draws together the members of an ethnic émigré community in the Australian metropolis. Again, Martin is instructive.[10] In her study of Adelaide residents, she observes three distinct patterns, variously described as community-type networks, clustered networks and loose-knit networks. The community-type network, as recognised by Gillian Bottomley in her subsequent study of Greek Australians, holds particular appeal for immigrant groups as it offers 'positive reinforcement ... and self-respect based on familiar cultural understandings'.[11] The person living within a community-type network will experience a series of institutional connections with other community members through attendance of the church, the soccer match, the social club and the family gathering. Informal networks of association tend to connect formal institutions resulting in an 'interwoven web of relationships'.[12]

The network model of community contact provides a useful means for considering the social interaction of the various communal groupings and the individuals within them that make up the Croatian community within and across Australian cities. The community-type network is likely to have relevance to a large majority of people with a Croatian background – indeed, all those who maintain some sense of attachment to the 'Croatian community'. Some members will live within rather tight confines of the community-type network, experiencing only passing contact with Australians from a non-Croatian background. Their non-Croatian cultural experiences will occur mainly through mediated means, principally via television. Other Croatian Australians who have achieved social mobility through education and work are less closely encapsulated within the community-type network and, indeed, experience more of a 'loose-knit' association with the Croatian community. The term 'symbolic ethnicity' as used by the American sociologist Herbert Gans helps to explain the lived relationship of Croatianness exhibited by Australian Croatians who maintain a loose-knit association with their ethnic community.[13] Gans had in mind upwardly mobile young people who dip into their ethnic background at will and who associate with their ethnic community on occasions of their own choice. Although helpful, this interpretation does not entirely explain the situation of a loose-knit affiliation to the Croatian community in Australia. Even for the loose-knit affiliate, certain cultural customs are likely to be more demanding than Gan's understanding of 'symbolic ethnicity' would allow. Regular attendance at the Croatian Roman Catholic Church, for example, is likely to be a feature of not just the community-type network but also the loose-knit network. Accordingly, the loose-knit affiliate is likely to find him/herself in regular contact with community-type affiliates through at least one institutional avenue. Engagement with the Croatian community is an everyday affair for the community-type network affiliate. Being a Croatian in Australia comes into every facet of their social activity and, therefore, in Gansian terms they live out a 'practised culture'. I subsequently consider the BBB in relation to these terms and see how they fluctuate between engagements with 'symbolic ethnicity' and 'practised culture', and how their expression of religion bridges these modes of cultural engagement.

Central places: the church and the soccer club in the Croatian community network

The institutional relationship between religion and soccer provides a stark, even tangible, example of the connection between the sacred and profane. The differences between the two are, to an extent, blurred in the lived reality of social relations within the Croatian community network, both being central places of common 'worship', albeit to different gods. The overriding similarity is that both serve as key gathering points for Croatian people and as institutional sites that allow the proud public display of a collective social identity based on ethnic partisanship. Although followers of the Roman

Catholic faith, Australian Croatians have financed the building of churches for their own community, and the apparently exclusive attendance at these particular edifices by Croatian people reinforces a significance that goes beyond religion alone. This again denotes similarity between the church and the soccer stadium, as the stadia built by Croatian people in the suburbs of Australian cities have been clearly used as a means of association and identity expression that exceeds an interest in sport. This is not to suggest that there is an explicit organisational link between the two institutions and their physical structures. Each stands in its own right and the connection is largely symbolic in the manner described. It should also be noted that the BBB and other parochial Croatian soccer fans invoke religion into soccer support. I would not suggest that this invocation is reciprocated by Croatian churchgoers with disinterest or a less passionate interest in soccer.

Given the particular émigré experience of Croatians in Australia it is not surprising that, as a people, they put great value on pride of place. By this, I mean physical spaces that they are able to claim as their own. This extends from a high degree of home ownership amongst Croatians in Australia to the collective ownership of community sites such as the church and soccer and social clubs. More than many other immigrant groups Croatians have felt a sense of displacement and dislocation, being unable to claim a 'legitimate' sense of home until the independence of Croatia was established in 1991. Accordingly, key institutional sites within Australia, such as the church, have served as a collective proxy for the homeland. This special role of the church has assisted with the strong continuing allegiance afforded to the Roman Catholic faith across generations of Croatian Australians. As Mato Tkalcevic notes, the enduring strength of the church within the Croatian community has contributed to the preservation of 'bonds which might otherwise dissolve'.[14] Primarily, he has in mind the way in which the church is able to establish a sense of moral authority that allows for the reproduction of some traditional ways of Croatian life. This pertains particularly to the family, which is organised according to a patriarchal hierarchy known as the *Zadruga*. Although some features of the domestic relations within the *Zadruga* have become redundant in contemporary Australia, it is still customary within Croatian households for the male to be regarded as the family head. The strictest sanction that is likely to arise from this situation is a demand on the progeny to marry within the Croatian community. To the extent that this occurs, a sense of Croatian kinship within Australia is fostered and the community-type network is strengthened. The church itself is used as a point of introduction for young Croatian people of opposite sexes and therefore plays a direct role in the continuity of endogamy within the Croatian community in Australia. The major Croatian Roman Catholic churches are located within metropolitan areas with the largest populations of Croatian Australians. Prominently, churches are found in the outer-western Sydney suburbs of Blacktown and St Johns Park and the Melbourne outer-western suburb of Sunshine.

Within the Croatian community network the quotidian takes an institutional place of importance alongside the sacred. Accordingly, the major soccer grounds and social clubs are found in close proximity to the Croatian churches in the outer western suburbs of both Sydney and Melbourne. Next to the church service the soccer match offers the most frequent occasion on the social calendar for the collective gathering of Croatian people. It also provides the opportunity for the largest gathering and is capable of drawing together Croatians from different parts of the respective cities. A home match at Sydney United's Edensor Park ground is something of a national fete day, as various items of Croatian popular culture – cassettes, t-shirts, magazines – are sold along the walkway to the entrance, prior to the match. On occasion, dance troops and singers will perform items of Croatian folk culture before the match and during the half-time break. Following the match supporters will adjourn to the King Tomislav social club, which sits adjacent to the football ground. The club is open to people of all ages and both sexes and serves as an extension of the Croatian social experience offered by the soccer match. This experience is usefully described by the term 'topophilia', love of place. This term has been imported into sport scholarship by the cultural geographer John Bale to capture the sensual experience of sports fans and participants associated with sporting sites such as football grounds. *Inter alia*, Bale suggests that 'topophilia may involve ... "fondness of place because it is familiar, because it is home and incarnates the past, because it evokes pride in ownership or of creation"'.[15] This characterisation precisely describes the sense of place felt by many Croatian Australians during their home ground soccer supporting experience.

The BBB, home and away

The converse of 'topophilia' is 'topophobia' – fear of place. There is evidence to suggest that such a fear resides in rival fans and non-Croatian visitors to grounds such as Edensor Park. In a more innocuous sense some writers of letters to the pages of soccer journals have expressed a sense of alienation upon visiting the home grounds of Croatian community-sponsored premier league teams. The tenor of the complaint by these assumedly Anglo-Australians is that they are made to feel like 'strangers in their own country'. Perhaps these people do experience at least a dislike of place from their visit to Edensor Park, but this would appear ascribable to their own ethnocentrism and a concomitant inability to come to terms with lived collective expressions of multiculturalism.[16] More convincing are the complaints from rival fans claiming to have been verbally, even physically, harassed by volatile elements within the Sydney United crowd. Such complaints have been directly slated to the BBB and have resulted in pleas to the ASF to ban the group from premier league stadia.[17] For their part the BBB unashamedly admit to adopting a hooligan presence within the soccer stadium, albeit one steeped in macho bravado rather than serious physical menace. However, the group would take delight in knowing that they were responsible for the intimidation of rival supporters on their home patch.

The BBB see themselves located within a proud tradition of parochial support for Croatian community-associated teams within Australian soccer. As with most mythology, there is some truth behind the mist. There has certainly been a history of crowd disorder at Australian soccer matches involving Croatian-supported teams. This history has been studied by Philip Mosely who reports that between 1968 and 1978 there were sixteen newsworthy episodes of crowd violence at matches involving the former Sydney Croatia.[18] BBB members are aware of this history, having received it by way of oral tradition rather than documentary reportage. A number of BBB members boast of knowing a male relation who participated in one or another of the battles from 'the old days'. Whatever the accuracy of stories from the past and the credibility of BBB claims of lineage to the violent tradition, there is a decisive generational distinction between the modes of soccer support exhibited by the young men of the BBB in the 1990s and their 'uncles' in the 1960s and 1970s. The BBB has emerged since the phenomenon of football hooliganism gained prominence in Britain and Europe in the 1970s, and they have come into existence as a self-proclaimed and self-styled hooligan group, borrowing their name from the identically named BBB of Dinamo Zagreb. As such they represent a distinct subcultural formation similar to other male subcultural groupings studied by ethnographers associated with the former Centre for Contemporary Cultural Studies at the University of Birmingham.[19] There is no evidence of the previous generation of parochial Croatian soccer supporters in Australia being a subculture in such defined terms. Rather it would seem that groups of young men became involved in clashes with rival fans, often Serbians, on a given afternoon at the soccer. In contrast, the BBB talk more about violence than they engage in it. Accentuated aggression (rather than violence) tends to be part of the stylistic ensemble of the subculture and it is mixed with a number of other codes and symbols of hyper-masculinity. The group performs its masculinity during the soccer-supporting occasion via the verbal expression of bigoted broadsides steeped in homophobia, sexism, racism and ethno-centrism, as well as religious intolerance.

The chant serving as the title for this paper is part of an imprecatory repertoire that is voiced by the BBB at both home and away matches. The chants are directed at rival supporters and primarily at gatherings of young male supporters who provide a tangible and direct opposition for the BBB on match days. Many of the chants contain obscenities and are highly unoriginal, having been used on British soccer terraces over the years. For example, when entering a stadium for an away match the BBB will launch into their version of an old chestnut by declaring, 'Jingle bells, jingle bells, Bad Blue Boys are here, here to shag your women and here to drink your beer'. More original are the chants related to their cultural background, including: 'We are red, white and blue, we are Catholic, why aren't you?' As with other culturally related chants this imprecation is pitched at an imagined other, specifically the enemy Serbian. However, a related frustration is that the premier league does not offer young Croatians the opportunity to physically confront rivals of Serbian background. This opportunity ended in the 1980s with the establishment of a premier league that included Sydney Croatia but not the Serbian community-sponsored team Avala, which remained in the New South Wales state competition. It is likely that soccer officialdom used this bifurcation of the professional soccer competition to separate these two clubs, as their matches had resulted in some of the crowd disorder discussed above. Consequently, the BBB use the rival fans available to them as a proxy for venting against the absent Serbians. Particular targets are the young male supporters of Sydney Olympic, a soccer club supported by Sydney's Greek community. The BBB perceive a cultural and political affiliation between nationals of Greece and Serbia and on this basis have conjured a hostility, which is reciprocated by the opponent. A particular point of affinity between the Serbians and the Greeks as perceived by the BBB is religion; both are associated with the Orthodox Church of Eastern Europe. Religion thus provides a clear binary distinction from the enemy and can be used in the soccer-supporting context as a key mode of abuse of the proxy enemy.

Within the BBB collective mindset, religion is irrevocably linked to politics. Again a binary opposition to the politics of the enemy is at work. BBB members associate Serbians with communism and they completely reject the politics of the left even in social democratic guise. Indeed, they go to the other extreme, expressing sympathy for far-right politics. Most members exhibit a keen interest in a version of modern Croatian history that is passed down by word of mouth from the males of the parent generation. Although the narratives in question, and the manner in which they are subsumed into the subcultural ideology, appear as folklore to an objective outsider, they are digested as hard fact by the BBB member. Historical veracity is ultimately of marginal importance to the purchase of narratives as a justification for interpretations of the lived contemporary reality. As James Fentress and Chris Wickham point out, the 'power' of the narrative is in the ability to 'legitimise the present'.[20] The historical narratives of the parent generation have provided the BBB with a useful means of interpreting the world and how they should fit into it. They believe that the Croatians are an oppressed people who have engaged in a justifiable struggle for independence against aggressive powers over hundreds of years. From such an understanding BBB members are unashamedly respectful of the Nazi collaborator Ante Pavelic, who is regarded as a 'freedom fighter' rather than a war criminal. The fascination with Pavelic extends into soccer support and the associated stylistic display. A number of members wear t-shirts emblazoned with transfers of Pavelic's stern countenance, others with emblems they associate with right-wing youth groups in Croatia from the present and the past.

The inconsistencies in the connection between politics and religion made by the BBB become apparent in their related positions on international and domestic matters. A notable example is their support for the IRA and the general issue of Irish nationalism. Support for the IRA is based on religious affinity shared by the Irish and the Croats for Roman Catholicism. However, the BBB completely ignore the political ideological dimension of Irish nationalism, particularly the general anti-Tory sentiments of the movement, let alone the IRA. In a converse example, the BBB express preference for the conservative Australian Liberal Party over the Australian Labor Party (ALP). They regard the ALP as a socialist party and blame it for the victimisation of the Croatian community during the period of the Whitlam Government between 1972–5, an era when the suspected terrorist activities and guerrilla-training by some Croatian men resident in Australia were being investigated.[21] Yet, in their readiness to condemn the ALP, the BBB over-look the entrenched relationship between that political party and the Roman Catholic Church in Australia and the traditional Protestantism of the Liberal Party.

As indicated, the interest in fascist iconography takes a prominent place in the BBB soccer-supporting ensemble. This interest and the resultant public image accord with a familiar collective hooligan persona, but one reminiscent of a bygone era of urine-drenched terraces in Britain rather than the glitzy steel and plastic stadia of today. The fascist symbolism of the BBB evokes an old-style British brand of hooliganism with National Front connections and calling cards in the back pocket. The symbolic likeness is not lost on the BBB, and although many are quite fashion-conscious young men, they resist the post-1980s 'casual' tendency in football hooligan support to opt for designer sportswear on match day rather than any trace of team colours. As one member put it, 'without our colours, we don't stand for anything'. As already indicated, the BBB are more prone to aggressive displays of masculinity than they are to actual fighting, and this distin-guishes them from football hooligan subcultures that maintain fighting with like-minded rivals as a core activity. However, if applying a broad defi-nition of violence to include extreme verbal insult, then the behaviour of the BBB on any given match day is undeniably violent. The repertoire of chants is designed to offend and is loaded with racist, misogynistic and homo-phobic taunts. Symbolic allusion to fascism appears most notably by way of a Nazi-type salute which follows chants voiced in Croatian.

This type of behaviour has, understandably, upset many people, not only those to whom it is directed, but even other Croatian people who do not want their community represented in this way. The behaviour has been particularly criticised by other Croatian cohorts of similar age, those who are socially mobile and resent the Croatian community being depicted as violent hooligans. To young urban professional Croatians, the BBB merely perpet-uate an image of Croatians in Australia as thugs and terrorists, an image from which they are keen to distance themselves. The BBB are not unaware of this complaint; however, it is one they reject. Indeed, they express some resentment towards young professional and 'university types' within the Australian Croatian community, who they believe have sold out on the 'peasant tradition'. The tradition as the BBB want to live it involves a simplistic evocation and combination of history, politics, religion and kinship, a tradition they continue to associate with their parent generation. To some extent this involves a 'magical recovery of community' in the manner discussed by the Birmingham researchers Phil Cohen and John Clarke in relation to working-class youth resident in London East End housing estates in the late 1960s and early 1970s.[22] A related irony for the BBB is that their parents are inclined to give strong moral and material support to their progeny attaining tertiary educational qualifications and thus moving beyond the 'peasant tradition' that the BBB so revere. Ultimately, the BBB appear to be engaged in a quest for a lost tradition, and their collective social persona might be viewed with sadness from this perspective. However, it is preferable from a position within contemporary social science to suspend judgement and to view the BBB as a group of collective social actors who construct a meaningful and relevant identity from the cultural resources they have available to them. To this end, the concluding part of the paper considers the BBB with reference to the theoretical work of Michel Maffesoli on neo-tribes and re-interprets the social and cultural significance of religion within the neo-tribal context of the BBB.

The BBB meet Maffesoli: enter the neo-tribe

Maffesoli uses the term neo-tribe to explain certain forms of communal gatherings in contemporary society.[23] One of his ambitions is to move beyond the traditional understanding of community within sociology with the tendency to focus on the rational nature of communities. Like other theorists of postmodernity, such as Zygmunt Bauman, Maffesoli introduces Georg Simmel's notion of sociality to describe contemporary social relations.[24] This is to emphasise the expressive rather than the rational quality of collective decision-making and choice. Maffesoli's brief is neatly captured in the summation offered by Kevin Hetherington:

> the important thing to recognise is that this concept of a neo-tribe, and the groupings and identifications it is used to describe, is associated not with rationality and its modes of identification and organisation but with sentiment, feeling and shared experience – with affectual forms of sociation.[25]

This emphasis on sentiment and feelings is not to suggest that the neo-tribe is a rabble, and Maffesoli would not accept Gustave Le Bon's position on the irrational and therefore chaotic nature of the crowd. Maffesoli would

question the very relevance of looking for rationality within social gatherings. His position is largely derived from a debate with the ghost of Weber.
Whilst jettisoning the rationalist precepts of Max Weber's social theory,
Maffesoli sees Weber's idea of the 'emotional community' as inspirational to
his own thoughts on the neo-tribe. Unlike Weber, however, Maffesoli is
unequivocal in his endorsement of the neo-tribe as an emotional community that *exists in its own right*. Although 'ill-defined in nature', 'changeable
in composition' and 'lacking in organisation', the neo-tribe represents a
form of association derived from free choice and based on affectual commitment and instinct.[26] Maffesoli envisions a range of social gatherings as
neo-tribes, from anti-nuclear protesters to clubbers; however, the neo-tribal
category is not exclusive to the young – some neo-tribes may embrace
people across age groups whilst other neo-tribes may be formed by people
within age cohorts beyond their twenties. Similarly, the neo-tribe cannot be
confined as a terminology to describe political groupings with particular
ideological leanings or missions; however, neo-tribes tend to be political in
one way or another. As Hetherington observes, neo-tribes evince a 'troubled
politics of identity in which people try to renegotiate their identities'.[27]
This may involve neo-tribal affiliates engaging in a 'cut-n-mix' of cultural
symbols drawn from the cornucopia of their life experience. Whilst
Maffesoli has tended to play down the importance of traditional sociological
structural dimensions such as class, ethnicity, gender and religion to the
formation of neo-tribes, it is possible to see such dimensions having a
bearing on the choices made by collective groups in their neo-tribal or
subcultural activities and representations.

The very basis of the BBB's existence is to be found in social structural
factors with ethnicity overarching gender, class and religion. The BBB are
brought together by their Croatianness, which is at once reminiscent of the
coercive aspects of community and of the affectual and free-choice aspects of
the neo-tribe. The BBB constantly exhibit the pressure that comes to bear
from the parent culture, the need to marry a Croatian bride, the duty to
family relatives and the obligation to attend church. But rather than rebel
against these potentially coercive aspects of community the BBB incorporate
them into their neo-tribal culture. They do this by amplifying the obliga-
tory aspects of their ethnic background so that endogamy, family loyalty and
religiosity become collective character traits that distinguish the BBB from
other Australian age cohorts. Each of these traits is performed via a hyper-
masculinity – liaisons with non-Croatian women are regarded as sexual
conquests, female family members are to be protected from would-be suitors
of non-Croatian background, and religion is used as a means of vilification
in public settings such as the soccer stadium.[28] The BBB certainly live
according to a 'practised culture' in that they have been strongly socialised
by their parent culture and in most cases their daily routines remain
connected to the Croatian community in some way. Even as far as work is
concerned, a good number of BBB members have blue-collar jobs, particu-

larly in the building industry, and are hired by Croatians who employ mainly other Croatian men. Their collective existence, however, is at once indicative of 'symbolic ethnicity', if not in the yuppyish manner portrayed by Gans. It would be overstating the case to say that they dip into their ethnicity at will, but the BBB certainly engage in a strategic usage of their ethnicity in ways relevant to the subcultural personae they have constructed. A related way of viewing their selective adaptation of ethnic background is with reference to the terms 'strategic essentialism' and 'strategic hybridity'. These terms have been used by Greg Noble and his associates in their study of Lebanese youth in western Sydney to show the strategic manner by which the youth slip between expressions of ethnicity that reinforce tradition on the one hand, and the desire to move beyond it on the other.[29] The particular strategy used will reflect the situation and the desired outcome. Strategic essentialism is more likely to be used in a public context as a means of marking out cultural and ethnic difference and, therefore, staking a claim of distinctive collective identity. Strategic hybridity has particular pertinence in the domestic context as youths attempt to create a space for themselves removed from parental constraint. The freedom obtained if the strategy is successful results in a move back into the public domain – for example, the nightclub – and from here further strategic decision-making occurs.

If the BBB are a neo-tribe, they are at once a 'sensual solidarity', a term used by Phillip Mellor and Chris Shilling to describe social groupings that give the appearance of being traditional but are very much of their time.[30] Sensual solidarities are a response to the preponderance of banal associations in contemporary life; they offer a consumption-oriented rather than a production-oriented form of sociality, and are based on 'feelings, emotions and the effervescence which can derive from *being with* others'.[31] Whilst not promoting technophobia, the sensual solidarity craves physical immediacy and sponsors co-presence and interdependence. The gathering point is most significant, and this connects with Maffesoli's interest in the 'proxemics' or proximity of neo-tribes. On a related note, Hetherington refers to 'social centrality' to emphasise the importance of a particular place as the focal point for the enactment of neo-tribal ritualism.[32] The central place will, of course, differ from one neo-tribe to another, but all central places will be used as performance sites where neo-tribal gatherings express their collective identity either privately to each other or publicly to onlookers. For the BBB, the soccer stadium at Edensor Park is the central place around which neo-tribal life gravitates. For the BBB this is both a private and public place. Private in that it was literally built by the hard toil of Croatian people, and it is a home owned by the community in a collective private sense. Public in that the home is open on match day to visiting soccer teams and their supporters. The confusion between the private and public nature of the home ground further explains the hostility of the BBB to visiting/rival supporters.

Overwhelmingly, the home ground is a sacred place and the playing pitch is the most sacred preserve within the arena. In terminology not unfamiliar to soccer supporters generally, the BBB refer to the pitch as 'sacred turf' and any attempt by rival fans to run onto the playing field at Edensor Park is adjudged akin to desecration. The particular reverence held for the soccer ground by the BBB needs also to be understood with a view to their particular location within the Croatian community. Of the various institutions within the community network, the soccer stadium is the one to which the young men of the BBB can make special claim. They are not scholars at school or in church but they do know about soccer and the soccer stadium provides a place of worship that affords them simultaneous expression of the sacred and the profane. There is no contradiction in this expression as the blurring of the sacred and the profane is the hallmark of sensual solidarities. Even the most profane practices on the soccer terrace may be interpreted as a sense of sacrifice whereby the social actor operates with an extreme momentary 'recognition of other' and a partial 'loss of self'.[33] This is not meant to condone the seemingly anti-social behaviour of the BBB, but rather to understand their practices from a perspective that gives insight into the nature of their collectivity. Their aggressive masculine posturing on the soccer terrace is at once an expression of mutual hyper-sensuality that can only be understood as a ritualistic engagement with both the sacred and the profane. Such is the religious order which is the BBB.

Conclusion

It is important to reiterate that this account of the BBB is in no way intended to cast aspersions on their particular religious practice, nor on that of the Croatian community more generally. In relation to the broader Croatian community, the intention has been to show the way in which religion is an integral marker of identity and difference. In particular, religion was a key means of publicly asserting difference from the rival Serbian community during the long period when both Croats and Serbs were officially recognised in Australia as Yugoslavians – and the Serbs were the politically ascendant ethnic group in Yugoslavia. The BBB offer a hyperbolic version of antagonistic Croatian identity, one that draws on various aspects of symbolic identification taken from the parent culture, including religion, and is mixed with a kaleidoscope of imagery from contemporary youth culture. This wilful hybridity – the blending of the old and new along with the sacred and the profane – is indicative of a postmodern collective identity, hence the discussion of the BBB as a neo-tribe.

Notes

1   The empirical data for the paper is based on my doctoral thesis, J.A. Hughson, *Feel for the Game: An Ethnographic Study of Soccer Support and Social Identity*, unpublished PhD thesis, School of Sociology, University of New South Wales, 1996, which involved an ethno-

graphic study of the BBB. Fieldwork was conducted over a period of two years and covered the 1993/4 and 1994/5 national soccer league seasons. At the time of the study the BBB had an 'official' membership of forty, but on match days against key rivals the number of their rank would swell beyond one hundred in the gathering point behind goal. Since the conclusion of the study the encroachment of soccer officialdom against the ethnic affiliations of premier league teams has intensified, further marginalising supporters of teams such as Sydney United and groups such as the BBB in particular. However, as long as soccer support remains at the core of subcultural life for groups of young men from non-English-speaking ethnic backgrounds, the study of the BBB will hold more than historical relevance.

2 M. Maffesoli, *The Time of the Tribes*, London, Sage, 1996.

3 J. Hughson, 'The Croatian community', in P. Mosley, R. Cashman, J. O'Hara and H. Weatherburn (eds), *Sporting Immigrants: Sport and Ethnicity in Australia*, Sydney, Walla Walla Press, 1997, p. 53.

4 See P. Mosely, *Ethnic Involvement in Australian Soccer: A History 1950–1990*, Canberra, Australian Sports Commission, 1995.

5 J. Hughson, 'Australian soccer: ethnic or Aussie? The search for an image', *Current Affairs Bulletin*, vol. 68, no. 10, 1992, pp. 12–16.

6 J. Martin, *Community and Identity: Refugee Groups in Adelaide*, Canberra, Australian National University Press, 1972.

7 R. Unikoski, *Communal Endeavours: Migrant Organisation in Melbourne*, Canberra, Australian National University Press, 1978, p. 305.

8 R. Wild, *Australian Community Studies and Beyond*, Sydney, Allen & Unwin, 1981, pp. 39–40.

9 Ibid., p. 40.

10 J. Martin, 'Suburbia: community and network', in A.F. Davies and S. Encel (eds), *Australian Society: A Sociological Introduction*, second edition, Melbourne, Cheshire, 1970, pp. 301–39.

11 G. Bottomley, *After the Odyssey: A Study of Greek Australians*, St Lucia, University of Queensland Press, 1979, p. 171.

12 Ibid., p. 176.

13 H. Gans, 'Symbolic ethnicity: the future of ethnic groups and cultures in America', *Ethnic and Racial Studies*, vol. 2, no. 2, 1979, pp. 1–20.

14 M. Tkalcevic, *Croats in Australia*, Canberra, AGPS, 1989, p. 27.

15 J. Bale, *Landscapes of Modern Sport*, Leicester, Leicester University Press, 1994, p. 121.

16 J. Hughson, 'Australian soccer: ethnic or Aussie? The search for an image', *Current Affairs Bulletin*, vol. 68, no. 10, 1992, pp. 12–16.

17 J. Hughson, 'The Bad Blue Boys and the "magical recovery" of John Clarke', in G. Armstrong and R. Giulianotti (eds), *Entering the Field: New Perspectives in World Football*, Oxford, Berg, 1997, p. 250.

18 P. Mosely, 'Balkans politics in Australian soccer', *ASSH Studies in Sports History*, vol. 10, 1994, p. 36.

19 P. Cohen, 'Subcultural conflict and working-class community', in S. Hall, D. Hobson, A. Lowe and P. Willis (eds), *Culture, Media, Language: Working Papers in Cultural Studies, 1972–79*, London, Hutchinson, 1980, pp. 78–87; J. Clarke, 'The skinheads and the magical recovery of community', in S. Hall and T. Jefferson (eds), *Resistance Through Rituals: Youth Subculture in Post-war Britain*, London, Hutchinson, 1976, pp. 99–105.

20 J. Fentress and C. Wickham, *Social Memory*, Oxford, Blackwell, 1992, p. 88.

21 J. Hughson, 'Football, folk dancing and fascism: diversity and difference in multicultural Australia, *Australian and New Zealand Journal of Sociology*, vol. 33, no. 2, 1997, p. 171.

22 J. Hughson, 'The Bad Blue Boys and the "magical recovery" of John Clarke', in G. Armstrong and R. Giulianotti (eds), *Entering the Field: New Perspectives in World Football*, Oxford, Berg, 1997, p. 250.

23 M. Maffesoli, *The Time of the Tribes*, London, Sage, 1996.

24 Z. Bauman, *Intimations of Postmodernity*, London, Routledge, 1992.
25 K. Hetherington, *Expressions of Identity: Space, Performance, Politics*, London, Sage, 1998, p. 52.
26 M. Maffesoli, *The Time of the Tribes*, London, Sage, 1996, p. 12.
27 K. Hetherington, *Expressions of Identity: Space, Performance, Politics*, London, Sage, 1998, p. 53.
28 J. Hughson, 'The boys are back in town: soccer support and the social reproduction of masculinity', *Journal of Sport and Social Issues*, vol. 24, no. 1, 2000, pp. 8–23.
29 G. Noble, S. Poynting and P. Tabar, 'Youth, ethnicity and the negotiation of identities'. Paper presented to the Australian Sociological Association Annual Conference, Hobart, 1996.
30 P.A. Mellor and C. Shilling, *Re-Forming the Body: Religion, Community and Modernity*, London, Sage, 1997, p. 173.
31 Ibid., p. 174.
32 K. Hetherington, *Expressions of Identity: Space, Performance, Politics*, London, Sage, 1998, p. 106.
33 P.A. Mellor and C. Shilling, *Re-Forming the Body: Religion, Community and Modernity*, London, Sage, 1997, p. 175.

5 Women, sport and American Jewish identity in the late nineteenth and early twentieth centuries[1]

Linda J. Borish

Introduction

The *American Hebrew* in January 1915 printed an article titled 'Jews in sport' and commented on Jewish women athletes: 'In any mention of golfers, the name of Miss Elaine Rosenthal of the Ravisloe Country Club [Illinois] should be included. Miss Rosenthal's sensational play on the Nassau links last summer [the site of the USA Women's Amateur Golf Championship] is still a favorite topic in golfing circles, and we expect great things of her next season'. The *American Hebrew* also commented on other Jewish women in sport: 'In the tennis world, too, our women players show great promise. Miss Erna Marcus, paired with Mrs Pouch, won the Long Island doubles championship'.[2] Other sports featured the athletic skills of Jewish American women; from the basketball courts of Young Men's and Young Women's Hebrew Associations to the swimming pools in competitive swim clubs and even national level events, Jewish women have played a part in the sporting culture in American history. The story of Jewish women in American sport remains scarcely explored in women's history, sport history and American Jewish history, yet Jewish American females, as participants and administrators, altered and expanded sporting opportunities for Jewish American women and girls. In some cases, Jewish women even pushed for greater access to sports for women generally, increasing sporting pursuits for Jewish and non-Jewish women and girls alike, whilst maintaining and at times strengthening their Jewish identity. In the late nineteenth and early twentieth centuries, at Jewish settlement houses and at Young Men's/Young Women's Hebrew Associations, middle-class reformers designed programmes to promote Jewish American women's physical health and sport as part of the Americanisation of lower-class female immigrants within Jewish social and religious contexts.

Whether engaging in sports for physical health, competition between Jewish or non-Jewish teams, or representing athletic prowess on national teams, Jewish American women's sporting activities provide a valuable lens through which to investigate the multifaceted place of sports for women in American culture and history as well as offering insight into the ways that gender, ethnicity, religion and social class shape sporting experiences. Jewish organisations in the USA and other countries, formed for various reasons including immigration aid, the promotion of Jewish religiosity, and the preservation of ethnic practices in leisure and foodways, also provided opportunities for women and girls to participate in a range of sports.

Jewish women themselves campaigned for physical culture and sporting activities despite limited autonomy and control of resources at some Jewish settlements and Young Men's and Young Women's Hebrew Associations. Yet most studies on immigration and ethnicity, such as those focusing on Jewish men and sports, corellate with historian Donna Gabaccia's characterisation of gender and immigrant life: 'most histories of immigrants in the United States begin with the experiences of migratory men disguised as genderless human beings'.[3] By probing materials about Jewish immigrant women, however, it becomes evident that some Jewish American women demonstrated extraordinary leadership and shaped women's sports in their local communities, Jewish and mainstream organisations and even the Olympics, influencing sport in the larger American culture and international athletic environments. For Jewish immigrant women in the USA, the tension between maintaining Jewish ethnic and religious practices and becoming oriented to new American traditions emerged in the way some women experienced sporting activities. This historical research expands understandings of intersections of gender, ethnicity, class and religion within sporting contexts. Yet sports historical studies often focus on Jewish men in sport, to explore how Jewish immigrant men, from the 1880s to the 1920s, 'through sport ... could be more American and not any less Jewish', especially in urban areas with large Jewish populations.[4]

Jewish women coming to America encountered new cultural values and practices; however, the preservation of Jewish identity became part of negotiating their places as Jews within the process of adapting to American culture. For Jewish women their life in America encompassed elements of their religion within the context of exposure to sporting practices as they participated in Jewish organisations and associations designed to aid them in the transition to American society. These separate Jewish associations, such as the Young Women's Hebrew Associations and ladies' auxillaries of the Young Men's Hebrew Associations, or Jewish settlements such as the Young Women's Union or Irene Kaufmann Settlement, provided a forum for preserving religiosity for Jewish women and autonomy to create a Jewish environment whilst incorporating physical activities and sport for their physical wellbeing and to gain access to American practices. The Young Women's Hebrew Association, the oldest existing organisation for Jewish women, founded on 6 February 1902 in New York City by Mrs Israel Unterberg, was organised 'for Jewish working girls and students' and when the YWHA's building was dedicated at 1584 Lexington Avenue, 'here classes, clubs, religious services and recreational activities attracted a large number of members'.[5] As the number of Jewish girls at this YWHA increased, so too did the need for greater space and expanded programmes in religion, education and recreation. The new home for the YWHA was dedicated on 22 November 1914 at 31 West 110th Street. The new YWHA encompassed the Jewish identity of the girls as the building 'contained a synagogue', in addition to a 'gymnasium, swimming pool, class and club rooms, dining room, and residence quarters for more than 170 girls'. Over the years this impressive YWHA 'served the spiritual, education, recreational and housing need of Jewish girls in New York City'.[6] Sport, under the auspices of these kinds of organisations, served to enhance and uphold the spiritual and religious identity of women and girls as members of a Jewish team, organisation, or club, yet at the same time offered occasions for them to participate in the growing sporting culture in American society.

Jewish women in America pursued a broad spectrum of sporting activities from physical culture training to competitive endeavours. In various venues, at times affiliating with other Jewish young women in the new American environs, and for some interacting with non-Jewish women in society, Jewish women athletes gained access to American cultural knowledge and activities. Yet these women learned about sport within dedicated Jewish organisations and forged an American Jewish identity. Using diverse primary materials, including archival sources, the American Jewish press and the American press, reports from Jewish associations and material culture evidence yields information about the ways Jewish American women played sport and pursued physical activities. Jewish American women and girls engaged in sport and expressed interests in promoting their physical health, deriving enjoyment from sports participation and participating in competitions with both Jewish and Gentile women. The Jewish organisations for women, emphasising both religion and recreation as part of their mission, provided access to sports such as calisthenics, basketball, swimming, tennis, track and field events and bicycling for Jewish women and girls, revealing the need to look beyond Protestant Anglo-Saxon ideals of sport for white, middle-class women in the early twentieth century. As sports studies scholar Jennifer Hargreaves has written: 'There is a tendency for generalizations to be made about all women in sports from examples of white women', and these stereotypically refer to white, western bourgeois women.[7] Moreover, some American Jewish women at times challenged traditional gender boundaries in sport to secure sporting opportunities for women in American Jewish ethnic institutions, as well as in more mainstream sites in American society in the late nineteenth and early twentieth centuries.

Settlement houses and physical exercise programmes

For Jewish immigrant women, exposure to American life and sporting forms occurred at settlement houses and immigrant aid associations in the latter decades of the nineteenth century. East European immigrants came to

America and populated urban areas such as New York, Boston and Philadelphia. German Jews, who by the 1880s had become wealthier and oriented to American culture and institutions, sought to help the newest Jewish immigrants to adjust to American culture; German Jews opted to promote assimilation rather than nurturing the ethnic identities and religiosity of these Jewish immigrants.[8] For example, reformers wished to solve urban problems of poverty, poor sanitation and overcrowding in urban areas. Some of these women reformers organised playgrounds for immigrant children in cities. Reformer Jane Addams, founder of Hull House in Chicago, and Jewish Americans such as Lillian Wald, founder of Henry Street Settlement in New York City, Lizzie Black Kander, founder of The Settlement in Milwaukee, and Lina F. Hecht, founder of Boston's Hecht House, were alarmed at the vice and danger they perceived in the chaotic city culture and street life of lower-class Eastern European Jewish immigrants. These reformers sought to inculcate immigrant youth into middle-class gender roles and cultural values, and believed women in particular needed physical stamina to fulfill domestic responsibilities.[9] The immigrants wanted to preserve their religious observances and use of Yiddish, maintain kosher laws about food and retain traditional customs of dress for men and women. The German Jews from the earlier decades of migration asserted that these Jewish newcomers needed to become more like them to assimilate to American culture. The institutions founded by the philanthropic and reform-minded German Jews, however, did retain a Jewish context in order to bring the immigrants under their influence.

Those who spearheaded settlement house programmes advocated that Jewish women and girls engage in sporting and recreational pursuits as part of their provisions for the wellbeing of the immigrants. In 1885, Miss Fannie Binswanger and other young philanthropically oriented Jewish women founded the Young Women's Union in Philadelphia, the oldest Jewish settlement in the USA, which served the social needs of Russian Jewish immigrants. The settlement initially opened a kindergarten to assist working mothers and their children. Soon other programmes followed at Philadelphia's Jewish settlement house, including a school for domestic instruction, classes in English and reading, and recreation and sports to give children a chance to escape the congested city.[10] Miss Caroline Massman and Miss Sadie Kohn instructed young Jewish women and girls in calisthenics and gymnastics, and when the new building opened in 1900, 'the gymnasium was used by girls as well as boys' for 'Gymnasium Class'.[11] When the Young Women's Union moved into this larger facility in 1900, the President reported the need to construct a new gymnasium. Reorganised as the 'Neighborhood Centre' in 1918, the director of the agency explained that the Centre's schedule featured added activities in art, dramatics, embroidery, cooking and athletics.[12]

To promote the spiritual and bodily wellbeing of Jewish females, philanthropists who founded the Irene Kaufmann Settlement House in Pittsburgh in 1895 incorporated 'many social, civic, health, recreational and educational activities', thus integrating women's sport and physical education into their offerings. Perceptions persisted in mainstream middle-class Protestant views about immigrants, such as the stereotype that Jewish women came to America with poor health, posture and physical strength. To counter stereotypes about the frail and sickly immigrant with a weak physical constitution, middle-class reformers strove to renovate their physical health and guide the women immigrants in a wholesome Jewish environment. Whilst some historians have explored how stereotypes about Jewish men's bodies persisted, and physical activities for Jewish men existed at some institutions to redress this, historians have overlooked the concerns articulated by reformers about Jewish women's health, and in turn, the strategies implemented to improve their physical wellbeing.[13] At the Irene Kaufmann Settlement (IKS), activities in wholesome physical exercise and athletics were conducted. In the settlement's house organ, *IKS Neighbors*, a writer noted: 'Many of our girls have asked for the use of the gymnasium and their requests have been granted'. Classes were held in 'dancing, gymnasium, and swimming'. In short, for the IKS females, 'Gym and a Swim for Vigor and Vim'.[14]

In Boston, one of the earliest Jewish settlements in the city considered the health and physical welfare of Jewish immigrant females to be of importance in offering services to these newcomers to America. Lina F. Hecht founded the Hebrew Industrial School in 1899; her husband, Jacob, was a philanthropist in Boston. Following her death in 1922, the School changed its name to the Hecht Neighborhood House. For the physical wellbeing of the Jewish youth, Hecht explained that when the Public Evening Schools closed: 'This school is to serve as a recreation house and yard for those who live in the ill-favored streets of the West End'.[15] To promote the physical health of girls, the Hebrew Industrial School in 1900 featured the 'Soap and Water Club', designed to achieve 'personal cleanliness' for the immigrants. In the 'Pledge of the Soap and Water Club', the member promised to keep ten rules of 'health and hygiene', linking both physical and moral wellbeing for Jewish females.[16]

From the early emphasis on physical wellbeing, the Hecht House expanded its physical education and sporting activities for Jewish youth, though Jewish identity remained a concern for women workers at Hecht House. For example, at one meeting, staff 'discussed question of taking children swimming during Jewish Holiday, "Tish a Ba Ov". Decided that Miss Kramer shall ask advice of Mrs Caploe'. If she approved the youngsters swimming, 'Then each child will ask his parent's consent before we take him'.[17] Those Jewish youngsters participating in sport needed to preserve Jewish holiday observance according to their family practices. Sport could be used to bring these Jewish females into the arm of the Hecht House but the Jewish customs would be sustained. In a 1930 report a Hecht house worker stated that in the Junior Mass Activities for boys and girls, activities consisted of baseball, basketball, track meets, camping trips and prize walks.[18]

At settlement houses, sporting activities and vocational training became a means to foster the American Jewish identity of the many young women and girls encountering the dangerous, unsafe and unsanitary city environs in coming to America. Jewish women who served as administrators in settlement houses therefore integrated physical health and wholesome active recreations along with education into their mission to aid young lower-class Jewish females coming to cities. For example, The Settlement in Milwaukee, founded in 1896 by Lizzie Black Kander and a group of thirteen women, was referred to as the Jewish Settlement. When it wished to expand its building in 1900, Mrs Simon Kander, author of the well-known *The Settlement Cook-Book: The Way to a Man's Heart* (1901), a selection of kosher recipes from her cooking classes, used the money from the cookbook sales to pay for larger quarters, to which they relocated in 1911. The Settlement's programme featured 'classes in English and other branches, some in sewing and domestic science, gymnastics, dancing or other kinds of recreation'.[19] The Milwaukee press described the new home: 'The gymnasium is provided with all apparatus necessary and has Instructors, both for boys, girls, young men and women', and the settlement served as the forerunner of the Jewish Center in Milwaukee, which opened in 1931.[20]

The Chicago Hebrew Institute and women's active participation in sport

At other Jewish institutions, women indicated their desire to participate in more vigorous and competitive sporting forms. The Chicago Hebrew Institute (CHI) on the lower West Side of Chicago, organised in 1903 by a group of young men, promoted the moral, physical, religious and civic welfare of Jewish immigrants and residents. The CHI, in its Americanisation of Eastern European immigrants, offered a comprehensive range of classes in citizenship, English, commerce, domestic science, Jewish culture, literature, art, physical culture, drama and music.[21] Jewish philanthropist and businessman Julius Rosenwald helped secure property for the Institute. President Jacob M. Loeb, elected in 1912, and Dr Philip L. Seman, Director of the Institute from 1913 to 1945, guided the expansion and programme development to create a thriving Jewish institution, the forerunner of today's Jewish Community Centers. In 1922, the CHI changed its name to the Jewish People's Institute, and it moved into a new building in Lawndale in 1927.[22] Dr Philip Seman explained: 'The Institute is frankly Jewish and staunchly American'.[23] The Institute's officials wanted to serve the Jewish population as it moved to new areas of Chicago. Still the mission of the institution incorporated preserving the Jewish cultural elements whilst exposing Jewish women and men, girls and boys, to the American activities of sport, physical education and league competitions. This dual agenda of serving the Jewish religion and at the same time teaching Jewish people about American culture became embodied in the sport and physical culture programmes from the early days of the CHI.

The CHI emphasised the importance of physical fitness for males and females. In 1914, in an article in the American Jewish paper *The Sentinel*, titled 'The temple of the body. How the Hebrew Institute is laboring to make Jews physically fit', journalist Bertha A. Loeb drew on the prevailing conception about Jews, sport and physical health in the early twentieth century, asserting: 'The undersized, anaemic "Jewish weakling" will soon be a recollection of by-gone days'.[24] The CHI aimed to ensure that 'one of the first activities to be set into being was a gymnasium for the youth of both sexes'.[25] In the report of the *CHI Observer* in 1913–14, Dr Seman explained the health and social benefits of the Ladies of the English School for Foreigners Gymnasium Class:

> The girls could not quite see what exercise and calisthenics had to do with the study of English, but it did not take very long before they felt a new life entering their tired, wornout bodies. ... We recognized that the girls, who work hard in shops or in factories all day long needed physical instructions to invigorate them.[26]

The history of the new gymnasium and swimming pool at the CHI, which opened in June 1915, reveals debates about gender and the level of resources that should be devoted to women's physical culture, as well as the kinds of sports women should engage in. Initially the physical pursuits of girls and women did not receive much attention in the new building plans. But President Loeb wanted to serve the needs of Jews of both sexes and battled to construct equal athletic facilities for men and women. Loeb and James Davis, the athletic committee chairman at the time of the quest for a new building, believed separate gyms and swimming pools, or 'tanks' as they were called, should be included in the new building. Loeb appealed to Jewish philanthropist Julius Rosenwald who donated $50,000 for the new gymnasium. Loeb wrote to Mr and Mrs Julius Rosenwald in October 1913: 'We can build a gymnasium for $100,000 if we build it for men and boys alone but we cannot build it for $100,000 if we wish to give service to *women, girls and children* (this is for Mrs J.R. to think about)', and Loeb asserted, 'I have repeatedly in the last year in public and through the *Observer* promised the people in the neighborhood that they would have a gymnasium for both girls and boys'. Loeb urged Rosenwald to consider the plans for the larger gymnasium: 'I impress upon you the great need of the gymnasium, especially of the women's and girls' departments. The women and girls who are to avail themselves of the benefits which a gymnasium affords in that particular neighborhood', Loeb explained, 'are of the working class. They can get the very much needed recreation to revive their physical strength for the morrow's hard task in the evening only'. Loeb and the women's committee made their case to secure adequate space for women in the new gymnasium, although Rosenwald turned down the petition to donate the additional funds. Other Jews in the community made donations to support the effort to build strong Jews, women and men, physically and spiritually.[27]

A battle ensued between Loeb and Rosenwald about the funds to be spent for the gymnasium. President Loeb appealed to 'the supreme court in the gymnasium case, namely to the honorable judges Mr and Mrs J.R. [Julius Rosenwald] sitting en Banc'.[28] Indeed, on 1 November 1913, Loeb filed a 'Petition for Rehearing on Behalf of Appellee *Chicago Hebrew Institute Gymnasium Case*' based on the conviction that the conclusions reached by Rosenwald were 'in error'. Loeb presented an 'Assignment of Errors' with four points, some related to gender issues: 'First: The court erred in not rendering an opinion as to the argument relative *gymnasium* for *both* sexes. ... Four: ... we fail to see that the "Better Half" of this Honorable Court either affirmed in or dissented from the decision rendered'.[29] Despite this appeal, in his letter dated 3 November 1913, Rosenwald disclosed that he would not allot any more funding.[30]

Although the lack of this financial support delayed the construction of the CHI's new gymnasium, Loeb raised the needed extra funds, and the CHI offered some of the best athletic facilities for Jewish men and women. In Loeb's address to the CHI on 31 March 1914, he assured members of the benefits of sport facilities accessible to both genders: 'If our boys and girls have shown such wonderful results as I have stated, in antiquated and old gymnasiums what will they be able to do in a building of their own?' Loeb highlighted that the CHI had opted for innovative plans for a gymnasium because 'Our demands were different than any YMCA or social center building in as much as we wished to accommodate all of our people, namely boys and girls, men and women', and to achieve this 'it was necessary to draw plans for practically two gymnasiums'. Two gymnasiums, two swimming tanks, 'one for the men and boys and the other for the women and girls', required more funding, contributed by the Jewish community members.[31]

The opening of the new $125,000 gymnasium in 1915 drew praise, especially for the athletic facilities offered to Jewish women and girls. At the 9 June 1915 dedication for the women's day of the events, Mrs Julius Stone lauded the New Gymnasium Building and expressed thanks to Loeb and his co-workers 'for the consideration they have given to the needs of women and girls. We consider it a gift and a tribute to all womankind'. Superintendent Dr Philip L. Seman proclaimed: 'For the first time in the history of American Jewish social service, an Institution is fitted to meet a great Jewish need by having a gymnasium second to none in the United States'. In the 1915 *CHI Observer*, Seman declared the Gymnasium offered 'equal facilities for men and women'.[32] One journalist even remarked that the gym 'Is Boon for Women. ... In a city where the women have as little athletic opportunity as Chicago this is a great step forward. It is only another instance of the aggressiveness', he stated, that 'has placed the Hebrew Institute where it is on the athletic map'. The reporter observed that because women have their own swimming pool and gymnasium, 'At no time need they be inconvenienced by the activities of the men'.[33] The gymnasium provided girls with a place to develop their basketball ability and competitive spirit. The 1921 team compiled an impressive record: 'The Girls' Basketball Team has played 26 games and has not a single defeat against its name'.[34] The Institute girls won the Central AAU Girls' Basketball Championship, and in their outstanding season: 'The Chicago Hebrew Institute girls made 447 points and their opponents only 116 points'. In 1922, the team again repeated their excellent performance.[35]

At the CHI's natatorium, females obtained proper swimming instruction from Miss Sara Hanssen, a noted Olympian from Denmark. Over 300 girls and young women, aged from 5 to 30 years, swam at the pool, and many learned to swim from instruction by Miss Hanssen. And with the new ladies' swimming tank getting regular use, the *Chicago Herald*, in the article 'Mother, may I go out to swim?' (1916), asserted: 'The Jewish girls make particularly good swimmers', commenting, 'It is a well known fact that women learn to swim quicker than men. There is more flesh and less bone, consequently her body is more buoyant'.[36] Girls at the Hebrew Institute demonstrated their athletic prowess in swimming, practising their strokes in the ladies' swimming tank. In 1921: 'The girls' swimming team has made a very splendid record for itself during the season. The team won the Open City Swimming Championship of Chicago' hailed as the 'biggest of its kind ever held in the city'.[37] In team competitions, too, the Jewish People's Institute compiled an impressive record, beating the YWCA Girls' Team in a dual meet at the Institute's swimming tank in front of over 300 spectators.[38]

Sporting experiences for women at the YWHA

From its beginning, those Jewish women spearheading the YWHA of New York City, the model for other YWHAs, incorporated sport and physical education into the institution's mission and religious context. Mrs Israel Unterberg not only served as president of the New York City YWHA but was also chairman of the Women's Work Committee of the Council of the Young Men's Hebrew Kindred Associations, and provided advice to various Jewish communities about extending the work of the YWHA. Mrs Unterberg explained to women workers how to be successful at YWHAs in carrying out 'suggestions for social and athletic work that I have intimated. ... The distinguishing feature is the religious work and the religious activity that you bring into existence'. In establishing the New York YWHA, Unterberg emphasised that 'the organizers felt the need of establishing some center where Jewish ideas and Jewish ideals will be developed'.[39]

The YWHA implemented its plan to serve Jewish American women in New York City and provided classes in physical education and athletics. President Unterberg reported in the *Annual Report* for 1916 that: 'The Young Women's Hebrew Association is unique. It is the largest if not the only association of its kind that is devoting itself exclusively to the religious, mental and physical life of the Jewish young women of our city.' The YWHA classified its activities in four areas: 'Religious work, gymnasium, social work and educational work'.[40]

The YWHA was an autonomous organisation distinct from the YMHA of New York City and female directors of the YWHA maintained their policy of providing a Jewish environment where Jewish young women and girls could enjoy sport and physical culture activities. In 1908 the YWHA reiterated its purpose: 'We are striving to raise the standard of Jewish Womanhood', and in addition to classes such as dressmaking, stenography, typewriting, Hebrew and Bible they supervised 'a gymnasium with average attendance of twenty-four'.[41] In the 1911 Class Report the chairlady stated that the girls devoted time to 'apparatus work, jumping, and folk dancing, and Thursday evening to basket ball, athletic games and drills'.[42] For upholding their Jewish identity, the YWHA declared that on the 'question of the observance of the Sabbath in the building' staff and teachers 'create just an atmosphere in the association which distinguishes it from any other social or communal activity and which justifies the existence and makes of your work a Young Women's *Hebrew* Association'.[43]

Mrs Bella Unterberg reminded her fellow YWHA workers: 'it is the finest thing a Young Women's Society can start with, with the gymnasium and the basket-ball teams for your recreational work'.[44] Indeed, the New York YWHA records reveal the sport and physical culture activities available to Jewish women and girls. The new home featured 'a swimming pool, 20 feet by 60 feet, a gymnasium' and 'a roof garden with tennis courts'. In fact, President Unterberg emphasised the importance of physical culture in describing the new building. She stated, 'We have made ample provision for the physical welfare and the recreation needs of our girls', and detailed the Association's new home:

> The large gymnasium, connecting lockers and the shower baths in the basement, will hold a class of 200, in, say, Swedish floor work. We are planning regular gymnasium classes under competent instructors, and there will be organized sports, activities that were not possible in our former crowded quarters.[45]

One New York newspaper hailed the Association as 'the most comprehensive programme of physical education in the country for Jewish women and girls'.[46] The indoor swimming pool opened in October 1916 and girls enjoyed contests in water sports.[47]

Yet, in most of the YWHAs, autonomy of funding, decision-making, and employment of female staff trained in physical education and sports supervision did not exist, and their history differs from that of the New York City YWHA. During the first decades of the twentieth century, at most YWHAs that were affiliated with YMHAs, women secured only limited access to the use of the gymnasium and they lacked female physical training instructors; as such, these YWHAs, as auxiliaries, typically struggled for funding and athletic spaces. For example, the Louisville YMHA was founded in 1890 and remained mainly a male domain. A picture of the gym class in the 1890s termed it Ladies 'Gym' Class as if this hardly qualified as the type of sport pursued by men.[48] In San Francisco the YMHA was formed in 1877 and held separate quarters for Jewish men. The YWHA organised in 1914, and the women originally lacked access to the YMHAs quarters for gymnasium activities. However, the San Francisco YWHA used various clubrooms and included gym classes, basketball and swimming as well as vocational training for young women. For Jewish women, in 1918 'the YMHA gymnasium was used for their physical activities', with the YWHA's Monday night gym classes taking place at the Haight Street building of the YMHA, which housed a new gymnasium.[49]

Whilst Jewish women wanted to participate in sport and active recreation, limited use of gymnasia and athletic fields hampered their opportunities. In 1921, the National Jewish Welfare Board (JWB) was founded and it became the national governing body for YMHAs and YWHAs, and the National Council of Young Men's Hebrew and Kindred Associations. The JWB actively promoted the merger of YMHAs and YWHAs and sought to develop them into Jewish Community Centers (JCCs) by the middle decades of the twentieth century. A national campaign to improve Jewish community life for Americans of all social classes and religious backgrounds occurred in the first decades of the twentieth century; the call to provide physical recreations in Jewish cultural settings within the larger American culture prompted staff of the JWB to work with numerous local communities that wished to renovate YM/YWHAs or build new JCCs. New York Supreme Court Justice Irving Lehman served as President of the JWB from 1921 until 1940. The JWB mission integrated Jewish life, education, social activities and sports for both sexes in YM/YWHAs, with varying degrees of success.[50]

Most situations explored by the JWB revealed that women wanted physical culture classes and sports, but faced restraints from male personnel who limited women's use of popular athletic facilities. In several cases, the national Field Secretary for Women's Work, Emily Solis-Cohen, recorded hardships faced by Jewish women in the YWHA organisation and programmes. In South Brooklyn, plans to merge the YWHA with the YMHA in November 1923 were presided over by Solis-Cohen as the YWHA voted to reorganise and merge with the YMHA. On 8 January 1924, Solis-Cohen reported: 'The girls also said they had no use of the gymnasium and therefore were not holding their members and had difficulty in collecting their dues'.[51] In fact, Mr Harris, the Executive Secretary of this YMHA, informed the YWHA: 'The gymnasium schedule is full, for evenings, being given to the boys, and Monday evenings to lectures. Consequently, for this season', Harris stated, 'the women cannot have the gymnasium.'[52] Yet, the YWHA members wanted to use the gym. Solis-Cohen asserted in her correspondence that she and Mr Samuel Leaf, a JWB worker, 'would take up the matter of the women's gymnasium' in communicating with Mr Harris.[53] Women confronted the power of gender and the YMHA board's effort to constrain their activities. Solis-Cohen explained: 'It is apparent that there is a feeling among some of the members that the building is a man's building and the association a man's association.'[54]

As some YWHAs procured space for their female members' use, they offered physical training classes and athletics such as gymnastics, swimming, tennis, basketball, volleyball, badminton, track and field, bicycling and bowling. The Hartford YWHA was founded in 1915 by a group of young Jewish women at the city's YMHA rooms. The association grew fairly quickly, and the members wanted to secure a place for YWHA work. The leadership of Miss Marion Scharr, Executive Secretary, enabled the Hartford YWHA to administer a full range of programmes, and the Athletic Department became a success even though the girls lacked 'proper quarters'.[55] The *Connecticut Hebrew Record* commented on the Hartford YWHA, 'There was good and enthusiastic material for several basket ball teams', but not until the Brown School gymnasium 'was procured, and then for but once a week'. Despite this handicap, the YWHA team was good enough to play the YWCA, and the 1920 Hartford YWHA basketball team wore uniforms with 'YW' on the front of their gym shirts to identify their squad. Miss Lee Gersman, athletic director, offered other sports to the Jewish girls, such as swimming, despite the need to go to the YWCA pool, and soccer and tennis.[56]

In fact, athletics expanded with the female autonomy of this association. The Hartford YWHA boasted in 1920 that 'there are two basket ball teams and the girls have picked out the five best players and challenge any team in the State'. These Jewish girls wanted to play and win. Other Connecticut YWHAs preferred 'playing with YWHA organizations', and a game with great significance took place between rival Ys. 'December 14 will establish a new precedent in the history of the YWHA's of this State', a journalist explained, 'when two associations will meet in battle on the basketball court', the Hartford team representing 'the State Capitol' and the New Haven team representing the 'City of Elms. As both Hartford and New Haven are confident of winning, the contests will afford many thrills to spectators'.[57] Whilst admission to the game cost 50 cents, Jewish charities benefited: 'the entire net proceeds will be divided equally and contributed to the Jewish Home for Orphans and the Home for the Aged'. The game was won by the YWHA of New Haven over the YWHA of Hartford but proved a success for players and spectators alike: 'An audience as large as ever turned out for any men's basketball game witnessed the match.'[58]

By 1921, these YWHA girls were practising twice a week, still using Hartford-area school gyms. But playing in a keen competition appealed to the basketball players of this YWHA, and 'the association expects to join the basketball leagues comprising the Travelers Insurance Company, the Aetna Fire, the Simsbury Independents, the New Departure of Bristol and the YWCA'.[59] The athletic prowess of the Hartford YWHA team continued when the YWHA team, coached by Morris N. Cohen, won the State Championship in 1930 and 1931. Working-class Jewish women often participated in the same sporting endeavours as did other working-class women; in their Jewish organisations, designed to promote wholesome recreation and Jewish identity, indeed, some young women excelled in basketball and achieved victories in their team competitions. These Jewish associations, at times promoting preservation of Jewish life, and at times offering Americanisation programmes, furthered access to sporting opportunities for women and girls, especially those gaining exposure to sports and physical recreation at these ethnic institutions.

Advocates of competitive sports in the early twentieth century

In the early twentieth century some Jewish American women emerged into the public eye as successful athletes. These women sustained ties to Jewish cultural institutions and they excelled in American sporting contests. As in the particular cases of the Jewish women discussed below, some women athletes triumphed in national settings, and a few even triumphed in international settings such as the Olympic Games. Even though these women pursued high-level athletics they still maintained their Jewish identity. In some cases, these Jewish American women influenced sport and expanded the opportunities for other women, both Jewish and Gentile. The success of American Jewish women competing in public in sports drew the interest of the American Jewish press and mainstream American newspapers. The accomplishments of these female athletes, and the earlier generation of Jewish women in YWHAs or Jewish settlements, indicate the ways sport in the religious and ethnic culture has played a role in the lives of Jewish women.

Some women gained competitive sporting experiences at the Jewish country clubs formed in the progressive era, and gained prowess in elite sports such as golf and tennis. For upper-class Jewish families, the Jewish country clubs provided a place for elite sports and social networks for the males and their families. As anti-Semitism prohibited these wealthy German Jews from joining the country clubs of Anglo-Saxon Protestants, country clubs for Jews fostered athletic activities, and these, at times, also catered for females. For example, Elaine Rosenthal Reinhardt, born in 1896, became one of the most prominent female golfers in the early twentieth century, playing at the Ravisloe Country Club in Homewood, Illinois. In 1914,

Rosenthal competed in the US Women's National Golf Championship in Nassau, New York, reached the finals against Mrs H. Arnold Jackson and earned high praise. 'Miss Rosenthal made it clear that she will have to be reckoned with in future championships, for she has many shots in her bag, a nervy player, and a heady one, and she is only 18 years old', remarked the *New York Times*.[60] Rosenthal's mother, Mrs Bernard J. Rosenthal, played competitive golf, and her sister Mrs Gladys Byfield was also a championship golfer, sometimes competing against Elaine.[61] Rosenthal continued her outstanding golf play in numerous tournaments. In 1917 she won the Western Women's Golf Championship; in fact, she won this prestigious title in 1918 and 1925, becoming the first woman to wear the 'triple crown'. Although she married S.L. Reinhardt from Texas in 1921, she did not give up her golf.[62]

Rosenthal earned national acclaim in golf with such victories in 1916 and 1917 at the Women's Golf Championship of Florida, and in 1917 she won the Women's North and South Amateur Championship at Pinehurst, NC Country Club. During World War I, golf matches were halted, but Rosenthal was amongst the elite golfers invited to participate in Red Cross golf exhibitions to raise funds. In 1917 and 1918, golfers from Atlanta – US women's national champion Alexa Stirling, and stars Bobby Jones and Perry Adiar – and Elaine Rosenthal, the best female golfer in the Midwest, who were known as 'The Dixie Kids', played patriotic golf exhibitions and raised over $200,000 for the American Red Cross.[63] Rosenthal continued her high performance on the links in tournaments after the war. The *Chicago Tribune* covered her golf contests, given her ties to the Chicago area: 'Miss Rosenthal in Golf Finals', the paper reported in August 1919 whilst covering a tournament in Shennecossett, Connecticut.[64] In the final of the golf contest on 9 August 1919, 'Mrs Ronald H. Barlow of Philadelphia won the Shennecossett championship today when she defeated Miss Elaine Rosenthal of Chicago in the final, 1 up.'[65] In the description of the match, the journalist wrote, 'In the early stages it looked as if the Chicago golfer was going to have things pretty much her own way', but she lost some later holes, and then 'Miss Rosenthal encouraged her followers by winning the seventeenth', and Mrs Barlow prevailed with the one-stroke win.[66] Rosenthal, the best Jewish woman golfer in the first part of the twentieth century, displayed her outstanding skills and gained the attention of both Jews and non-Jews.

In sports such as swimming, Jewish American females benefited from their predecessors in water sports for women. In fact, Jewish and Gentile women seeking to pursue competitive swimming in a range of settings, from club level to national and international levels, in the first decades of the twentieth century, benefited from the impressive leadership and reform activism of Charlotte Epstein. Thus, an article in the 1915 *American Hebrew* titled, 'Jewesses in Athletics', featured Charlotte Epstein, one of the most important women in the history of US women's swimming: 'For the first time the AAU has permitted women to enter the ranks of competitive amateur athletics and at the Sportsmen's show at the Madison Square Garden. In the swimming and diving events Jewesses have been taking a prominent part.'[67] *American Hebrew* commented: 'Among the entries are Miss Lucy Freeman 440-yard champion; Miss Rita Greenfield, Miss Sophie Fruitage and Miss Frances Ricker.' The article identified: 'All of these young ladies are members of the National Women's Life Saving League, of which Miss Charlotte Epstein is chairman of the Athletic Branch'.[68] In fact, Epstein, known as the 'Mother of Women's Swimming in America', joined the recently formed National Women's Life-Saving League in 1911, and in 1912 became a member of the Athletic Committee, responsible for directing all competition. In 1913, Epstein became chairman of the Athletic Branch of the National Women's Life-Saving League. 'She and her associates have devised several spectacular events and swimming contests which will bring out not only the utmost speed and skill of the young women contestants, but will demand that they show proficiency in running, life-saving, and other endeavors.'[69] Epstein swam in competitions and won in some of the 'Plunges', diving events, in her career.[70]

Several events sponsored by the National Women's Life Saving League attracted skilled swimmers and gained wider recognition of Charlotte Epstein's outstanding leadership. Epstein's work in affiliating the National Women's Life Saving League with the Amateur Athletic Union in particular promised better competition and organisation of women's meets. To officially sanction women's swimming, Epstein promoted the sport to be under the jurisdiction of the Amateur Athletic Union in 1915. The *New York Times* explained that women swimmers permitted to register in AAU-sanctioned meets 'may be regarded as a brilliant victory for the fair natators particularly as it opens to them the long sought opportunity of bidding for honors in Olympic Games'.[71] Advocates such as Epstein believed women should supervise women's water sports and the Life Saving League 'would place things in its hands' to provide competition for the fair contestants.[72] The press still described the women swimmers in gender terms, stating: 'Woman, the life giver, is life saver too', or 'Men, here's rare chance to have a fair maiden hug you.'[73] Not only did Epstein and these swimmers advocate competitive contests, they claimed the right to wear 'one-piece bathing suits, which they draped with skirts' when not racing for the prizes.[74]

To advance the sport of women's swimming, Charlotte Epstein founded the renowned Women's Swimming Association of New York City in October 1917. Epstein and a few other members, also businesswomen interested in swimming for exercise and securing pools for women to swim, resigned from the National Women's Life Saving League to form the Women's Swimming Association (WSA), a non-profit club. Epstein explained that the new swimming club was organised 'because the members felt that thereby they could best further the interest of all women desiring to learn how to swim and those of the competitors as well'.[75] Epstein became swimming club team manager of the WSA in 1917, served as Chairman of the Sports Committee, and was then made club President in 1929, demonstrating her excellent administrative ability and determination to enable the WSA to prosper. As founder of the WSA, Epstein, known as 'Eppie', launched the national and international fame of American women swimmers in the early twentieth century. WSA members in 1917 held impressive swimming credentials: 'among some of the members are Claire Galligan, holder of the world's 500-yard record, National champion at 500-yds, one-half mile and one mile, and who is considered to be the best all around swimmer in the country; Lucy Freeman, national long distance champion, holding the record for swimming from Spuyten Duyvil to the Battery'; another member was Charlotte Boyle, one of the best sprinters in the USA.[76] In fact, Eppie's WSA members gained great success in diving and swimming competitions producing prominent Olympic champions such as Aileen Riggin, Helen Meaney, Ethelda Bleibtry, Gertrude Ederle, Alice Lord, Eleanor Holms and the Olympian and first all-around US swimming champion Charlotte Boyle. In 1923, Epstein reported in the *WSA News*, the monthly periodical of the club, that WSA girls 'have held the all-around championship of the United States continuously',[77] referring to the National Championships in the senior AAU competitions. The team remained an amateur club. Epstein encouraged the team with the club slogan: 'Good Sportsmanship is Greater Than Victory'.[78] Eppie commented on the club's achievements in 1920: 'The WSA team maintained its leadership in this country, and established its right to supremacy throughout the women's swimming world.'[79]

Charlotte Epstein provided extraordinary leadership and promoted the competitive swimming of WSA teammates, becoming the team manager-chaperon of the 1920 Women's Olympic Swimming Team, the first time females were allowed to compete in the sport in the Olympic Games. One of Eppie's WSA club members, Aileen Riggin, the 1920 gold medal Olympic Fancy Diving Champion and 1924 Olympic medalist in diving and swimming, recalled Eppie's crucial role in giving WSA members the chance to compete in the Olympics. As a 14-year-old girl competing, Riggin remembered how 'this seemed to cause great commotions with the officials'. Epstein battled the Olympic officials: 'They had a bitter session but finally we won and the Committee members said they would allow us to go.'[80] Indeed, Eppie's swimmers triumphed at the 1920 Olympics in Antwerp: 'Six of our members earned the right to represent the United States in Antwerp, out of a total of thirteen girl swimmers and divers selected', Epstein recalled.[81]

During Epstein's leadership at the WSA and time as Olympic manager, 1920–36, WSA members accomplished tremendous swimming feats, earning world records in competitions. At the 1924 Olympics in Paris, WSA stars were again a strong group with Gertrude Ederle, Helen Wainwright, Aileen Riggin, Helen Meany and others contributing to the US victory in women's swimming events. Epstein gained recognition for her work on behalf of US women's swimming in 1924: 'Miss Epstein is the first woman to have been honored by being appointed an Olympic judge.'[82] WSA members praised Eppie's activism in supporting competitive swimming for them and leading the club members to dominance in swimming in the early twentieth century.

Charlotte Epstein's influential swimming career continued until her death in 1938. She achieved the official position of Olympic team manager of the US women's swimming team for the 1920, 1924 and 1932 Games. Eppie worked with Jewish organisations with suitable swimming pools. So the WSA team of Olympians such as Aileen Riggin and Gertrude Ederle swam at the YWHA of New York for national championship meets in the 1920s.[83] The public acclaim of these women's swimming champions appeared in the Jewish and Anglo press; Eppie's advocacy of swimming reached Jewish youth at the YM/YWHAs and American youth at the AAU and national swimming meets in which many of her WSA teammates triumphed in competitions.

Epstein maintained her Jewish identity and excellent guidance in swimming as Chair of the Swimming Committee at the 1935 Maccabiah Games. The Maccabiah Games, also known as the Jewish Olympics, promoted athletics and Jewish culture in an international forum; the first Maccabiah was staged in 1932 in Tel Aviv, Palestine, and the swimming events took place in the Mediterranean Sea. This first Maccabiah consisted of 390 participants representing eighteen countries competing in sixteen sporting events, and was held in a newly built stadium. By the second Maccabiah Games, held in 1935, the number of athletes had increased. These games featured 1,350 participants from nearly thirty countries, in eighteen sports. The 1935 Maccabiah included improved swimming facilities; swimmers used the 'Bat Galim' swimming pool in Haifa for the swimming competitions instead of the sea. The British Mandate government disapproved of the Maccabiah but the Games still took place in 1935. For the second Maccabiah, Lord Alfred Melchett served as Honorary President of Maccabi and sponsored the Games: 'In defiance of the British government's strict limitations on aliyah [seeking permanent residence], many competitors took advantage of their being in the Holy Land and decided to stay.'[84] It was reported that the entire Bulgarian delegation 'unanimously decided to make aliyah and shipped their musical instruments back to Bulgaria instead of themselves'.[85]

At the second Maccabiah in 1935, tens of thousands crowded into the Tel Aviv Stadium for the opening ceremony. The festivities featured the hoisting of the Maccabiah flag and expressions of Jewish identity manifested in the 'Blue and White clad Maccabi' and the singing of 'Hatikvah', the Jewish national anthem: 'Every building, every shop and every home proudly displayed the Zionist colours.'[86] In his opening address in Hebrew, translated into English, Lord Melchett proclaimed, 'We represent here today a movement of 200,000 young men and women imbued with high ideals and with the knowledge that the physical development of Jewry, the inculcation in the heart of Jewry of the love of athletics, is a necessary element in the upbuilding of our nation and of our land.'[87] To the Jews who came from the diaspora, Maccabiah officials stated that they must return to their countries after the Maccabiah; but despite a plea by Melchett: 'I wish to remind all Maccabis of the solemn promise which I have given upon their behalf, to leave this country before the period allowed by the authorities expires', many simply stayed.[88]

Just as at the Olympic Games, Epstein's swimmers achieved victories in the Maccabiah Games. One of Eppie's WSA team members, 16-year-old Janice Lifson, triumphed in the Maccabiah try-outs held at the WSA pool.[89] Of the meet, the *American Hebrew* asserted: 'Janice Lifson, who scored first in the 100 metre free style and back stroke races at the Maccabiad, was the outstanding Jewish woman swimmer of the year. A member of the WSA, she is one of America's fine divers.'[90] *The Palestine Post* recorded: 'Miss Lifson, the young American diving champion, was again high scorer for the day.'[91] The Jewish athletes returning to America after the Maccabiah were feted at New York City's 92nd Street YMHA.[92]

Epstein sustained her affiliation with Jewish organisations throughout her swimming career and continued promoting women's competitive aquatic sports. Her WSA and Olympic swimmers appeared at swimming exhibitions such as at the opening of the new Jewish Community Center in Yonkers, New York in 1929. The WSA Captain Doris O'Mara, 1924–8 Olympian and national champion, and sister Eileen O'Mara, a national champion, performed in the swimming pool as part of the celebration of new athletic facilities at the Jewish Community Center.[93]

To advance women's competitive swimming, Epstein served on other important athletic committees. She was appointed Chair of the USA Olympic Women's Swimming Committee as well as Chair of the Amateur Athletic Union, National Women's Swimming Committee. Yet despite her contributions to women's sport generally, her religious and cultural identity remained central. In 1936, she refused to attend the Olympic Games in Berlin because she opposed American participation, and, as a Jewish American she withdrew from the American Olympic Committee as a protest against National Socialist policies. She thus clearly articulated her American Jewish identity by publicly communicating her support of an American boycott of the Nazi Olympics. Her stance reveals the significance of her religious identity even within the sporting arena, and placed her in the company of other Jewish athletes and administrators who advocated American non-participation. To recognise Epstein's distinguished services to the American Olympic Committee, on 26 June 1939 the American Olympic Committee issued a 'Resolution on the Death of Miss Charlotte Epstein'. Epstein 'received national and international recognition for the part she played in the development of many swimmers and divers, as well as for her outstanding executive ability'.[94]

Track and field engaged the athletic ability of Jewish females at Jewish YM/YWHAs and the Olympics. In the 1920s, Jewish American Lillian Copeland attended the University of Southern California, and became an outstanding track and field athlete winning nine national titles and setting world records in the javelin throw and the discus toss. Copeland excelled in an international meet in Brussels, Belgium in August 1928: 'Miss Lillian Copeland of the United States broke the world's record for the shot put with a toss of 11.71 meters and also won the discus and javelin throws', the *New York Times* reported.[95] Copeland led 'the American women's Olympic team to victory over the leading European stars in an international meet' with the American women's team winning 'the meet by taking four first places of the nine events contested'.[96] Copeland competed for the American women's Olympic team in the summer 1928 Olympic Games, earning a silver medal in the discus. At the 1932 Los Angeles Olympic Games Copeland won the gold medal in the discus throw, setting another world record.[97] Copeland excelled in the 1935 Maccabiah Games and won her events. According to the *American Hebrew*: 'Outstanding was Lillian Copeland of Los Angeles, 1932 Olympic champion, who scored first in the javelin throw, shot put and discus at Tel Aviv.'[98] Copeland, a leading competitor for the 1936 American Olympic team, also decided to boycott the Berlin Olympics, confirming her position as a Jewish American sportswoman.[99]

Another female track and field star at the 1935 Maccabiah, Sybil Koff, contributed to American victories. Sybil (Syd) Koff Cooper of New York (1913–98) was a star at the first Maccabiah in 1932 at 19 years old when she won four events in track – the 100-metre race, the high jump, the broad jump and the women's triathlon – winning the 100 metres in front of 25,000 spectators. In the 1935 games Koff excelled again; she won three first places in the 60-metre dash, 400-metre hurdle and 200-metre dash, and took second in the broad jump. In total, Koff won seven gold medals in these first two Maccabiads.[100] The *American Hebrew* in 1935 remarked 'Miss Koff, the Maccabiad star, was the leading Jewish girl athlete of the year winning the 200 Metre Metropolitan AAU title'.[101] Koff was also a contender for the 1936 Olympics, qualifying for the track team, but boycotted the Nazi games with other Jewish athletes. During their careers, these Jewish track athletes Lillian Copeland and Sybil Koff competed against the great Mildred 'Babe' Didrickson and other world-class athletes. Koff almost earned a place on the 1932 American Olympic track team, narrowly being eliminated in the sprints and hurdles. In 1940 Koff won the woman's 80-yard hurdles at the national championships, the Olympic trials for the upcoming Olympic Games; she qualified for the 1940 Olympic Games in Helsinki, but the games were subsequently cancelled.[102]

Conclusion

The history of Jewish American women in sports reveals that as athletes, advocates and administrators, these women shaped the sporting landscape in the USA and in some cases, the sporting landscape in international contexts. From the early efforts for physical culture and healthful exercise for women at Jewish settlements, to sport programmes at Jewish YM/YWHAs, and to contests at the Maccabiah Games and even in the Olympic Games, Jewish women have played a significant role in sport in American history. Moreover, Jewish institutions, seeking to conserve religious traditions and ethnic culture as well as communicate important lessons about American society, influenced the access to sport of Jewish female youth; as young Jewish women interacted with Jewish and non-Jewish women in situations in sport they gained access to American cultural traditions. Their Jewish identity remained a component of their participation in sport in American life.

Sporting activities, therefore, held a considerable place in the lives of numerous Jewish women. Jewish women in the USA as proponents of physical training for immigrant women and girls, as participants in a variety of sports and as leaders in local, national and international sporting events, reveal the considerable impact of Jewish women within their ethnic culture and women's roles in the majority culture. Gabaccia remarks that the 'construction of ethnicity and the construction of identity were intertwined, not conflicting, cultural processes of change'.[103] Jewish women engaging in sports exist as part of the historical reality of US and international sport. These women, who participated in a range of sporting practices, were introduced to American culture whilst simultaneously preserving their Jewish identity, contoured by their gender and ethnic roles in American society. The President of the YMHA and YWHA of New York City, Louis M. Loeb, remarked on the achievement of this notable institution on its seventy-fifth Anniversary. Loeb asserted: 'The young people who come under the influence of the Young Men's and Young Women's Hebrew Association will continue to be molded and forged into better Jews and more useful citizens'.[104] Participating in sport, and advocating competitive sporting experiences for women in their Jewish associations and in wider organisations, Jewish women nurtured ethnic and gender identities and constructed their place as American Jews in American culture.

Notes

1   An earlier version of this essay was published in *International Sport Studies*, vol. 22, no. 1, 2000, pp. 5–24. I thank Tara Magdalinski for her valuable suggestions on my chapter. At the New York Public Library, Dorot Jewish Division, librarian Faith Jones provided me with considerable assistance on my visits and offered insightful comments on my search for sources; I appreciate the important help the archivists gave me for my research with the various collections.

2   'Jews in sport', *American Hebrew*, vol. XCVI, 29 January 1915, p. 347.

3   D. Gabaccia, *From the Other Side: Women, Gender and Immigrant Life in the US, 1820–1920*, Bloomington, Indiana University Press, 1994, p. xi.

4   See M.R. Nelson, 'Basketball as cultural capital: the original Celtics in early twentieth-century New York City', in M. Cronin and D. Mayall (eds), *Sporting Nationalisms: Identity, Ethnicity, Immigration and Assimilation*, London, Frank Cass, 1998, p. 74. This collection of essays focusses on men in sport and issues of ethnicity in various countries.

5   *Building Character for 75 Years: Published on the Occasion of the 75th Anniversary of the Young Men's and Young Women's Hebrew Association*, New York City, 1969, p. 20. For information on this New York City Young Women's Hebrew Association see L.J. Borish, 'Jewish American women, Jewish organizations and sports, 1880–1940', in S.A. Riess (ed.), *Sports and the American Jew*, Syracuse, Syracuse University Press, 1998, pp. 105–31.

6   *Building Character for 75 Years: Published on the Occasion of the 75th Anniversary of the Young Men's and Young Women's Hebrew Association*, New York City, 1969, pp. 21, 22.

7   J. Hargreaves, *Sporting Females: Critical Issues in the History and Sociology of Women's Sports*, London, Routledge, 1994, p. 255.

8   For information on immigrants to America during the Progressive era focussing on Jewish immigrants, see G.R. Sorin, *A Time for Building: The Third Migration, 1880–1920, Volume III. The Jewish People in America*, series ed. Henry L. Feingold, Baltimore, The Johns Hopkins University Press, 1995; N.W. Cohen, *Encounter With Emancipation: The German Jews in the United States, 1830–1914*, Philadelphia, The Jewish Publication Society of America, 1984. Selected works on Jewish women in America include P.E. Hyman, *Gender and Assimilation in Modern Jewish History*, Seattle, University of Washington Press, 1995; R. Glanz, *The Jewish Woman in America: Two Immigrant Generations, 1820–1929*, Volumes I and II, place of publication unknown, KTAV Publishing, House and National Council of Jewish Women, 1976; H.R. Diner, *A Time for Gathering: The Second Migration, 1820–1880, Volume II. The Jewish People in America*, series ed. Henry L. Feingold, Baltimore, The Johns Hopkins University Press, 1995; B.A. Schrier, *Becoming American Women: Clothing and the Jewish Immigrant Experience, 1880–1920*, Chicago, Chicago Historical Society, 1994; A.R. Heinze, *Adapting to Abundance: Jewish Immigrants, Mass Consumption, and the Search for American Identity*, New York, Columbia University Press, 1990; E. Ewen, *Immigrant Women in the Land of Dollars: Life and Culture on the Lower East Side, 1890–1925*, New York, Monthly Review Press, 1985; J.D. Sarna (ed.), *The American Jewish Experience*, second edition, New York, Holmes & Meier, 1997.

9   On social reformers' perceptions of immigrant youth's need for healthful play and sport as an alternative to the temptations and evils of urban, consumer culture see J. Addams, *Twenty Years at Hull House*, New York, New American Library, 1960 [1910]; J. Addams, *Spirit of Youth and the City Street*, New York, Macmillan, 1923; L.D. Wald, *The House on Henry Street*, New York, Dover Publications, 1971 [1915]. Historical works on reformers, immigrants and proper leisure and sport include K. Peiss, *Cheap Amusements: Working Women and Leisure in Turn-of-the-Century New York*, Philadelphia, Temple University Press, 1986; G.R. Gems, *Windy City Wars: Labor, Leisure, and Sport in the Making of Chicago*, Lanham, Scarecrow Press, 1997; G.R. Gems, 'Working class women and sport: an untold story', *Women in Sport and Physical Activity Journal*, vol. 2, 1993, pp. 17–30; L.J. Borish and B.L. Tischler (eds), *Rethinking History: The Journal of Theory and Practice*, 'Labour, Leisure and Sport' special edition, vol. 5, no. 1, 2001; J.F. McClymer, 'Gender and the "American way of life": women in the Americanization movement', *Journal of American Ethnic History*, vol. 10, 1991, pp. 3–20; N.B. Sinkof, 'Education for "proper Jewish womanhood": a case study in domesticity and vocational training, 1897–1926', *American Jewish History*, vol. 77, 1988, pp. 572–99; E. Ewen, *Immigrant Women in the Land of Dollars: Life and Culture on the Lower East Side, 1890–1925*, New York, Monthly Review Press, 1985; C. Goodman, *Choosing Sides: Playground and Street Life on the Lower East Side*, New York, Schocken Books, 1979; S.A. Riess, *City Games. The Evolution of American*

Urban Society and the Rise of Sports, Urbana, University of Illinois Press, 1989; D. Nasaw, *Children of the City: At Work and at Play*, Garden City, Anchor Press/Doubleday, 1985.

10 History, Young Women's Union, Neighborhood Centre Records, MSS 10, Philadelphia Jewish Archives Center at the Balch Institute (hereafter cited as the PJAC); E. Bodek, ' "Making do": Jewish women and philanthropy', in M. Friedman (ed.), *Jewish Life in Philadelphia, 1830–1940*, Philadelphia, Institute for the Study of Human Issues, 1983, p. 156.

11 Young Women's Union of Philadelphia, *Twenty-Fifth Anniversary Report, 1885–1910*, pp. 7–8, 28, Neighborhood Centre Records, MSS 10, PJAC.

12 Young Women's Union of Philadelphia, *Annual Report, 1916–1917*, pp. 6–7, Neighborhood Centre Records, MSS 10, PJAC; *Director's Report, April 1917 to April 1918*, pp. 1–2, Neighborhood Centre Records, PJAC; Young Women's Union of Philadelphia, *Twenty-Seventh Annual Report*, p. 15, Neighborhood Centre Records, MSS 10, PJAC, 1912, cited in J.L. Greifer, 'Neighborhood centre – a study of the adjustment of a culture group in America', unpublished PhD thesis, School of Education, New York University, 1948, pp. 249–50.

13 See P. Vertinsky, 'The "racial" body and the anatomy of difference: anti-semitism, physical culture, and the Jew's foot', *Sport Science Review*, vol. 4, no. 1, 1995, pp. 38–59; G. Eisen, 'Jews and sport: a century of retrospect', *Journal of Sport History*, vol. 26, no. 2, 1999, pp. 225–39; S.L. Gilman, *The Jew's Body*, New York, Routledge, 1991; G. Pfister, 'Physical culture and sport among Jewish women in Germany at the turn of the century', in L. Laine (ed.), *On the Fringes of Sport*, Finland, The Finnish Society for Research in Sport and Physical Education, 1993, pp. 164–74.

14 '1895–GREETINGS–1925; a brief history of the Irene Kaufmann Settlement', *IKS Neighbors*, vol. 3, 15 January 1925, pp. 1–3; 'Gym work for girls', *IKS Neighbors*, vol. 1, 1 April 1923, p. 4; 'Dancing! Gymnasium! Swimming!', *IKS Neighbors*, vol. 1, 25 October 1923, p. 4.; 'Girls play volley ball', *IKS Neighbors*, vol. 4, 15 May 1926, p. 53; 'Gym and a swim for vigor and vim', *IKS Neighbors*, vol. 3, 15 October 1925, p. 96.

15 L.F. Hecht, 'Synopsis of Report of the Boston Industrial School, 1899', Hecht House Collections, American Jewish Historical Society Library, Waltham, MA (hereafter cited as AJHSL). For philanthropic efforts and the Hecht family's contributions to aid Jews in Boston, see J.D. Sarna and E. Smith (eds), *The Jews of Boston: Essays on the Occasion of the Centenary (1895–1995) of the Combined Jewish Philanthropies of Greater Boston*, Boston, Combined Jewish Philanthropies of Greater Boston, 1995.

16 Report of the Hebrew Industrial School, 1900–1901, pp. 4–5, Hecht House Collections, AJHSL.

17 'Staff meetings report, Hecht Neighborhood House', 22 July 1938, Hecht House Collections, AJHSL.

18 'Draft of the report of the Hecht House Neighborhood House', 15 May 1930, Jewish Welfare Board, New York City, p. 10, Hecht House Collections, AJHSL.

19 Lizzie Black Kander Collection, Near Print Box; Lizzie Black Kander Papers, President's Reports, Microfilm 482, American Jewish Archives, Cincinnati (hereafter cited as AJA). For information on Lizzie B. Kander's philanthropic work and leadership in aiding Jewish immigrants in Milwaukee, see L.J. Swichkow and L.P. Gartner, *The History of the Jews of Milwaukee*, Philadelphia, Jewish Publication Society of America, 1963.

20 H. Abrams, 'A Jewish Settlement House and Its Practical Mission', *Milwaukee Free Press*, 10 November 1912; Lizzie Black Kander Collection, Near Print Box; Lizzie Black Kander Papers, Letter to Mrs Kander, 28 May 1934, Microfilm 482, AJA.

21 L.J. Borish, 'The Chicago Hebrew Institute', in J. Grossman and A.D. Keating (eds), *Chicago History Encyclopedia*, Chicago, University of Chicago Press, forthcoming.

22 H.L. Meites, *History of the Jews of Chicago*, Chicago, Jewish Historical Society of Illinois, 1927; I. Cutler, *The Jews of Chicago From Shetl to Suburb*, Urbana, University of Illinois Press, 1996; G.R. Gems, 'Sport and the forging of a Jewish-American culture: The Chicago Hebrew Institute', *American Jewish History*, vol. 83, 1995, pp. 15–26; Jewish

Community Center of Chicago Papers, Archives and Manuscripts Department, Chicago Historical Society, Chicago, IL; S.L. Levine, 'The Jewish Community Center Movement', *The Sentinel's History of Chicago Jewry, 1911–1961*, Chicago, Sentinel Publishing Co., n.d., pp. 184–6.

23 P.L. Seman, 'Democracy in action', *Chicago Jewish Forum*, 1943, pp. 49–54, Philip L. Seman Collection, Scrapbooks, AJA.

24 B.A. Loeb, '"The Temple of the Body". How the Hebrew Institute is laboring to make Jews physically fit', *The Sentinel*, 1 May 1914, Jacob M. Loeb Collection, Chicago Hebrew Institute (hereafter cited as CHI), AJA

25 Ibid.

26 P.L. Seman, 'Report of the Superintendent', *CHI Observer*, 1913–1914, pp. 10–11, Philip L. Seman Collection, Scrapbook, Vol. I, AJA.

27 Jacob M. Loeb to Mr and Mrs Julius Rosenwald, 28 October 1913, Jacob M. Loeb Collection, CHI, AJA.

28 Ibid.; Julius Rosenwald to Jacob M. Loeb, 29 October 1913, Jacob M. Loeb Collection, CHI, AJA.

29 Jacob M. Loeb, 'Petition for rehearing on behalf of appellee Chicago Hebrew Institute gymnasium case to the Hon. Rosenwald, presiding', 1 November 1913, Jacob M. Loeb Collections, CHI, AJA.

30 Julius Rosenwald to Jacob M. Loeb, 3 November 1913, Jacob M. Loeb Collection, CHI, AJA.

31 Jacob M. Loeb, Address, 31 March 1914, Chicago Hebrew Institute; 'Break ground for new gymnasium at Hebrew Institute', *Chicago Israelite*, 15 August 1914, Jacob M. Loeb Collection, CHI, AJA.

32 Addresses on the Dedication of the New Gymnasium Building, June 1915, Jacob M. Loeb Collection, CHI, AJA; *CHI Observer*, vol. 3, February 1915, p. 46, Philip L. Seman Collection, Scrapbook, AJA.

33 'Hebrew Institute dedication is the result of hard work and optimism', ca. June 1915, Chicago Hebrew Institute 'News Letter No. 11', on Physical Culture Activities, Jacob M. Loeb Collection, CHI, AJA.

34 *CHI General Director's Report*, 1921, pp. 56–7, Philip L. Seman Collection, Scrapbook, AJA.

35 *JPI General Director's Report*, 1922, p. 80, Philip L. Seman Collection, Scrapbook, AJA. The JPI senior women also excelled at volleyball, and in 1931, 1932 and 1933 the women won the Amateur Athletic Federation Volleyball Championship.

36 Chester Foust, 'Mother, may I go out to swim?' *Chicago Sunday Herald*, 2 January 1916; and 'Imported from Europe – a swimming instructor', *Chicago Tribune*, 8 July 1915, Philip L. Seman Collection, Scrapbook, AJA; B.A. Loeb, 'A gala day at the Institute', *The Sentinel*, 11 June 1915, Jacob M. Loeb Collection, CHI, AJA.

37 *CHI General Director's Report*, 1921, pp. 58–9, Philip L. Seman Collection, Scrapbook, AJA.

38 *JPI General Director's Report*, 1922, pp. 90–1, Philip L. Seman Collection, Scrapbook, AJA; W. Smith, 'JPI enters 53 in Tribune swim events', *Chicago Tribune*, 11 July 1930, p. 22; 'Seek badges and prizes in Tribune 100 yard swim races at Lincoln Park', *Chicago Tribune*, 13 July 1930, p. 3, photo; W. Smith, 'Tribune 100 yard swim races draw entries of 400 boys, girls', *Chicago Tribune*, 13 July 1930, p. 6; '1,470 girls and boys swim today in Tribune races', *Chicago Tribune*, 27 July 1930, p. 5; W. Smith, 'Claudia Eckert wins senior girls' crown', *Chicago Tribune*, 28 July 1930, pp. 21, 23; Philip L. Seman Collection, Scrapbook, AJA.

39 Mrs Israel Unterberg, 'The YWHA', *Publications of the Council of YMH and Kindred Associations*, July 1919, pp. 57, 59.

40 Young Women's Hebrew Association, *Thirteenth Annual Report*, February 1916, pp. 12, 13, YWHA Records, 92nd Street YM/YWHA Archives; see L.J. Borish, '"An interest in physical well-being among the feminine membership": sporting activities for women at

Young Men's and Young Women's Hebrew Associations', *American Jewish History*, vol. 87, no. 1, 1999, pp. 61–93 for material on the founding of the New York City YWHA and programmes for women at YMHAs and YWHAs.

41 Young Women's Hebrew Association, *Fifth Annual Report of the President*, February 1908, YWHA Records, 92nd Street YM/YWHA Archives, pp. 2, 12.

42 Young Women's Hebrew Association, 'Class Report', 1 January–1 February 1911, YWHA Records, 92nd Street YM/YWHA Archives. See L.J. Borish, ' "An interest in physical well-being among the feminine membership": sporting activities for women at Young Men's and Young Women's Hebrew Associations', *American Jewish History*, vol. 87, no. 1, 1999; D. Kaufman, *Shul with a Pool: The 'Synagogue-Center' in American Jewish History*, Hanover, Brandeis/University Press of New England, 1999, for information about the philosophy of YM/YWHAs and this early YWHA in New York City.

43 Young Women's Hebrew Association, *Fifth Annual Report of the President*, February 1908, YWHA Records, 92nd Street YM/YWHA Archives, pp. 2, 12; Mrs Israel Unterberg, 'The YWHA', *Publications of the Council of YMH and Kindred Associations*, July 1919, p. 59.

44 'Second triennial convention. Conference: girls' and women's work', *Publications of the Council of YMH and Kindred Associations*, November 1916, AJHSL.

45 'New Home for Girls' Club', 92nd Street YM/YWHA Archives; see also Frances Kahn, 'Live a Little Longer', *Kol Alamoth*, 1 June 1915, p. 10; Young Women's Hebrew Association, *Twenty-Fifth Anniversary, 1902–1927: Twenty-fourth Annual Report*, January 1927, pp. 16–17, YWHA Records, 92nd Street YM/YWHA Archives.

46 'Hows and whys of Big Burg's Y's. 110th Street YWHA has most comprehensive physical education system of type in entire country', *New York Post*, 17 January 1936, Newspaper Clippings, YWHA Records, 92nd Street YM/YWHA Archives.

47 Young Women's Hebrew Association, *Thirteenth Annual Report*, February 1916, pp. 36–7, YWHA Records, 92nd Street YM/YWHA Archives; 'The story of six years' work of the Young Women's Hebrew Association 1919 through 1924', February 1924, p. 21, YWHA Records, 92nd Street YM/YWHA Archives.

48 'Louisville, KY', *American Israelite*, vol. 37, 22 January 1891, p. 7; C. Memser, 'Letter on the history of the Louisville, YMHA, February 17, 1950', Louisville, KY, YMHA, National Jewish Welfare Board Archives (hereafter JWB Archives), AJHSL; T. Levitan, 'The physical aspect: a history of athletics in the YMHA', *The Chronicler, 40th Anniversary Number, 1890–1930*, January 1930, pp. 9, 17, 20; *Jewish Community Center, 75th Anniversary*, 1965, Louisville, KY, YMHA, JWB Archives, AJHSL; H. Landau, *Adath Louisville: The Story of a Jewish Community*, Jewish Community Federation of Louisville, 1981, discusses the founding of the YMHA and the development of the Jewish Community Center.

49 L.H. Blumenthal, 'History of YM and YWHA 1877–1933 and the San Francisco Jewish Community Center – 1933–38', San Francisco, 1938, pp. 1, 4–5, San Francisco, JWB Archives, AJHSL; see also R.K. Rafael, 'The YMHA and the YWHA of San Francisco', *Western States Jewish History*, vol. 19, 1987, pp. 212–14.

50 L. Popkin, 'The problem of the Jewish youth in America', *American Hebrew*, vol. 109, 1921, pp. 196–7; L. Kraft, 'Center, the Jewish', in I. Landman (ed.), *The Universal Jewish Encyclopedia*, New York, The Universal Jewish Encyclopedia, Inc., 1941, pp. 84–8; 'Report New England Section, Jewish Welfare Board', 3 June 1948, p. 1, JWB Archives, AJHSL; L.J. Borish, 'Young Women's Hebrew Association', in G.B. Kirsch (ed.), *The Encyclopedia of Ethnicity and Sports in the United States*, Westport, Greenwood Press, 2000, pp. 502–4. For information on the National Jewish Welfare Board, see L.J. Borish, 'National Jewish Welfare Board Archives, Young Men's-Young Women's Hebrew Association Records, A Research Guide', American Jewish Historical Society, Archives and Manuscript Collections, Waltham, November 1996, pp. 1–16.

51 'Report Young Women's Hebrew Association, South Brooklyn, NY', 8 January 1924, pp. 1–3, Brooklyn YM/YWHA, JWB Archives, AJHSL.

52 Ibid., pp. 1–2.

53 Ibid., pp. 1–3.

54 'Report Young Women's Hebrew Association, Brooklyn, NY', 15 April 1924, p. 1, JWB Archives, AJHSL; Even Field Secretary Mr Leff mentioned that the YWHA President seemed concerned about losing members, and Mr. Harris 'promised to let the YWHA have as much space in the building as it could use', again, 'with the exception of the gymnasium' in the Report for 9 October 1924, Brooklyn YM/YWHA, JWB Archives, AJHSL.

55 'History of Hartford YWHA', *Connecticut Hebrew Record*, vol. 1, 21 May 1920, pp. 1, 3, 5, JHSGH.

56 Ibid.; S.H. Becker and R.L. Pearson, 'The Jewish Community of Hartford, Connecticut, 1880–1929', *American Jewish Archives*, vol. 31, 1979, pp. 184–214.

57 'Hartford YWHA challenges teams', *Connecticut Hebrew Record*, vol. 2, 10 December 1920, p. 13, JHSGH; 'New Haven', *Connecticut Hebrew Record*, vol. 2, 10 December 1920, p.12, JHSGH.

58 'New Haven YWHA', *Connecticut Hebrew Record*, vol. 2, 24 December 1920, p. 13, JHSGH.

59 'Hartford YWHA', *Connecticut Hebrew Record*, vol. 4, 30 September 1921, p. 18, JHSGH. Articles about this women's basketball team also appear in 'Hartford YWHA Athletics', *Connecticut Hebrew Record*, vol. 4, 25 November 1921, p. 19, JHSGH; 'YWHA girls victorious', *Connecticut Hebrew Record*, vol. 4, 9 December 1921, p. 16, JHSGH.

60 'Mrs. Jackson wins golf championship', *New York Times*, 20 September 1914, p. 4; See also 'Chicago girl plays fine golf and wins', *New York Times*, 19 September 1914, p. 8.

61 L.J. Borish, 'Jewish American women, Jewish organizations and sports, 1880–1940', in S.A. Riess (ed.), *Sports and the American Jew*, Syracuse, Syracuse University Press, 1998, pp. 127–8; 'Miss Elaine V. Rosenthal', *American Hebrew*, vol. XCV, no. 23, 2 October 1914, p. 653; 'Jews in Sport', *American Hebrew*, vol. XCVI, 29 January 1915, p. 347; 'Sisters rivals on Palm Beach Links', *New York Times*, 18 February 1921, p. 12; B. Postal, J. Silver and R. Silver, *Encyclopedia of Jews in Sports*, New York, Block Publishing Co., 1965, pp. 294–5; *Fifty Years of Ravisloe, 1901–1951*, Homewood, Ravisloe Country Club, 1951, courtesy of Ravisloe Country Club. For information on golf at country clubs, and women golf players on the links, see R.J. Moss, *Golf and the American Country Club*, Urbana, University of Illinois Press, 2001.

62 'Thrice Western Women's Golf Champion', *American Hebrew*, vol. 117, 6 November 1925, p. 828.

63 'Miss Rosenthal in form', *New York Times*, 15 February 1917, p. 8; 'Miss Rosenthal gets cup, Chicago golfer retains Florida title by beating Mrs. Bragg', *New York Times*, 18 February 1917, p. 1; 'Miss Rosenthal is victor', *New York Times*, 27 March 1917, p. 8; 'Miss Rosenthal wins golf trophy', *New York Times*, 30 March 1917, p. 8; 'Highlights on Links and polo fields', *American Hebrew*, vol. 123, 1 June 1928, pp. 104, 106; N.H. Gibson, *The Encyclopedia of Golf*, New York, A.S. Barnes & Co., 1958, pp. 42, 70, 156; D. Gleason, 'Alexa Stirling', *Millionaire Magazine*, 2000. Retrieved October 2000 from the World Wide Web http://www.millionaire.com.

64 'Miss Rosenthal in golf finals', *Chicago Tribune*, 9 August 1919.

65 'Miss Rosenthal loses final, 1 up', *Chicago Sunday Tribune*, 10 August 1919, p. 2.

66 Ibid.

67 'Jewesses in athletics', *American Hebrew*, vol. XCVI, no. 11, 8 January 1915, p. 279.

68 Ibid.

69 'Women life savers', *American Hebrew*, vol. XCVII, no. 16, 20 August 1915, p. 390.

70 'Indoor swim for girls', *New York Times*, 12 November 1916, p. 4; L.J. Borish, 'Charlotte Epstein', in P.E. Hyman and D.D. Moore (eds), *Jewish Women in America: A Historical Encyclopedia*, New York, Routledge, 1997, pp. 380–2.

71 'Women swimmers and AAU', *New York Times*, January 1915; 'Ladies' night now in view for AAU', Women's Swimming Association, Scrapbooks 1915–17, newspaper clippings,

Women's Swimming Association Archives, The Henning Library, International Swimming Hall of Fame, Ft Lauderdale, FL (hereafter WSA Archives, ISHOF).

72 'Women swimmers and AAU', *New York Times*, January 1915; 'Ladies' night now in view for AAU', Women's Swimming Association, Scrapbooks 1915–17, newspaper clippings, WSA Archives, ISHOF; See L.J. Borish, 'Charlotte Epstein', in P.E. Hyman and D.D. Moore (eds), *Jewish Women in America: A Historical Encyclopedia*, New York, Routledge, 1997, pp. 380–2; L.J. Borish, 'Charlotte Epstein', in G.B. Kirsch (ed.), *The Encyclopedia of Ethnicity and Sports in the United States*, Westport, Greenwood Press, 2000, pp. 148–9; I am currently writing a paper about Charlotte Epstein in which I discuss her interests in swimming and water polo, as well as the other dimensions of her work with the National Women's Life Saving League and her efforts to develop women's competitive swimming.

73 Women's Swimming Association, Scrapbooks 1915–1917, newspaper clippings, WSA Archives, ISHOF; 'Woman, the life giver, is life saver too', *New York Evening Sun*, 13 August 1915; 'Swim meet for women', *New York Times*, 8 August 1915, WSA Archives, ISHOF.

74 'Kid M'Coy's rainbow bath suit outshines girl lifesavers, who drag ducks and fruit from the sea', *New York Tribune*, 15 August 1915; 'Men, here's a rare chance to have a fair maiden hug you', *New York Evening Telegram*, 14 August 1915, WSA Archives, ISHOF.

75 'Heights girl, leader of "mermaids", praises home news campaign for swimming pool', ca. 1917, Women's Swimming Association, Scrapbooks 1915–1917, WSA Archives, ISHOF.

76 'A brief history of the Women's Swimming Association of NY', Charlotte Epstein File, WSA Archives, ISHOF. Additional material on prominent swimmers in the Women's Swimming Association can be found in P.D. Welch and H.A. Lerch, 'The Women's Swimming Association launches America into swimming supremacy', *The Olympian*, March 1979, pp. 14–16.

77 'Report of sports committee', *WSA News*, vol. III, November 1923, pp. 4–5, WSA Archives, ISHOF. The *WSA News* was first published in January 1921 to inform members of news and events, and the purpose of the club.

78 'A brief history of the Women's Swimming Association of NY', Charlotte Epstein File, WSA Archives, ISHOF. See also Charlotte Boyle Scrapbook, WSA Archives, ISHOF; R. Wettan, 'Charlotte Epstein, women's emancipation, and the emergence of competitive athletics for women in the United States', *Proceedings, Second International Seminar on Physical Education and Sport in Jewish History and Culture*, Wingate Institute, Netanya, Israel, 1977, pp. 98–103.

79 'Team notes, manager's report for 1920', *WSA News*, vol. I, February 1921, p. 2; 'WSA wins fourteenth national team championship in water sports', *WSA News*, vol. IV, October 1924, p. 1; Charlotte Boyle Scrapbook, WSA Archives, ISHOF. Several WSA swimmers like Aileen Riggin, Helen Meany, Gertrude Ederle, Charlotte Boyle, and other champions, as well as Charlotte Epstein have been inducted in the International Swimming Hall of Fame.

80 Aileen Riggin Soule, interviewed by Linda J. Borish, Kalamazoo, MI, USA, June 1995.

81 'Team notes, manager's report for 1920', p. 2; Aileen Riggin Soule discussed the success of the 1920 US Olympic Women's Swimming Team and her WSA teammates, Aileen Riggin Soule, interviewed by Linda J. Borish, Kalamazoo, MI, USA, June 1995.

82 'Dinner to WSA Olympic team', *WSA News*, vol. IV, July, August, September 1924, p. 10. For information on the WSA members on the Olympic swimming team, see also 'WSA girls big factor in Olympic triumphs', *WSA News*, vol. IV, July, August, September 1924, pp. 1, 4, WSA Archives, ISHOF.

83 Aileen Riggin Soule, interviewed by Linda J. Borish, Kalamazoo, MI, USA, June 1995; 'Program of the National Championship Meet, Women's Swimming Association of New York at the Young Women's Hebrew Association, March 13, 1920', WSA Archives, ISHOF; see also National Swimming Championship Flyer and Entry Form 1923, YWHA Scrapbook, 92nd Street YM/YWHA Archives.

84 'History of the Maccabiah Games', in R. Rabinowitz (ed.), *16th Maccabiah, One People, One Dream*, Israel, July 2001. Archival Material from the Pierre Gildesgame Maccabi Sports Museum, and Maccabi World Union, Ramat-Gan, Israel. Booklet in possession of L.J. Borish who attended the Opening of the 16th Maccabiah in Jerusalem, Israel, 16 July 2001.

85 'History of the Maccabiah Games', in R. Rabinowitz (ed.), *16th Maccabiah, One People, One Dream*, Israel, July 2001. Archival Material from the Pierre Gildesgame Maccabi Sports Museum, and Maccabi World Union, Ramat-Gan, Israel.

86 Quotes from 'Second Maccabiah flag hoisted', *The Palestine Post*, Tel Aviv, 2 April 1935, p. 1, and 'Gay pageantry marks opening of Maccabiah', *The Palestine Post*, Jerusalem, 3 April 1935, p. 1, New York Public Library (NYPL), Jewish Division.

87 'Second Maccabiah flag hoisted', *The Palestine Post*, Tel Aviv, 2 April 1935, p. 1, NYPL, Jewish Division.

88 'After the Maccabiah', *The Palestine Post*, Jerusalem, 9 April 1935, p. 5, NYPL, Jewish Division. For additional information on athletes wanting to stay in Palestine see 'History of the Maccabiah Games', in R. Rabinowitz (ed.), *16th Maccabiah, One People, One Dream*, Israel, July 2001.

89 'Miss Lifson takes swimming honors', *New York Times*, 18 February 1935, p. 22.

90 'Jewish who's who – 1935, sports', *American Hebrew*, vol. 138, 20 December 1935, p. 193. Lifson also appears in the piece 'Jewish sportsmen on parade', *American Hebrew*, vol. 136, 7 June 1935, p. 94.

91 'Maccabiah sports end – swimming meet', *The Palestine Post*, Jerusalem, 11 April 1935, p. 5, NYPL, Jewish Division.

92 'Maccabi team feted', *New York Times*, 6 June 1935, p. 30.

93 'Hark ye athletes', *Community News*, 7, September 1925, p. 5, New Haven, CT YM/YWHA, Jewish Welfare Board Archives; 'Athletic night Monday, April 15th at 8:00 PM', *Jewish Community Center, Yonkers, New York, Dedication Week Program, April 14–21, 1929*, Jewish Welfare Board Archives, American Jewish Historical Society, Waltham, MA.

94 Charlotte Epstein File, WSA Archives, ISHOF; 'Miss Epstein dead; Olympics official', *New York Times*, 27 August 1938, p. 13; L.J. Borish, 'Charlotte Epstein', in P.E. Hyman and D.D. Moore (eds), *Jewish Women in America: A Historical Encyclopedia*, New York, Routledge, 1997, pp. 380–2.

95 'Miss Copeland sets mark in shot-put', *New York Times*, 13 August 1928, p. 12.

96 Ibid.

97 L.J. Borish, 'Lillian Copeland', in G.B. Kirsch (ed.), *The Encyclopedia of Ethnicity and Sports in the United States*, Westport, Greenwood Press, 2000, p. 110; 'Lillian Copeland, 59, dies; won Olympic medal in 1932', *New York Times*, 8 July 1964, p. 35.

98 'Jewish who's who – 1935, sports', *American Hebrew*, vol. 138, 20 December 1935, pp. 192–3.

99 L.J. Borish, 'Lillian Copeland', in G.B. Kirsch (ed.), *The Encyclopedia of Ethnicity and Sports in the United States*, Westport, Greenwood Press, 2000, p. 110; M. Wacks, 'Copeland, Lillian', in P.E. Hyman and D.D. Moore (eds), *Jewish Women in America: A Historical Encyclopedia*, New York, Routledge, 1997, pp. 288–90; 'Lillian Copeland, 59, dies; won Olympic medal in 1932', *New York Times*, 8 July 1964, p. 35; D.H. Pieroth, *Their Day in the Sun: Women of the 1932 Olympics*, Seattle, University of Washington Press, 1996.

100 'Miss Koff scores in Jewish Games', *New York Times*, 1 April 1932; 'Jewish sportsmen on parade', *American Hebrew*, vol. 136, 7 June 1935, p. 94; 'Jewish who's who – 1935, sports', *American Hebrew*, vol. 138, 20 December 1935, p. 193.

101 Ibid., p. 192.

102 'Sybil Cooper, track star, 85', *Forward*, 29 May 1998, p. 10; S. Cooper, 'The story of Sybille – true and complete', *Sybille Gallery Newsletter*, Premiere Issue, Summer 1998, pp. 1–2; 'Miss Koff scores in Jewish Games', *New York Times*, 1 April 1932; L.E. Cohen,

'Sport chats: Syd Koff – she suddenly became an athlete and rose to champion', *Brooklyn Daily Eagle*, 22 August 1934. Articles and news clippings courtesy of Doris Beshunsky, Philadelphia, PA.

103 D. Gabaccia, *From the Other Side: Women, Gender and Immigrant Life in the US, 1820–1920*, Bloomington, Indiana University Press, 1994, p. 124.

104 *Building Character for 75 Years: Published on the Occasion of the 75th Anniversary of the Young Men's and Young Women's Hebrew Association*, New York City, 1969, p. 3.

6 Manly Catholicism
Making men in Catholic public schools, 1945–80

Timothy J.L. Chandler

The Puritan and the Catholic
Both thought they were promoting
God's kingdom, but they thought it
Had to be promoted in a different
Manner. And the different manner
Made it quite a different kingdom.[1]

There is a well-known story of a young master, new to Sherborne, who is due to make his first visit to Downside as the coach of a school rugby team. As he waits at the school entrance for his team to board the bus, the young man sees the imposing figure of the headmaster approaching him. The headmaster stops and, speaking quietly but firmly, says to the young master, 'if you lose to "the papists" you needn't come back'. Whilst the story is probably apocryphal, it is recounted over and over again to new masters, handed down to them by senior members of staff. It is but one small part of the folklore that surrounds the Sherborne/Downside rivalry, and is considered an important part of the socialisation of new rugby coaches at Sherborne.

This anecdote reveals tensions between Catholic and Protestant public schools that are played out, in part, on the sports field. Shirburnians refer to Downside as Doomside (pronounced Dooooomside): a name that connotes both humour and foreboding; a term portentous of the feelings and thoughts that surround both individuals and teams as they prepare to grapple with the old enemy; a reminder that if your team should lose you are doomed to face the failure, humiliation, even depression that a loss to 'the papists' would auger. Whilst it has been popularly likened to a 'war without weapons', in this sense, sport operates as a marker of religious difference and as a mechanism to instil a particular devotional identity in the boys attending Catholic and Protestant public schools in the United Kingdom.

Attempts to retain the integrity of Catholic communities are not without precedent. Steven Fielding suggests that the Catholic Church in England has attempted to raise structural fences around Catholics in order to reinforce a sense of belonging to a separate culture whilst reinforcing the importance of the centrality of the Church in the lives of Catholics.[2] As such, organised games, particularly in 'total environments' such as boarding schools, may provide an additional avenue to confirm faith amongst participants. Although at Catholic public schools, such as Ampleforth and Downside, some of the original structural fences of location and insularity have been broken down by playing inter-school contests against non-Catholic public schools, the symbolic and ritual markers that Catholics have used to differentiate themselves from their Protestant counterparts remain powerful. In particular, the role of sport in the embodiment of Catholicism and the physical practice and expression of religious identity is an area that has received little attention and may reveal the myriad ways that physical culture contributes to the performance of religious identity. Indeed, a sense of the centrality of the Church in the lives of Catholics, and the significance of the Benedictine family and community, is evident at both Ampleforth and Downside.[3] Whilst many have considered the role of organised games in English public schools, few have taken into consideration the religious differences that have served to distinguish Catholic and Protestant faiths. In this sense, it is appropriate to examine the role of sport in the service of religion within these institutions.

The term 'English public schools' has been used as a short-hand to describe a set of institutions for which there is no generally agreed or clear-cut definition.[4] It is generally accepted, however, that such schools have long provided a private and often expensive education for the scions of England's upper-middle classes; and one of the best-known characteristics of this group of schools has been the significant role assigned to organised games and sports as a cornerstone of the education they provide.[5] Such a description highlights both the class-centred tradition of English education and the broader emphasis on the centrality of class sentiment within English society. It is also indicative of the fact that historians have tended to identify English public schools, as a group, as being part of a culturally and politically homogeneous upper-middle class. As Fielding and others have noted, 'the general bias towards this type of class interpretation is partly a reflection of the relatively homogeneous nature of English society'.[6] The significance of issues surrounding this small group of schools is crucial because 'interests of class and status, power and advantage, familial continuity and social integration are at stake'.[7]

Yet, if we look at English society through a religious rather than a class lens, and focus on Catholics and Puritans/Protestants, as the earlier quote from Richard Peters has suggested,[8] we get a rather different picture. Edward Norman has suggested that anti-Catholicism and hostility towards the Catholic Church have been one of the first defining qualities of modern 'Englishness' shared by all members of society.[9] Whilst such hostility to Catholics may have been less marked amongst Protestant[10] members of those 'relatively homogeneous' upper-middle classes who attended public schools than amongst their working-class counterparts, it is certainly the case that, in general, the Catholic English public schools can be characterised by a 'cultural, geographical, religious and educational distance from mainstream public school life'.[11] Many of the major English houses of Catholic religious orders and their associated schools, including Ampleforth and Downside, spent time in isolation on the European continent, to avoid persecution. On returning to England at the end of the eighteenth and the beginning of the nineteenth centuries, following the passing of the Catholic Relief Acts beginning in 1778, these houses remained very much in isolation as sanctuaries for Catholics.

Whilst Catholic public schools have been both distant and different, such distance and difference have been declining since 1945, especially in the final decades of the twentieth century as public schools collectively have faced changing economic and political realities. John Rae has called the changes such political and economic pressures have wrought a 'revolution',[12] typified by an increased academic competition between schools, which is exemplified by an emphasis on examination results. Despite Rae's classification, others, such as Geoffrey Walford, with the benefit of greater distance from such events, have suggested that the second half of the twentieth century has seen both continuity and change in public schools.[13] Change in these institutions has come in the shape of reform in order to preserve their position and status. Walford cites as major changes and reforms the emphasis on examination results to try to ensure access to the best universities and high-status careers for Old Boys, along with the declining influence of the Combined Cadet Force and the broadening of sporting opportunities. Continuities, in the form of the on-going stress on community living, organised games and the house system, however, are also readily apparent. Christine Heward's detailed description of public school life between 1929 and 1950 differs only in degree rather than in kind from the one offered by John Wilson in the early 1960s.[14] And even Rae admits that 'if a man who had entered his public school in 1960 could repeat the process in 1980 he would probably find more that was familiar than unfamiliar'.[15]

Ampleforth and Downside had their own distinct games culture, playing their own forms of cricket and football. Because of their isolation and insularity, however, these unique activities and the culture that supported them remained strong and undiluted well into the twentieth century. And yet, even when they did become less isolated, adopting the rugby football code and participating in 'foreign' matches with non-Catholic institutions, the impact of this extended athleticism was unlike that found generally in Protestant Public Schools; devotion to Christianity was not completely subsumed by the worship of muscle. Ampleforth and Downside were able to reject the extreme forms of 'both the animus and emblems of athleticism' which typified so many of the Protestant public schools even in the inter-war years.[16] I have argued elsewhere that muscular Christianity was, *in extremis*, a combination of the morality of the monk and the manliness of the beast.[17] It appears that the constant presence of the monks limited the extent to which the beast was manifested in the muscular Christianity of

Ampleforth and Downside games at the institutional level well into the twentieth century.

Although, as Walford has noted, sporting opportunities have increased for boys since 1945, the emphasis on team games, particularly rugby and cricket, has remained strong in all of the leading public schools. Given that sport was, and still is, a large part of the education offered by these institutions, Catholic public schools are provided with opportunities to contest the religious terrain with their Protestant counterparts, since sporting success remains a readily understandable and obvious measure of a school's status.[18] As such, I argue that the manner in which certain core religious values have been constructed in Catholic public schools, both in and through sport, has helped differentiate them from their Protestant counterparts, and has contributed to the embodiment of Catholicism in their young men. Indeed, there is a sense in which religion has been used in the service of sport in the Catholic schools, almost as much as sport has been used in the service of religion. In this regard, I stress how differences, reinforced by the fact that Catholic public schools are deemed 'other' by Protestant institutions, have been perceived in Protestant schools, and suggest that 'otherness' functioned as a psychological 'weapon' for Catholic schools on the playing field – a case of religion in the service of sport. Finally, I show how sport in general, and rugby in particular, provided Catholic school communities with sites where masculinity-making for individuals could be made explicit,[19] as well as with opportunities for marking out 'correct' or 'appropriate' styles of being.[20]

I present much of the material in the form of a case study of the relationship between two schools: Downside (Catholic) and Sherborne (Protestant).[21] I outline two specific examples of perceptions of and interactions between boys and masters at Downside and its 'Old Firm' rival Sherborne, and provide an insight into the way that Protestants signify religious difference by inscribing the Catholic (sporting) body with distinctive characteristics. My purpose in providing these examples is to highlight how bodily labelling, significant of pertinent religious and sporting difference, has been maintained. And whilst Pierre Bourdieu contends that the privileged classes see sport as a means of self-development and are less inclined to physically abuse their bodies than the 'dominated classes',[22] I suggest that we need to broaden our view of 'privileged' and 'dominated' classes to include religion along with other factors such as class, gender and race, if we are to explain the character of Catholic public school sport.

The impetus for examining the relationship between Catholics and Protestants in the context of school sport derived in part from the work of Bill Murray and others on the 'Old Firm' rivalry of Rangers and Celtic in Glasgow as well as from my experiences in these diverse educational settings.[23] I am also intrigued by Richard Light's work, which suggests that 'bodily practices [operate] to embody a culture specific form of masculinity'.[24] Whilst Light focuses on cross-cultural differences, I contend that religious distinctions may also be embodied, such that playing styles, or indeed, the perceptions of difference in style, become markers of religious identity. In this case study, I argue that religious identity in Catholic schools, for example, influences the range and types of masculinities that sport is thought to embody in their students.

One final caveat is necessary. The Catholic public schools are no more a completely homogeneous group than are their Protestant counterparts in that each has been significantly shaped by factors such as history and location. It is for this reason that I have elected to present material in the form of a case study of two schools in order to tease out some of the more important themes rather than attempting to generalise across public schools. In the case of Catholic schools, there is the added issue of specific denominational affiliation. Thus Catholic public schools range from staunchly Jesuit institutions, such as Stonyhurst, to Rosminian-influenced schools, such as Ratcliffe. Yet, in their quest to be seen as public schools, all have adopted organised games, to a greater or lesser degree, as a central part of their educational programme. I focus on two of the best-known Catholic public schools, Ampleforth and Downside, paying particular attention to Downside. Both are Benedictine foundations and have strong and long-standing academic and athletic traditions; both are members of the Headmasters' Conference, placing them amongst the elite group of independent schools in Britain; and both participate in sporting competitions that are limited to elite public schools and their Old Boys, such as the Cricketer Cup.[25] These three pertinent characteristics suggest that Ampleforth and Downside are accepted by the leading Protestant public schools as being their equals in status, despite their religious differences and their past history of distance and isolation.[26]

Catholicism, masculinity and sport

> Young men situationally accomplish public forms of masculinity in response to their socially structured circumstances.[27]

The Catholic Church has adopted its educational role as a direct consequence of its mission to assert the primacy of Christian theology. Whilst the teaching of Catholic youth has been the task of both men and women, the education of the young necessarily reflects the ideas of their elders, and, in the cases of both the Catholic church in general and the Catholic public schools in particular, traditionally those elders have been men. Indeed, the Catholic Church remains a male-dominated and male-led institution, such that within Catholic public schools leadership positions have often been filled by monks, who have adopted a life of spiritual, emotional and physical devotion to God and service to humankind. Catholic theologians and educators agree that:

[T]he more surely any body of men adheres to a fixed conviction of positive principles and ways of life, the more purposefully will it seek to guide along clearly laid down lines the moral, intellectual and even physical development of its children. The Catholic Church is pre-eminently such a body of men.[28]

As such, we would expect that Catholic public schools would be bound up with the organic life of the Catholic Church and that its teachings would be 'lived in common and shared by pupils and teachers alike'.[29] And in that common experience life is but a preparatory stage for death. The aim of a Catholic education is to prepare for a life after death, and this requires the development of character, moral virtues and the best possible record of behaviour. In a male-oriented, male-dominated world in which a hair-shirt was not an unexpected mode of attire, in which 'creature-comforts' had been abjured, and in which the Crucifixion was the ultimate means of passing through the gateway of death to the life beyond, the dominant model of masculinity portrayed to Ampleforth and Downside boys was spartan and physical. Based on the principle of self-renunciation, these Catholic schools looked to promote a healthy asceticism as their model of masculinity, and to achieve that aim by giving it a concrete shape on the level of daily life.[30] This was their exemplar of male power and religious devotion. And although it shared many of the characteristics of the Protestant school system, the Catholic model was not the dominant educational or religious approach found in the elite public schools.

Tensions between Catholic and Protestant ideologies have a long history in Britain. As Mike Cronin points out elsewhere in this volume, in Ireland these tensions have clearly manifested themselves in sport in the past century, where power has resided largely with the Catholics. In England, the historical relations of religious power locate that power within a Protestant worldview and subordinate the Catholic to 'other'. From the 1550s, following Henry VIII's secession from Rome and the formation of the Church of England, life for Catholics in England became increasingly difficult. The suppression and dissolution of monasteries led to the departure to continental Europe of the vast majority of those priests and monks who remained loyal to Rome, although some staunch and wealthy Catholic households maintained their own priests – hiding them in priests' holes to avoid detection when necessary. The rising tide of Puritanism in the seventeenth century saw a further move away from Catholicism. The Bill of Rights (1689) declared that the monarch had to be a Protestant and the Act of Settlement (1701) required that the monarch had to be a member of the Church of England.

The Evangelical Movement of the late eighteenth century was balanced by the reaffirmation of the Catholic and apostolic character of the Church of England in the Oxford Movement, which saw the conversion of a number of highly placed clergyman such as Cardinal John Henry Newman to

Catholicism. The changing attitudes towards Catholics and Catholicism, particularly amongst the educated classes, had already effected the repeal of the Anti-Catholic Acts and the Penal Laws at the end of the eighteenth century. Such changes enabled the Jesuits of St Omer to return to Stonyhurst in 1794, and the two Benedictine houses of Ampleforth and Downside to take up residence in England in 1802 and 1814 respectively. Although originally very small, these two communities grew steadily with increasing contact with Oxford and Cambridge and under the patronage of some of England's wealthier Catholic families. They slowly adopted many of the characteristics of the English public schools, such as the house system and organised games, as they looked to compete more directly with them to offer a Catholic education for the sons of Catholic parents or, increasingly, of families in which only one parent was Catholic. Ampleforth and Downside became the communities that were responsible for the education of young upper-middle-class Catholic boys.[31]

Bob Connell has shown that schools are critical sites in the making of masculinities,[32] whilst Richard Light and David Kirk have demonstrated how the nature of young men's experiences of sport in schools contributes to the embodiment of a culture-specific masculinity. They have further shown how involvement in school sport can help identify the central role of the body in reproducing and maintaining a hegemonic form of masculinity. Furthermore, they demonstrate that the processes through which boys learn to become particular types of men need to be understood as having an important historical component. What it means to be a man in a particular school is as much a form of collective remembering as it is a form of individual attainment.[33] Likewise David Whitson has noted the time, effort and support given by schools to 'masculinizing practices' such as sport, and that 'becoming a man' is something at which boys must work. Furthermore, all-male boarding schools such as Downside and Sherborne provide ample opportunities for such self-discipline as well as a historical legacy of successes (and failures) from which boys can learn.[34] As such, in making men, schools and school sport shape not only class, race and gender relations, but also religious relations.

Sport, as a central facet of public school life, has provided an ideal terrain on which to contest such relations, and has offered opportunities for Catholic schools to challenge the 'religious order' every time they have played inter-school matches against their Protestant counterparts. Thus, constructing a religious identity is a feature of not only formal education; social or informal events, such as sport, are also complicit in defining and reaffirming Catholic masculinity for the boys who engage in them. In the case of institutions such as Ampleforth and Downside, where the schools are attached to monasteries and where the Abbot is in charge of education, religion is a critical feature of a student's lived experience. All forms of cultural practice are thus imbued with an essential 'Catholic' nature that is at once a marker of difference as well as a symbol of inclusion in a wider community. This is not to suggest that the religious identity operates independently of broader notions of masculinity. Indeed, the two reside simultaneously in sporting practices, but it is the expression of a specific Catholic masculinity as conveyed through sport that is of interest here.

The hegemonic masculinity that pervades public schools, whether Catholic or Protestant, is heterosexual, virile and uses success on the rugby field as one of its standard bearers and cultural markers. Yet that dominance is never completely secure and must be constantly negotiated. Thus, from a social relations perspective at least, the generalised form of masculinity exalted in the public schools during what might be termed the late-twentieth-century version of muscular Christianity, could, and coaches at the schools would argue *did*, differ within equally prestigious but religiously different public schools. In this context, as Tim Newburn and Elizabeth Stanko suggest, it is crucial to think about the power and variety of masculine values, the processes by which they become internalised, the processes of identification, and the ways in which certain core values become associated with specific groups, if we are to avoid thinking of an all-pervasive reified masculinity.[35] Therefore, if the manner and style in which rugby football is played characterises a school's dominant bodily culture and is one of the patterned ways in which masculinity is represented and internalised, then differences in playing style become important indicators of difference in masculinity and masculine identity,[36] even within what have typically been thought of as similar, even homogeneous, institutions.

Catholic corporeality

Given the significance of religion in such schools, organised sport, and rugby in particular, I suggest, is endowed with a particular 'Catholic way of playing'. As such, I argue that the body plays a central role in sport and religion at a school such as Downside, for it signifies, particularly to the non-Catholic, the corporeal relationship between physical discipline and religious commitment. Connell has noted the significance of the body in social processes reinforcing Bourdieu's view that the body is a central means through which culture is produced and reproduced.[37] More recently, Light and Kirk have observed the importance of the relationship between institutionalised regimes of physical activity in schools and lived experiences of class, culture and gender.[38] The ways in which sport is played in public schools are indicative of students' disposition, tastes and even beliefs, which in turn structure their behaviour and social action. Habitus, as the embodied social thinking of an individual, is developed as individuals engage in the social and cultural life of a school.[39]

Whereas researchers, such as Whitson, argue that hegemonic notions of manliness and masculinity are constructs that have developed within particular social and cultural fields over time,[40] I maintain that in these particular Catholic institutions, a traditional form of Catholic masculinity has been reproduced through discourse and corporeal practices not only as a result of internal drives but also in opposition to forces from outside the Catholic community. Thus, whilst Connell argues that masculinity in schoolboy sport is constructed around varying combinations of force and skill,[41] I propose that in the style of playing rugby, there is an added religious significance to the 'fearsome' and 'fearless' disciplining of the body and engendering of masculinity, suggestive of sacrifice, even transcendence. Indeed, there may even be reason to suggest that playing style may provide an important symbolic measure of religious inequality between Catholics and Protestants in what might be termed the 'religious order'. As one example, bodily differences are highlighted in the language used by Protestants to describe Catholics.

Amongst their Protestant counterparts Catholic public schoolboys are collectively referred to as 'left-footers', with all that term connotes in terms of difference: minority, strangeness, otherness. Where rugby football is concerned, this is obviously a particularly apposite term. Certainly in the past, it would not have been lost on public school boys, almost all of whom had at least a rudimentary understanding of Latin; the Latin word *dexter* meant on the right hand and had connotations of dexterity and skill as well as of normality. The opposite of *dexter* is *sinister*, meaning on the left hand. Left-handedness is not the norm, rather it is abnormal, even sinister. By implication then, left-footers are different, a minority, abnormal even sinister people. The term *sinister* has a variety of other connotations ranging from bad luck, to evil, witchcraft, idolatry and even the devil. Catholicism may not have been sinister but it was abnormal. Upper-middle-class left-footers may not have been sinister but they were certainly different. And they were thought to be different in bodily ways. They used their bodies differently – they used them fearlessly. Whilst in more recent parlance the term left-footer has become a label that is now more broadly used to denote difference of other sorts, most notably sexual preference, it is still a term that is applied to Catholics and particularly Catholics from public schools by their Protestant counterparts.

In preparing teams to play rugby against Downside, there had long been an expectation amongst the Sherborne masters that the game would be a particularly physical contest no matter what the level – under-14 or first fifteen[42] – but was particularly pertinent at the first fifteen level where adolescent boys were expected to perform like 'real men', an expectation held to as firmly by the boys as by their masters. The physical nature of these contests has also been noted by those outside the schools. The *Times* described one Downside/Sherborne match as being 'fiercely hard'.[43] There was something about the 'abandon' with which Downside boys played that both impressed and yet sometimes alarmed observers. It was not that Sherborne's other opponents did not play hard, and it was not that other schools did not have individual boys who could be very or even overly aggressive. Rather, as many Sherborne masters noted, it was just 'something' about the Downside approach, about their style of play. It was very physical, sometimes even feverish; and to many of the boys at Sherborne, it was intimidating. Like Ampleforth, its northern counterpart, Downside was known as a rugby powerhouse, and both established reputations as rugby strongholds. They each played in a manner that one senior master described as 'totally uncompromising', another as 'fearsome'. With regard to muscular Christianity, their adherence to principles of 'the beast' were as whole-hearted and visible as their adherence to the principles of 'the monk'.

From discussions with the masters who coached the Downside teams, it was clear that they were well aware of how their school was perceived by Shirburnians and the other schools against which they competed. They knew that the Downside style was viewed as very physical, and whilst they may not have associated this style with a belief system that promoted a particular form of masculinity, certainly they did not make such a connection explicit to the boys they coached, they did expect their teams to display a 'virile and healthy spirit'. They too used the term 'fearsome' to describe the style of rugby they favoured. It is also important to an understanding of the Downside style to know what they thought of as 'virile and healthy'.

Downside teams and their coaches expected that Sherborne teams would always be well-coached, play technically-sound rugby, be disciplined and play hard. Sherborne teams played a running and handling game premised on good organisation and team discipline. From the early 1960s onwards Sherborne had adopted a centralised system of coaching which emanated from, and was promoted by, the master in charge of (rugby) football, the legendary M.M. Walford, in consultation with team coaches.[44] It was implemented through ensuring that all masters who were coaching rugby, no matter what the level, would promote the principles and practices that Walford and his closest advisors felt would bring success to school teams.[45] This relatively uniform system of coaching was a distinctive feature of the bodily discipline to which Shirburnians were subjected. Indeed, it was also a central element of that discipline since rugby was compulsory for all boys. To this degree it could be viewed as part of the athletic technology used to provide bodily discipline.

With a history of appointing leading rugby players as teachers, many of whom were 'big names'[46] to ensure the continuing strength of Sherborne rugby, the expectations that Downside and other opponents had of Sherborne rugby teams were more than reasonable. To Shirburnians, playing well and playing hard meant playing technically well as a team, playing with spirit as a team, whilst giving of one's best as an individual. By contrast, when watching Downside boys play, it often appeared that for teams, playing well meant playing with passion – even playing as if their lives depended upon it. They tended to play in a manner that displayed enormous spirit and was indeed 'fearsome'. Their style might also be described as fearless in that boys often showed very little regard for their bodies.

Inventing traditions

These are of course nothing more than stereotyped images of the styles of rugby played at each respective school, which have been produced by Downside and Sherborne masters and boys over the many years of their rivalry. As such, we can regard these perceptions as something of an invented tradition, which was specifically negotiated to distinguish 'us' from 'them', thereby promoting and sustaining difference and distance between Protestant and Catholic corporeality. In my experience, it is clear that the respective demonstrations of physicality that I have observed and, indeed, the cultural meanings attributed to those displays, were deliberate and supported by these invented traditions at both Downside and Sherborne. Although the image of Downside's style being 'feverish' did not resemble the way that Downsiders viewed themselves or their style of play, Downside coaches agreed nonetheless that they coached their teams to be 'fearsome' and to play 'with a great deal of spirit'. At the same time, for successive generations of Shirburnians, their perception of Downside's feverish and fearsome style was indeed reality. Shirburnian masters and boys interpreted what they saw of their opponents on the field as being indicative of the Downside approach. To some degree then this rivalry provides an indication of how images of one institution can be developed, transmitted and sustained in another.

On 'crossing over' from Sherborne to Downside, it was evident to me that Downsiders viewed Shirburnians in an equally stereotypic manner. To them, Sherborne played a style of running game, which placed a premium on team play and coordination. In other words, they played 'scientifically'.[47] It appears therefore that the perceived style of play of one school even provided ongoing and necessary reinforcement to the 'style' of play of the other. With a history of well over 100 contests to reflect on, beginning in 1914, and at conservative institutions such as these where shared memory casts a long shadow, it was hardly surprising that stereotypes had become deeply ingrained; and that, for both schools, this had become 'the big game'.

When asked to reflect on the Sherborne/Downside rivalry, coaches at both schools identified two additional factors that may account for the differing styles. First, the grounds on which the two schools play seem to influence the style of play. Sherborne's playing fields are well-drained and generally dry, thereby favouring a fast, open running-and-handling game. Downside's fields, by contrast, are usually muddier, encouraging a more physical forward-based game.[48] A second factor is that Downside rugby coaches have allowed, even encouraged, individuals with talent to excel,[49] such that they have promoted the individual as well as individual skills. At Sherborne, where a team approach is preferred, combination and cooperation have been stressed rather than individual effort. And for the small number who had been teachers or coaches in both establishments or who had experience in coaching boys from both schools,[50] this difference in approach was tangible. In addition, on the basis of limited observations of other Catholic schools in which they also perceived amongst their teams a fearsome and feverish physical quality to the style of play, many of these coaches found confirmation for their generalised view that there was indeed a 'Catholic style of play' – a style based on extreme physicality and a bodily fearlessness; a style that could be extremely intimidating.

Theological considerations

The sporting ethos of Protestant public schools owes a large debt to muscular Christianity, an ideology premised on the Kingsleyan view that hardy team games could provide a 'physical armour-plating to withstand various potential threats to religious beliefs, bodily health and social stability' in mid-Victorian England.[51] The product of profound insecurity in an age that was 'deeply troubled with religious doubt, [and] acutely aware of weakness and frustration',[52] muscular Christianity stressed the values of physical prowess and spiritual aspiration. The athletic body was co-opted as an emblem of the spiritual which, when combined with a distrust of the flesh and the fears of the (in particular, adolescent) sexual body in all-male institutions, led to an emphasis on character-building as a hallmark of the English public school. As such, celebration of the advantages, both spiritual and secular, to be had from a disciplined and controlled self, marked originally by industry, temperance and morality in Kingsley's time, developed by the early twentieth century into manliness;[53] manliness in which sport became for many a significant source of bodily purification and an antidote to the development of adult male sexuality. Thus for the Protestant public schools, the vast majority of which 'took their religion as a cold bath', participation in team sports became a way of achieving the proper kind of manliness.[54] So whereas the manly athletic public school body came to represent Protestant public school belief, this was not so obviously the case in the Catholic schools. For whereas in the Catholic schools the athletic body has been used to *stand up* for a Catholic world view, in the Protestant schools the manly athletic body has been used to *stand in* for religion.[55]

Whilst many perceived a particular denominational physicality, theological precepts might also reveal significant differences between Catholic and Protestant styles of play. For Catholics, the central aim of life is to prepare for death,[56] and for those brought up in Benedictine public schools the path to transcending death lies through both faith and virtue. Transcendence is thus a central tenet of such an approach to life. It is of some interest then that the desire to achieve immortality through some extraordinary act – an act of transcendence – has been identified as one of masculinity's ultimate values.[57] What does this say about the likely effects of a specifically Catholic form of masculinity being promoted in schools? And what might the Catholic Church in general and, more importantly, Benedictine monks in particular, offer as appropriate theology for adolescent boys to promote faith and virtue and inspire transcendence? One potential source of information for Ampleforth students is to be found in a book of *Devotions and Prayers*.[58] Another more widely acknowledged source, is the popular and well-regarded set of *Meditations for Boys* written by the Benedictine writer, Bede Jarrett.[59] Whilst the meditations were dedicated to the boys of St Dominic's Parish, they have enjoyed far more widespread appeal amongst Benedictine institutions. They provide some indication as to how boys have been encouraged by their teachers to think about specific issues such as death, and of most interest here, their bodies and organised games.

Jarrett provided this meditation for boys regarding games:

> It is evident that, from the large place that games fill in my time ... that manner in which I take part in them must be of considerable importance to my soul. ... I should consider [what the] verdict [of others] would be if they were told to pass judgement on the spirit in which I play my games. ... It is the spirit rather than the result of my playing that matters. ... Here, then, let me turn to our Lord, ... and let me ask Him when I receive him in Communion to make me a follower of Him especially in my games.[60]

Whilst the proffered links between style or manner of play, the spirit with which games are played and the passing of judgement on a boy's soul, are ideas that might have been propounded in sermons by late-Victorian public school headmasters such as H.H. Almond, they are not notions that Protestant public schoolboys would have heard in the post-war years. The idea that displaying spirit, in terms of the way in which others perceive one's bodily actions, is commended as a way of baring one's soul and exemplifying virtue, however, may provide some insight into the very physical style of the Catholic schools' rugby players. With monks as constant reminders of the sublimation of the physical in favour of the spiritual, and an emphasis on spirit over everything else, it is perhaps possible to understand both how and why Downside boys played with such physical fervour, and why they appeared to delight in the physical and played in a manner that at times seemed fearless, or even reckless. The bodily spirit (the beast) promoted by coaches and displayed on the rugby field both mirrors and represents the religious spirit being inculcated by the monks in the school.

Further insight into such bodily action is provided by Jarrett's meditation entitled 'The Body'. Here he offers an example of how a set of seemingly disparate concepts – the body, the Rosary, sport and Easter, can be unified to provide a religious, even mystical, interpretation of how boys can transcend the pain and injury experienced in games and thus show reverence for God. He encourages boys to think along these lines by meditating as follows:

> When I turn to the sorrowful mysteries of the Rosary, I am taught to find in the suffering there displayed the means for sanctifying all my pains. ... His passion and death therefore take my pains and make them

blessed. The pains of my body, as well as my soul, can thus be sanctified, and the delights of my body, as well as my soul, thus turned to good account. ... The fine and wholesome feelings of life after a good sporting game ... are made blessed by the risen joys of Easter. This shows me how good a thing my body can be, ... the body will lead me to God. Of course, I must control and discipline it. ... But the body itself is a blessed thing, God's own make, to be reverenced and loved.[61]

This example of sport used in the service of religion highlights quite clearly a significant difference between Catholic and Protestant schools, despite the fact that, in both institutions, there was a long-standing expectation that sport was an integral part of education. But the disciplining of the Catholic body was very different from the disciplining of the Protestant body.

Another of the reasons for the differing approach in the two sets of schools is that in Catholic schools the emphasis was, and still is, very much on *esprit de famille*.[62] As a family, members are expected to develop themselves to the full; each is cared about as an individual. This is in contrast to the emphasis on *esprit de corps*, which was, and to a large degree remains, an underlying philosophy of Protestant schools. Whilst it is an over-simplistic contrast, in a Protestant school, such as Sherborne, the value of organised games was in the opportunity they provided for the outward display of conformity and cooperation, and for furthering allegiance to, and disciplining of, the corporate body. In a Benedictine establishment such as Downside, organised games were shaped, in part at least, to provide each student/member of the Benedictine family with an opportunity to reflect on their own body and their relationship with God. Games provided opportunities for meditation and (self-)confession such that, in Jarrett's terms, others could observe each family member's soul through the way they played and used their body, thereby offering opportunities to enrich an individual's understanding of the corporeal. The bodily discipline inherent in the playing of rugby was required to display a reverence for God. Playing without fear was a way of confessing appropriate reverence.

Debra Shogun describes the 'confessional' technology employed in sport and how coaches can and do use such technology both to increase self-awareness amongst athletes and to 'improve' the confessor/athlete.[63] The premise on which such techniques are based confirms the power and control that a coach has over an athlete, a system, which, in the public schools, is well-established, where masters in sport exercise a high level of control over their charges. In the context provided by the Catholic schools where religious goals are central, and at Downside and Ampleforth where Benedictine principles provide much of the discipline and its supporting ideology, the promotion of self-awareness and the improvement of the boy/player /confessor has a distinctive moral and religious flavour. As Jarrett has emphasised in his meditations, whilst providing an opportunity for *esprit de famille,* organised games have fulfilled the more important role of providing individual boys with a dedicated showcase for the display of Christian virtue and an enjoyable avenue for evaluating their individual worth. The style of play adopted is a means of confessing because it is a display of one's own worth. In Protestant schools, whilst organised games have also been a means of fostering individual value, there has always been a fear of what one famous headmaster referred to regularly in the late 1960s and early 1970s as 'the cult of the individual'.[64] As such, much more emphasis has been placed on fostering cooperation and providing a stage upon which *esprit de corps* and institutional health and worth could be fostered and demonstrated.

At Sherborne, the confessional technology was less focussed on individual boys and more focussed on the team and on the success of the coach in working with his team. Thus on a Saturday evening all coaches were expected to gather in Micky Walford's study and 'confess' to their team's performance. Micky invariably served his own home-brewed beer to the confessor/coaches on these occasions, but as the 'high priest' he always treated himself to twelve year-old scotch! Here again is further evidence to support an explanation of the differences in playing style noted by coaches at Downside and Sherborne on the basis of institutional emphasis. Downside concentrated on promoting individual talent, whereas Sherborne emphasised 'the team ethic'.[65]

Sportscapes and religious difference

Not only is the style of play emblematic of a Catholic corporeality, it is also possible to identify the way that God was manifested in the physical terrain at Catholic public schools. As John Bale observes, the sportscape is always subject to interpretation, and he suggests that they are 'mythical landscapes, projecting a particular image, sometimes with an explicit purpose in mind'.[66] At Protestant schools, images of God and reminders of religion are focussed almost entirely on the chapel alone – a chapel that from the 1970s onwards, many public schoolboys were required to visit only on Sundays. And whilst the chapel may have been physically located in the centre of a school, the rugby and cricket fields often provided a more important psychological, emotional and, some might argue, 'religious' focal point at schools such as Sherborne. Games invariably fostered more conversation amongst both masters and boys than religion. Thus for the boys at Protestant schools, and even some of the masters, there was a feel about institutions such as Ampleforth and Downside that they never experienced anywhere else. It was not the sense of secular humanism, which typified the religious stance of many boys in the Protestant schools in this period. These schools looked, felt, even smelt different, and for many, it was rather unsettling.

The exploitation of these physical and psychological differences on the playing field provided Catholic public schools in particular with a distinct advantage. The concept of 'home field advantage' is something with which all athletes are familiar, and playing away or 'on the road' has always meant entering enemy territory in a physical as well as a psychological sense. When competing away from home, there is a heightened sense of being in a place that is indeed different and 'other'. Certainly travelling to other schools, eating meals in their dining areas before playing, and having to deal with the strangeness of such places as athletes prepare to 'do battle' is never easy. Upon entering Downside or Ampleforth, Catholic schools inhabited by monks and filled with religious icons, such strangeness intruded into the preparation process for those unfamiliar with the Catholic church and its icons, rites and traditions. And for Protestant athletes entering one of these Benedictine establishments, those feelings were heightened to new levels. For some boys, there was an overwhelming sense that they were now in a completely unfamiliar place: a place where God seemed far more prevalent, and was conspicuously far more revered than at their school. Indeed, if there was a choice to be made, He was likely on their opponents' side rather than on theirs in the contest ahead.

But more than this, there were the monks. Even to self-confident youth there is something arresting about the sight of a monk in a dark habit wandering solemnly through the school grounds, head bowed, contemplative. It is a subtle antidote to the testosterone-charged aggression that the boys were expected (and invariably needed) to display in order to match their fearsome opponents on the rugby pitch. Did the monks know this? Did they go out of their way to impose their presence on their visitors, to proselytise? It seems unlikely. But certainly the masters who coached rugby at Downside (who were rarely monks but nearly always Catholic laymen) knew enough sport psychology to know that the greater the strangeness, incongruence and uncertainty that could be created in the minds of their opponents, the better Downside's chances of victory. And, from a Shirburnian viewpoint, what stranger and more incongruent act, when playing at Downside, than to see a monk visit the home team's locker room prior to the start of a rugby match to offer a blessing! (On very rare occasions, this happened when Downside was playing away from home and one of the monks who travelled with the boys would provide the same benediction in the visiting team changing room.)[67] At both Ampleforth and Downside, the presence of the monks, the monastery overseeing the school and having a monk as headmaster provided an atmosphere and a sportscape that embodied difference for Protestants – a difference based on religion.

When Sherborne teams travelled to Downside to play cricket, the situation was rather different. First and foremost, the physical intimidation which was so much a part of Downside's rugby style and tradition was not a factor. Furthermore, at the top level the teams did not even enter the school buildings but rather took both lunch and tea in the pavilion on the grounds and so did not experience the internal atmosphere of a Benedictine school. There were, however, two factors that helped heighten an awareness of difference and that were constant reminders to those non-Catholics present that this was a Catholic place. The first was that, as it was summer time, the monks were even more likely to walk around the grounds in contemplation and seemed to find the cricket grounds appealing places to enjoy the fresh air and bide their time.[68] As one boy suggested to me on playing cricket at Downside for the first time, it was bad enough having masters or even parents watching you play, but to have monks peering into your soul was far worse!

The second and perhaps more significant factor that helped emphasise the difference of playing cricket at Downside, at the senior level at least, was the Angelus bell. The ringing of the bell signifies a calling to all Catholics to remember that 'God so loved the world that He sent His only Son'.[69] The bell is rung three times a day, with the noon ringing being the one of most consequence to those visiting the school on match days, as teams would travel to Downside to begin play at 11:30am. Visiting masters-in-charge were encouraged to remind their teams that the Angelus Bell would be rung at noon at which time everyone should stop what they were doing, stand completely still, and be quiet until the bell was silent. It is perhaps hard to imagine the degree of consternation that such an intrusion into the time-honoured pattern of cricket could bring. As a new master-in-charge of Sherborne cricket, I was given a very general set of instructions by my opposite number at Downside. These guidelines outlined the expectations that the Downside community held as appropriate behaviour during the ringing of the bell. Having announced to my team that when the Angelus bell rang at noon, everyone should stand still and be quiet, the questions followed thick and fast: 'If the bell starts to ring when I am bowling and about to release the ball, should I try to stop in mid-delivery?' 'If I am batting should I ignore the ball if it is bowled as the bell begins to ring?' 'Should I face east?' 'Which way is east?' Trying to offer meaningful and appropriate answers to such questions posed by 16- and 17-year-olds was difficult. As visitors we did not wish to offend, but nor did we wish to be worrying so much about the bell that we did not give our full attention to the game! The uncertainty of the situation placed visitors at a distinct disadvantage. Whilst this was not perceived as a deliberate weapon to be deployed against opponents, for visiting teams the ringing of the Angelus was certainly a psychological problem. The Angelus intruded into the very important first half-hour of matches played at Downside, simply because it was an additional concern which a visiting team had to face. Furthermore it was an interruption that players could not grow accustomed to since they faced it at no other school. More importantly, a knowledge of the behaviours required at the sounding of the Angelus operated as yet another marker of difference between Protestant and Catholic. When I started coaching cricket at Downside, I realised that whilst the ringing of the Angelus was obviously unrelated to the playing of cricket, its strangeness to visiting schools was something that Downside's cricket coaches were not unhappy about. Thus, not only was it a means of enforcing religious distinctions, it also provided

Downside players with a psychological advantage about which they were not going to complain. Here was an opportunity for their 'different' religion to act in the service of sport.

Conclusion

Sporting success has long been seen as a measure of the success of the school as a socialising and disciplinary system. It has been a yardstick of the men made by the elite Protestant public schools for over a century. As contact between the Catholic and Protestant schools has grown through inter-scholastic competition, the Catholic schools have had the opportunity to use these sporting encounters as a means of displaying the success of their 'belief system' and religious affiliation every time they have defeated the old enemy. After all, the rehearsal and performance of an identity, be it Catholic or Protestant, is necessary to socialise newcomers and maintain a community. And as I have observed, socialisation in and through sport has long been at the heart of a public school education. Accordingly, sporting success has provided both religious and educational capital for the Catholic schools in their quest to become full members of the public school community.

The clear and established relationships between sport and religion at Downside and other Catholic schools makes it possible to suggest that, whilst sport has served religion in these institutions, religion has also served sport. Even in the late 1960s and 1970s, with the heyday of athleticism long past, sport was still very much a 'religion' at Sherborne for many boys and masters. Such an emphasis on sport made it possible for Downside to contest the religious terrain and order both in and through sport throughout the period covered in this chapter. And whilst since the 1980s results in public examinations have become the newest area of competition between the public schools, sport is still a significant part of a school's public image. Visit any public school website and sporting results are most certainly posted. And whilst Sherborne cricketers no longer have to deal with the Angelus,[70] I understand that new masters who are coaching a rugby team can still be advised not to return if they lose to 'the papists'. Catholic and Protestant public schools were, and in many significant ways still are, very different kingdoms.

Notes

1   R.S. Peters, *Authority, Responsibility and Education*, third edition, London, George Allen & Unwin, 1973, p. 131.
2   S. Fielding, *Class and Ethnicity*, Philadelphia, Open University Press, 1993.
3   A look at the websites of the two schools provides a clear indication of the importance of the Catholic church in the lives of students. See the home pages of Ampleforth College at www.ampleforthcollege.york.sch.uk and Downside at www.downside.ac.uk.
4   A. Percival, *Very Superior Men*, London, Knight, 1973.
5   J. Wakeford, *The Cloistered Elite*, London, Macmillan, 1969.
6   S. Fielding, *Class and Ethnicity*, Philadelphia, Open University Press, 1993, p. 4.

7 A.H. Halsey, A.F. Heath and J.M. Ridge, 'The political arithmetic of public schools', in G. Walford (ed.), *British Public Schools Policy and Practice*, London, Falmer, 1984.

8 R.S. Peters, *Authority, Responsibility and Education*, third edition, London, George Allen & Unwin, 1973, p. 131.

9 E. Norman, *Anti-Catholicism in Victorian England*, London, Allen & Unwin, 1968.

10 Rather than use the term non-Catholic, I have used the term Protestant to stand in opposition to Catholic. Whilst a significant number of the public schools describe themselves as non-denominational, most reflect Protestant principles and practices. Many are affiliated with the Church of England or other Protestant churches such as the Methodist Church.

11 J.A. Mangan, *Athleticism in the Victorian and Edwardian Public School*, Cambridge, Cambridge University Press, 1981, p. 60.

12 J. Rae, *The Public School Revolution*, London, Faber & Faber, 1981.

13 G. Walford, 'Classification and framing in English public boarding schools', in P. Atkinson, R. Davies and S. Delamont (eds), *Discourse and Reproduction*, Cresskill, Hampton, 1995.

14 C. Heward, *Making a Man of Him: Parents and their Sons' Education at an English Public School, 1929–1950*, London, Routledge, 1988; J. Wilson, *Public Schools and Private Practice*, London, George Allen & Unwin, 1962.

15 J. Rae, *The Public School Revolution*, London, Faber & Faber, 1981, p. 111.

16 J.A. Mangan, *Athleticism in the Victorian and Edwardian Public School*, Cambridge, Cambridge University Press, 1981, p. 60.

17 T.J.L. Chandler, 'The structuring of manliness and the development of rugby football at the public schools and Oxbridge, 1830–1880', in J. Nauright and T.J.L. Chandler (eds), *Making Men: Rugby and Masculine Identity*, London, Frank Cass, 1996, pp. 13–31.

18 Following the lead of Millfield School, a number of other 'minor' or less well-known schools such as Bryanston and Kelly College have begun awarding sport scholarships in the hope of increasing their sporting success and thereby raising their overall profile as a public school. One significant measure of a school's status is the quality of the opposing schools whose names regularly feature on its fixture lists.

19 C. Haywood and M. Mac an Ghaill, 'Schooling masculinities', in M. Mac an Ghaill (ed.), *Understanding Masculinities*, Philadelphia, Open University Press, 1996, pp. 50–60.

20 J. Butler, *Bodies that Matter: On the Discursive Limits of 'Sex'*, London, Routledge, 1993.

21 I should declare my own self-interest in this enterprise having taught and coached at the two schools in this case study. It was in trying to make sense of the experience of 'crossing over' from teaching and coaching in the Protestant school to coaching in the Catholic school that I began to look critically at the differences between the two institutions. I am indebted to all of the colleagues with whom I served in both of these schools, but I owe particular debts of gratitude to Derek Baty, Mike Beale and David Bulfield at Downside, and to Mike Davis, Phil Jones, Micky Walford and the late Paddy Whelan at Sherborne. My thanks also to John Willcox, former England rugby international and Ampleforth 'institution'.

22 P. Bourdieu, 'Sport and social class', *Social Science Information*, vol. 17, no. 6, 1978, pp. 819–40.

23 W.J. Murray, *The Old Firm: Sectarianism, Sport and Society in Scotland*, Edinburgh, Donald, 1984.

24 R. Light, 'Regimes of training, *Seishin* and the construction of embodied masculinity in Japanese university rugby', *International Sports Studies*, vol. 21, no. 1, 1999, p. 39.

25 An annual knock-out cricket competition organised by *The Cricketer* magazine for the Old Boys of the leading 64 public schools.

26 H.O. Evennett, *The Catholic Schools of England and Wales*, Cambridge, Cambridge University Press, 1944.

27 J.W. Messerschmidt, *Masculinities and Crime: Critique and Reconceptualization of Theory*, Lanham, Rowman & Littlefield, 1993, p. 82.

28 H.O. Evennett, *The Catholic Schools of England and Wales*, Cambridge, Cambridge University Press, 1944, p. 1.

29 Ibid., p. 3.

30 M. Broderick, *Catholic Schools in England*, Washington, Catholic University, 1936.

31 W.J. Battersby, 'Secondary education for boys', in G.A. Beck (ed.), *The English Catholics, 1850–1950*, London, Burns Oates, 1950, pp. 322–36.

32 R.W. Connell, 'Cool guys, swots and wimps: the interplay of masculinity and education', *Oxford Review of Education*, vol. 15, no. 3, 1989, pp. 291–303.

33 R. Light and D. Kirk, 'High school rugby, the body and the reproduction of hegemonic masculinity', *Sport, Education and Society*, vol. 5, no. 2, 2000, pp. 163–76.

34 D. Whitson, 'Sport in the social construction of masculinity', in M. Messner and D. Sabo (eds), *Sport, Men and the Gender Order*, Champaign, Human Kinetics, 1990, pp. 19–29.

35 T. Newburn and E.A. Stanko, 'Introduction: men, masculinity and crime', in T. Newburn and E.A. Stanko (eds), *Just Boys Doing Business?* London, Routledge, 1994, p. 2.

36 R. Light and D. Kirk, 'High school rugby, the body and the reproduction of hegemonic masculinity', *Sport, Education and Society*, vol. 5, no. 2, 2000, pp. 163–76.

37 R.W. Connell, *Gender and Power: Society, the Person and Sexual Politics*, Cambridge, Polity Press, 1987; R.W. Connell, *Masculinities*, Cambridge, Polity Press, 1995; P. Bourdieu, 'Sport and social class', *Social Science Information*, vol. 17, no. 6, 1978 pp. 819–40.

38 R. Light and D. Kirk, 'High school rugby, the body and the reproduction of hegemonic masculinity', *Sport, Education and Society*, vol. 5, no. 2, 2000, pp. 163–76.

39 Ibid.

40 D. Whitson, 'Sport in the social construction of masculinity', in M. Messner and D. Sabo (eds), *Sport, Men and the Gender Order*, Champaign, Human Kinetics, 1990, pp. 19–29.

41 R.W. Connell, *Which Way Is Up? Essays On Class, Sex and Culture*, Sydney, Allen & Unwin, 1983.

42 R. Hands, *Rugby Football at Sherborne School*, Sherborne, Alphabet and Image Press, 1991, p. 51.

43 Ibid., p. 86.

44 Known universally as Micky, Walford was an outstanding athlete. A triple blue at Oxford, he had captained England at hockey, had been on an MCC tour, and had been an England rugby final trialist.

45 D.F. Gibbs, *A History of Football at Sherborne School*, Sherborne, private, 1983, p. 13.

46 Sherborne made a habit of attracting former England international players to join the staff. In the years from 1960 to 1980 the list included: Richard Sharp, Mike Davis, Peter Knight, David Rosser, Charlie Hannaford and Alistair Hignell.

47 Indicative of this 'scientific' approach is the fact that Sherborne's most effective and undoubtedly best-known coach, Mike Davis, is the co-author of a well-known rugby coaching text. See M. Davis and D. Ireland, *The Science of Rugby Football*, London, Pelham, 1985.

48 D.F. Gibbs, *A History of Football at Sherborne School*, Sherborne, private, 1983, p. 13.

49 R. Hands, *Rugby Football at Sherborne School*, Sherborne, Alphabet and Image Press, 1991, p. 51.

50 Coaches from both schools took a combined Sherborne/Downside team on a tour of Canada in 1978.

51 Charles Kingsley has long been recognised as the most popular advocate of muscular Christianity. His ideal was a man who 'fears God and can walk a thousand miles in a thousand hours, breathes God's free air on God's rich earth, and at the same time can hit a woodcock, doctor a horse, and twist a poker around his fingers'. M. Bevington, *The Saturday Review, 1855–1868*, New York, Columbia University Press, 1941, p.188, cited in D.E. Hall, 'Muscular Christianity: reading and writing the male social body', in D. Hall (ed.), *Muscular Christianity: Embodying the Victorian Age*, Cambridge, Cambridge University Press, 1994, pp. 7–8.

52 W. Houghton, *The Victorian Frame of Mind, 1830–1870*, New Haven, Yale University Press, 1957, p. 216.

53 See T.J.L. Chandler, 'Morality, nationalism and health: rugby football's three faces of manliness at Oxbridge and the public schools, 1830–1880', in S. Bailey and W. Vamplew (eds), *Studies in Sports History*, Leicester, De Montfort University, 1998, pp. 32–8.

54 N. Vance, *The Sinews of the Spirit*, Cambridge, Cambridge University Press, 1985, p.178. See also R. Holt, *Sport and the British*, Oxford, Clarendon, 1989, pp. 89–92.

55 See D. Allen, 'Young England: muscular Christianity and the politics of the body in "Tom Brown's Schooldays"', in D. Hall (ed.), *Muscular Christianity: Embodying the Victorian Age,* Cambridge University Press, 1994, pp. 114–32. See also J. Mangan and J. Walvin (eds), *Manliness and Morality: Middle-Class Masculinity in Britain and America*, Manchester, Manchester University Press, 1987.

56 F.G. Baring and G.J. Ince, *The Catholic Faith in Public Schools*, London, Williams & Norgate, 1935.

57 D. Morgan, *The Demon Lover*, London, Methuen, 1989.

58 Ampleforth College, *Devotions and Prayers*, Ampleforth, private, 1933.

59 B. Jarrett, *Living Temples*, London, Burns, Oates and Washbourne, 1920.

60 Ibid., pp. 34–5.

61 Ibid., p. 70.

62 H.O. Evennett, *The Catholic Schools of England and Wales*, Cambridge, Cambridge University Press, 1944, p. 78.

63 D. Shogun, *The Making of High Performance Athletes*, Toronto, University of Toronto Press, 1999.

64 This was a phrase often used by Michael McCrum, a Shirburnian who was a housemaster at Rugby and Headmaster of Tonbridge before becoming Headmaster of Eton and Chairman of the Headmasters' Conference. The most famous occasion for its use was in a speech given at Tonbridge in June 1969 in honour of one of Tonbridge's most well-known sons, E.M. Forster. McCrum offered only two cheers for Forster because of what he saw as Forster's moral weakness of choosing friends over country in wartime – a choice Forster had championed in his *Two Cheers for Democracy*. McCrum likened this moral weakness to the 'cult of the individual', a growing trend in the late 1960s of choosing self over school.

65 R. Hands, *Rugby Football at Sherborne School*, Sherborne, Alphabet and Image Press, 1991, p. 106.

66 J. Bale, *Landscapes of Modern Sport*, Leicester, Leicester University Press, 1994, p. 13.

67 It would be interesting to know if the home team found this more or less unnerving because it happened on their territory.

68 Henry Coombe-Tennant, the monk responsible for caring for visitors to the Abbey at the time I was at Downside, confirmed that the cricket grounds provided the monks with a wonderful place for both exercise and contemplation. He also noted that it provided the monks a space where they could watch spirited displays of physical activity and dream a little of their own youth!

69 Dom Antony, personal communication, 6 April 2001.

70 The pressure of public examinations has made it necessary to discontinue cricket matches between the two schools. Dom Antony, personal communication, 6 April 2001.

7 Religion, race and rugby in 'Coloured' Cape Town

John Nauright and Tara Magdalinski

Much of the history of South African sport has focussed on the effects of apartheid and racial segregation on sporting structures and policies throughout the twentieth century.[1] Whilst these studies reveal the complexities of sport as a political instrument, sport has served other ideological imperatives within the nation, yet the relationship between sport and religious identity, for example, has not been considered in any detail. At the same time that rugby has been regarded as a surrogate Afrikaner 'religion', the role of sport in providing disadvantaged communities with alternative means of expression has been, for the most part, neglected. The muscular Christian ethos, popularised through British colonial institutions, influenced the predominantly working-class areas of Cape Town. Muslim and Christian teachers and parents alike promoted sports as a means of instilling discipline and responsibility into their sons and, on occasion, their daughters. This confidence in sport to generate a sense of community prevailed amongst parts of Cape Town's Coloured population,[2] where rugby, in particular, was thought to promote the generation of a kind of 'muscular Islam', which revered the potential strength and toughness that the sport could encourage in Muslims.

In South Africa, as in other British colonies, black communities were introduced to British sports through the extensive system of mission stations and schools, which sought to promote cricket, for example, as part of a 'civilising mission'. They had particular success in the eastern Cape region where organised sport had emerged by the 1860s with the first-known African cricket club formed in Port Elizabeth in 1869. Throughout the rest of the nineteenth century, the mission education system expanded rapidly, and British sports were increasingly incorporated into the curriculum. Organised, modern, physical activities were regarded as an important element of 'native' education, particularly as African recreational culture was thought to be 'incompatible with Christian purity of life'.[3] And despite apartheid claims that indigenous South Africans did not 'take' to sport,[4] by 1887 black sport had developed to the point that the African newspaper, *Imvo Zabantsundu*, devoted a section to it.[5] In addition to Africans, many urban mixed race or 'Coloured' South Africans started to play sport, and a

number of organised sporting competitions emerged during the late nineteenth and early twentieth centuries.

Within the Coloured community in South Africa's oldest city, Cape
Town, religion affected relations between Christian and Muslim sporting
organisations, whilst those African men who lived in District Six and the
Bo-Kaap played rugby in a separate competition based at Langa township
outside the city.[6] In a racially segregated society, discrimination *within*
disadvantaged groups may be somewhat unexpected, but it is important to
remember that despite the nomenclature that grouped a range of 'mixed
race' South Africans together under the homogenising 'Coloured' racial classification, this was a heterogenous group with differing ethnic, religious and
class backgrounds. In Cape Town, religion and culture as well as 'race' were
significant in distinguishing between groups within the Coloured communities. Whilst various groups were not detached from a common struggle
against racist oppression, religion and sport combined to highlight differences and rivalries between Christian and Muslim Coloured South Africans.
Before exploring the specifics of this case study, it is important to outline
the socio-political context for black Capetonians in the nineteenth and twentieth centuries.

Islam and 'Coloured' communities in Cape Town

Members of the Coloured community come from a variety of cultural backgrounds. Some were the mixed race descendents of European and African
sexual unions that occurred from 1652, whilst others had their ancestors
amongst the slaves brought to South Africa in the 1700s from parts of
present-day Indonesia, Malaysia, southern India and Sri Lanka. The first-
known Muslims arrived from the Indonesian islands in 1658 and were
brought to Cape Town where they were used to protect the Dutch settlement from indigenous groups or they became servants of early settlers.[7]
Many slaves were sent to work on farms, where they were typically
Christianised. Those remaining in Cape Town were generally better placed
to retain both their cultural networks and their faith, though it was not
until the nineteenth century that Muslims were allowed to establish their
own mosques and schools.[8] From 1657 to 1804 it was illegal to publicly
practice Islam, under the penalty of death; however, by the time the British
were installed as administrators of the Cape colony, a more 'liberal atmosphere' meant that Muslims had probably established their first places of
worship by the late 1790s.[9] In 1804 religious freedom was given to all Cape
citizens, which, according to Ebrahim Moosa, resulted from Cape leaders
adopting the ideals of the French Revolution. After their initial application
to build a mosque was turned down by Cape authorities, Muslims in the
area later known as the Bo-Kaap protested by holding open-air Friday
prayers. As a result of this action and the liberalising effects of international
ideas, the first mosque in South Africa was officially built by Imam Tuan

Guru in Dorp Street in 1804. Tuan Guru also founded the first Muslim school in Cape Town, which, by 1825, had over 491 students.[10] Thus a religious and educational base for Islamic culture was established by the end of the first decade of the nineteenth century.[11]

The creation of an Islamic quarter in Cape Town, as well as the foundation of cultural, religious and educational institutions within this community, assisted in the preservation of their religious identity. By 1810 freed slaves had begun to form a distinct Muslim community in Cape Town known as the Bo-Kaap, or the Malay Quarter, with many more settling there after all slaves in the Cape were freed in 1834. Some Muslim and many non-Muslim mixed race and African people also settled in Cape Town after the end of slavery, particularly in an area later called District Six. The Bo-Kaap existed on the side of a hill adjacent to Cape Town's central business district on the site of a disused quarry, whilst District Six, which housed many more Coloureds as well as some whites and Africans, was located on the other side of the city centre. The Bo-Kaap was almost exclusively Muslim and remained so into the post-apartheid era, whilst District Six was a mix of Muslims, Christians and the non-religious, though Muslims were the largest single group.[12] Whilst little has been written specifically about the impact of religion on the social and cultural history of Coloured communities in the Cape Town area, there was a strong Islamic community in the Bo-Kaap, as well as other Islamic pockets throughout the greater Cape Town region, as evidenced by the construction of mosques in most areas of Coloured settlement during the nineteenth century.[13]

District Six and the Bo-Kaap developed distinct, though closely related communities, and appear to have been South Africa's first real working-class areas. In 1838, more than 5,000 freed slaves sought homes in Cape Town alongside the few who had worked on the docks, in small-scale manufacturing or as labourers for whites. Based on population estimates, Moosa argues that by 1825 there were 3,000 Muslims in Cape Town, a number that had increased to 8,000 by 1850.[14] Overcrowding was already affecting District Six by the time the Cape Town City Council officially declared it the sixth district of the Cape Town municipality in 1867. In 1900, during the South African War, a concerted building programme began in District Six, which provided the physical structure for the community. The official population figures for District Six stood at 22,440 in 1936, and 28,377 in 1946, but by the early 1950s the population had passed 40,000 as urban influx increased throughout South Africa.[15] Don Pinnock describes the District Six of the 1940s and 1950s aptly as it was known for the

> ingenuity, novelty and enterprise of its residents, engaged in this mode of small-scale production and services. It was a vibrant area of cultural activities, and sport played an important part in the local community. By day it hummed with trade, barter and manufacture, and by night it offered the 'various pleasures of conviviality or forgetfulness'.[16]

which were common features of working class urban areas. In addition to District Six and the Bo-Kaap, by the early 1900s, Coloured South Africans also settled in areas further from the city. These newer suburbs were less cramped than their inner-city counterparts and were serviced by rail connections to central Cape Town. Though both Christians and Muslims moved to these outer areas, a strong Muslim presence remained in the inner city areas until the 1960s.[17]

Although there were differences between and within Muslim and non-Muslim communities, they nevertheless shared a number of cultural practices, particularly in music and sport. By the early 1900s, rugby had become the dominant winter sport; but, from the 1920s, soccer increased in popularity in Cape Town's suburbs. In District Six and the Bo-Kaap, however, boys almost exclusively played cricket in summer and rugby in winter.[18] The promotion of rugby union has parallels with other parts of South Africa where the game was actively encouraged in white and some Coloured schools, though it would be inaccurate to assume that the Coloured rugby culture was merely imitative of white structures and practices. Though connections between the two are evident, it is clear that the cultural practice of rugby within the Coloured community was culturally and organisationally distinctive.

Rugby in 'Coloured' Cape Town

The recorded history of Coloured rugby in Cape Town dates from the formation of the first rugby clubs in 1886 only a few years after the first white rugby clubs appeared. Five important clubs were founded in that year, including two of the most famous, Roslyns and Wanderers, yet the respective futures of these two clubs lay with two different rugby unions, which were established by the end of the nineteenth century. Roslyns, along with Good Hopes, Violets and Arabian College, came together to form the Western Province Coloured Rugby Football Union (WPCRFU) in 1886, whilst Wanderers became the prime mover behind a second union formed in 1898, the City and Suburban Rugby Union (CSRU), which included the founding clubs of California (1888), Perseverance (1889), Thistles (1891), Woodstock Rangers (1892), and Retreat (1898). Primrose joined in 1901, Progress in 1906 and Universal in 1931 to form the core of CSRU clubs into the 1960s. The WPCRFU clubs were all based in the Bo-Kaap and District Six, with CSRU clubs located in District Six, Woodstock and later in suburban Cape Town. The CSRU purchased its own ground in suburban Cape Town in the 1940s whilst the WPCRFU played at Green Point, walking distance from both the Bo-Kaap and the District.

The WPCRFU was well-connected with the national South African Coloured Rugby Football Board (SACRFB), founded in 1897, and was very successful in Rhodes Cup competitions,[19] but nearly collapsed in the early 1930s, with only Roslyn and Violets surviving from the original clubs.

Several new clubs emerged in the late 1920s and 1930s to revitalise the union, including Young Stars (1928), Orange Blossoms (1931), Caledonian Roses (1934) and Buffaloes (1936). By the 1940s, the additional clubs of Hamediahs, Evergreens, Watsonias, Young Ideas and Leeuwendale had joined the WPCRFU.

It is not clear why some clubs, such as Wanderers, did not join the WPCRFU in the 1880s or why a separate association was deemed necessary. The reputation of CSRU clubs as nominally Christian may have placed them at odds with the predominantly Muslim WPCRFU, and it is clear that there must have been antipathy between the Muslim and non-Muslim rugby communities, as the CSRU explicitly forbade Muslims from joining until the early 1960s.[20] CSRU minute books, which date from 1918, suggest that the CSRU decision to exclude Muslims from their competition may have been a motivating factor for the dual unions. Precisely when this ban came into practice is unclear, and the first indication of the 'Muslim issue' in these records appears in 1923 when a WPCRFU club applied to join the CSRU.[21] As there is no mention of a constitutional change to include Rule 22 after 1918, the ban on Muslims, if not created at the time of the CSRU's formation, certainly appeared early in its history.

The WPCRFU, by contrast, did not constitutionally exclude non-Muslim players or clubs from its teams or competitions. Winston Kloppers, a former District Six resident who played for the Muslim-dominated club Caledonian Roses in the 1960s, states that there was never any problem for non-Muslims such as himself to play on WPCRFU teams. Indeed, some non-Muslim players were attracted to leading WPCRFU clubs, which were regarded as the strongest in the Western Cape.[22]

Although the CSRU ban on Muslim players was effectively over by the 1960s, this perhaps had more to do with the emergence of a broader non-racial sporting movement than with any kind of religious accord. Within South African sport more generally, this meant the foundation in 1973 of the South African Committee of Sport, which preached 'no normal sport in an abnormal society'. Within rugby more specifically, the South African Rugby Union was formed as a non-racial rugby organisation, which developed, in part, due to a power struggle between rugby officials, such as Cuthbert Loriston and Abdullah Abass.[23] Whilst personality clashes were at times significant amongst leading officials, rugby served a vital role in the working-class areas of Cape Town and in the suburban areas in developing group solidarity and as a cultural release from the tensions of everyday life in a racially segregated society.

Rugby and community

Within Cape Town's Muslim community, rugby was important in generating community solidarity. Cultural performances provide members of any community with the opportunity to visibly display their allegiance to a particular group. Gerdien Jonker highlights that within Muslim communities in general, conduct is crucial to the performance of religious commitment:

> For observant Muslims, the central issue of religious life is expressed through conduct varying from correct moral behaviour to a methodical religious habitus. In the European diaspora, the issue of conduct has gained ever greater importance. Passing on the Islamic tradition from generation to generation in a society which does not reflect this tradition in any of its institutions has proven to be a difficult affair. This circumstance influences every decision on how to organize the details of one's life.[24]

Muslims in Cape Town, like those in Berlin referred to in Jonker's study, had to work to preserve their religio-cultural identity in the face of external influences and threats. The incorporation of a Muslim 'conduct' into daily routines meant that Muslims were able to communicate their commitment to shared cultural norms in a range of social settings, yet, at the same time, were able to mix easily with other non-Muslim Coloureds. Activities, such as rugby, were certainly useful tools in maintaining Muslim solidarity by providing spaces in which Muslims could recreate as Muslims, yet there was a recognition that sport, or any leisure activity for that matter, could only ever come second to religious devotion. Such a commitment to faith meant that the organisation of rugby, for instance, would need to accommodate the practice of Islam, which meant scheduling matches to not clash with prayer times or other religious expectations. A practical example of this was the suspension of WPCRFU matches during Ramadan, which meant that even if he were permitted to join a CSRU club, it would have been difficult for a practising Muslim to hold a regular place in its team. For this reason, the WPCRFU provided Muslims with more than simply an opportunity to play rugby; it was also an organisation that recognised the intricacies and priorities of Islamic culture in Cape Town.

In order to maintain its position within its community, the WPCRFU provided a number of ways that religious and social commitment could be performed. The physicality displayed through rugby provides some measure of the ways that Muslim players put their bodies on the line for the maintenance of community pride. District Six and the Bo-Kaap were tightly-knit communities where people lived in close proximity and where survival for working-class males often meant developing a sense of toughness centred on physical abilities. Rugby provided opportunities to develop physical and mental toughness as well as group solidarity. Indeed, the role of rugby in developing a Muslim consciousness cannot be underestimated, particularly when religious segregation was imposed on Coloured rugby by the rival union, and this community solidarity was expressed in the annual 'Rag' charity matches.

In addition to the famous 'Coon' Carnival, now named the 'Cape Carnival', that takes place annually at New Year, where colourful troops parade and sing in competition,[25] the Charity Rag match between Young Stars and Caledonian Roses became a focal point of annual community cultural celebration. The Charity Rag began in 1936, with proceeds that year donated to a hospital fund established by Cape Town's mayor. The event was staged every year afterwards with one exception into the 1980s, and always raised funds to support a nominated charity. The format of the competition was modelled on that used by the Universities of Cape Town and Stellenbosch during their annual match. Notable features included the colourful scarves knitted by female supporters, songs composed for the occasion as well as the sizeable crowds who came to the Green Point Track to spectate. Ten thousand or more people from the Bo-Kaap and District Six used to walk down for the matches, and processions from the District through the Bo-Kaap and down to the Track featured prominently.[26] As with Carnival, Rag matches provided a sense of cultural release, an event for community focus and solidarity and one where the wider system of oppression could be forgotten for at least a short period of time. Rag and Carnival were celebrations of the community's vibrant culture and its resilience in the face of wider social, economic and political domination by whites, and, in the case of Rag, allowed for the open expression of solidarity within the Muslim dominated areas of Cape Town.

But it was not only the Carnival or sporting organisations that contributed to the maintenance of community identity throughout the Bo-Kaap and District Six. By the mid-twentieth century, the working-class areas of Cape Town increasingly came under the influence of protection rackets. Often referred to generically as 'gangsters', these organisations initially operated to protect the community from robberies and violence, particularly incidents perpetrated by newcomers. By the 1950s, the dominant gang was the Globe Gang, which had emerged in the 1940s in response to the growing crime rate in District Six. As greater numbers of people moved into the area, the incidence of petty theft increased. In an effort to confront the problem, bricklayers, hawkers, painters and the sons of shopkeepers formed around a core from the Ishmail family, one of whom was a Cape Town City Councillor, and began to meet outside the Globe Furnishing Company in Hanover Street opposite the Star Bioscope. The Globe Gang had a close relationship with the police who counted on the gang to help control the District. They began by smashing a 'tax-racket' at the cinema where patrons were forced to pay a penny to youths before entering, yet were not averse to similar actions, forming a protection racket with all in their area forced to pay allegiance. Pinnock explains that by 1950 'the Globe was controlling extortion, blackmail, illicit buying of every kind, smuggling, shebeens, gambling, and political movements in the District'.[27] That the business interests of the group should have expanded should not be surprising given the mercantile background of its early members, and it is clear that their protectionist intentions were not purely noble in terms of safeguarding the community from external threats, but were centred on preserving the economic security of local merchants. Pinnock points out that as more people moved into the District, 'the Globe was an organisation that sought to assert and maintain the control of the more wealthy families and the hawkers'.[28] According to one Globe member:

> The Globe hated the skollie[29] element in town, like the people who robbed the crowds on [celebrations] or when there were those marches in town with the Torch Commando or Cissy Gool's singsong [demonstration] outside Parliament buildings. Mikey and the boys would really bomb out the skollie element when they robbed the people then. They tore them to ribbons.[30]

Gradually, though, more ruthless elements took control of the gang during the 1950s and direct acts of intimidation, theft and murder became a regular part of Globe activities.

Whilst mosques and churches played a pivotal role in community solidarity, organisations as disparate as the Globe Gang and rugby clubs also developed and preserved localised identity. Indeed, powerful or wealthy groups were given special treatment and were feared or respected. Nomvuyo Ngcelwane relates how the last two rows in the Star Bioscope were reserved for the Globe and no one else dared to sit there.[31] A number of the leading gangs aligned themselves closely with Muslim rugby clubs as part of their activities to promote their public presence. The Globe, for example, supported Roslyns, the most powerful and oldest club in the WPCRFU competition. Roslyns would also meet by the Globe Furnishing Company, side-by-side with the Globe Gang.[32] Montrose Rugby Club, which quickly established itself as the richest of the Muslim-dominated clubs, also had reserved seats at the Star, as the owner was a patron of the club. Montrose officials even had special parking spaces in front of the cinema, and ushers would wash their cars during movies.[33]

In an obvious reference to the relationship between the leading gangs and top WPCRFU rugby clubs, Richard Rive recounts the story of a gang, the Jungle Boys, and their links with rugby in his autobiographical novel, *Buckingham Palace, District Six*. In the book, three gang leaders comprised the front row of the Young Anemones Rugby Football Club's first team, and, according to Rive, they 'practised in Trafalgar Park and played hard and dirty. They turned up regularly with their team to fulfil fixtures but these seldom materialised because most of the teams they were scheduled to play would rather forfeit the match than meet the Jungle Boys head on.'[34] Rive's fictionalised account reveals the significance of the link between gangs and rugby in District Six. What is important for our analysis is that the development of protection elements within established Coloured communities in Cape Town drew upon a strong sense of community and worked initially to defend existing local and group interests against migrants to the area. Their relationship to leading rugby clubs cemented their social function in the community, whilst the clubs themselves achieved notoriety through their involvement with the gangs. Rough, intimidating play was a feature of Coloured rugby clubs from District Six and the Bo-Kaap, as well as of WPCRFU-representative sides.

The production and experience of Muslim toughness

Rugby was an integral part of the display of masculinity through physical performance. The physicality and brutality of Cape Town rugby gradually came to be associated primarily with the Muslim community, a result of the working-class, urban environment in which Muslim clubs found a foothold. These clubs contrasted, certainly by the mid-twentieth century, with the CSRU's more middle-class, suburban image. Muslim rugby clubs gained a reputation for their use of intimidating tactics whilst other representative teams feared Western Province because of its physically aggressive style of play coupled with the psychological terror waged against its opponents before matches even started. At the same time, their affiliation with protection rackets meant that their standing in the community was socially and politically linked to the gangs' threatening behaviours.

The display of aggression and competence amongst Muslim rugby players differed little from the tenets of muscular Christianity that had started to take hold in British colonies by the latter part of the nineteenth century. Timothy Chandler refers to this as tensions between the 'beast' and the 'monk' and in the early history of British rugby, the debate over the issue of 'hacking' led to new definitions of acceptable levels of violence in the game.[35] Vigorous play has always been a part of rugby, and different groups have interpreted the game in a variety of ways.[36] In Cape Town, perhaps there was more to 'muscular Islam' than to 'muscular Christianity', at least in terms of the muscular part, though it is clear that Muslim men in Cape Town had a number of motivating factors that encouraged their robust play. The dedication to communicating religious imperatives through sport would have been of greater consequence to the relatively homogenous Muslim community compared with the 'Christian' community in Cape Town, whose main claim to being 'Christian' was simply that they were not Muslim.

As in the English public school system, where the ethos of muscular Christianity energised the organisation of sports and games, 'muscular Islam' emerged in Cape Town's Coloured educational institutions, particularly during the late nineteenth century, after Muslims had established their own schools. 'Coloured' schools in Cape Town before the 1960s were located largely in District Six and were denominational with most being Lutheran, Catholic, Methodist or Anglican.[37] And whilst Muslim mission schools operated, there were fewer of these institutions. Muslim schools had reappeared in the early twentieth century, largely due to the efforts of Dr Abdullah Abdurahman, a Muslim who studied medicine at the University of Glasgow. Dr Abdurahman was the long-time leader of the African People's Organisation (APO) and also served for many years on the Cape Town City Council.[38] For Dr Abdurahman and many other Muslims, education was vital for both community and individual development.

The preservation of Muslim identity was significant in these educational sites, particularly when it came to introducing new players to the sports and games regarded as critical for the development of an appropriate masculinity. Generations of rugby players were identified and nurtured in the school system, and leading WPCRFU players typically came from a handful of schools, including those where leading WPCRFU players and later administrators, such as 'Meneer' Abdullah Adams and Magamoed 'Meneer' Effendi, taught or were principals. Muslim schools, such as the Muir Street Moslem School, Chapel Street Primary School, the Rahmaniyeh Institute and Trafalgar High School, quickly developed a reputation for producing the most successful rugby players in the Coloured community.

Muslim school teachers and sports administrators, even those teaching at non-Muslim schools, regarded rugby as the most effective means to instil discipline and masculinity into the community's youth, which, in addition to the fierce style of play amongst some WPCRFU clubs, contributed to the overall image of the physically capable Muslim rugby player.[39] Rugby replicated the 'hard' qualities that resonated with the toughness needed for survival in the cramped working-class areas of District Six and the Bo-Kaap and allowed for the physical release of tensions created in a segregated and highly unequal society. Gassan Emeran, a former school principal and cricketer from the Bo-Kaap, states that culture, politics and even life itself revolved around rugby, and for the Islamic majority of District Six and the Bo-Kaap, rugby was the 'second religion'.[40] Magamoed 'Meneer' Effendi, a long-time District Six school teacher and rugby administrator, argues that the 'non-white community as such was a very sport loving community' and that rugby 'brought the whole community together'.[41] As such, rugby provided for social cohesion as well as individual physical development.

Despite the desire to produce healthy, robust athletes, the Coloured rugby fraternity was often accused of extremely violent play. Indeed, evidence from the *Cape Standard* and the *Cape Sun*, the two newspapers serving the Coloured community, from the 1930s and 1940s suggests that violent play on the field occurred regularly. Despite this, CSRU Minute Books show that the Union took a hard line with those found guilty of rough play with suspensions ranging from a couple of matches to two years. The WPCRFU also suspended players for exceedingly rough play, but the documents do not exist to establish whether there was a consistent policy of punishment or whether it matched the CSRU in its sanctions. Former WPCRFU-representative player Rajab Benjamin recounts that violence was part of the tactics of rugby, but insists that any roughness or violence stayed on the field of play and did not spill over into the community more broadly.[42] What is clear, however, is that a culture of rough play was an accepted part of the game, though there were limits to the levels of violence tolerated. Despite these caveats, Coloured rugby was regarded as significantly more violent than white rugby. The differences in what is considered appropriate on-field behaviour have led to a number of problems since the unification of rugby in 1992, particularly in the Western Cape, as the provincial tribunal has been faced with conflicting perceptions of acceptable violence.[43] In the late 1950s, Benjamin took a white rugby-playing friend to see a WPCRFU match at Green Point Track and recounts his shocked reaction to the vigorous play:

> You know I had a friend who used to play for the European Western Province Union who was playing wing for them for the union and one Saturday I said him, ' you come with me man. Come and have a look at our rugby.' That day, I think, Roslyns was playing Rangers and they were playing at Green Point Track on the B ground. So I said to come and we will look at this match. So he has looked at this match and afterwards he said to me 'you know, if was a Coloured I would never play rugby' and I said 'why?' and he said 'look how they are playing it'. I said 'no, but it is rugby man. That is how rugby should be played. After the match then they praise one another and they kiss but they play the game hard, hard, hard.' So he said to me he would never play rugby if he were a Coloured, the way they play rugby.[44]

Of course, not all clubs were equally feared. Roslyns developed a reputation for intimidating their opponents, their opponents' spectators and referees. In fact, not only were Roslyns' players considered a threat, but so too were their spectators, such as the Globe Gang. Former Young Stars players reveal that they had trouble finding referees for matches against Roslyns during the 1950s as 'the referees were frightened because Roslyns must win, if Roslyns doesn't win, it's a fight because they got their stones and their chains ready and their big swords ready that means they're going to attack'.[45] In one game between Stars and Roslyns, Benjamin, then playing for Stars, scored a try near the end of the match, and his team only needed to convert the try to win. Benjamin says he knew that Roslyns' spectators would arm themselves with chains and other weapons as soon as he made the extra point: 'we passed the Globe corner and they had their table decorated because they were winning the trophy back this year'.[46] Some fans had pangas (large knives) and chains, and Benjamin readied himself for a quick escape after the match by moving to the opposite side of the field from where the Globe Gang was located.

The on-field violence was not, however, restricted to competition within either the WPCRFU or the CSRU but was a feature of representative matches between the two unions. These inter-union games regularly attracted large crowds, regardless of whether they played at the Green Point Track or the CSRU grounds at Mowbray. The CSRU rarely defeated the WPCRFU, though there was often little difference in playing ability between the two, and a number of informants have suggested that the Western Province team generally prevailed because they could effectively intimidate their opposition, usually beginning months in advance of the actual contest.[47] The rivalry between the WPCRFU and the CSRU was certainly fierce and whilst the difference between the two cannot be explained simply in terms of religion, the denominational conflict between the largely Muslim WPCRFU and the strictly non-Muslim CSRU meant that religion was certainly a source of friction, if not the overarching reason for their disputes.

Tensions between 'Muslim' and 'Christian' rugby

It is unclear when or why the ban on Muslim players in the CSRU was implemented; however, the documentary evidence reveals that certainly by the 1930s, the CSRU had adopted a militant stance against the inclusion of Muslims in their affiliated clubs, conducting what can only be described as extensive inquisitions into the religious background of some of its registered players. Of course, it was difficult to determine the religion of every player, so more often than not the CSRU Executive Committee relied on gossip and hearsay to locate Muslims amongst their ranks. Any team found to have a Muslim player had to forfeit any matches in which that player participated and faced a stiff fine, and the player himself was expelled from both the club and the union.

The severity of the CSRU ban was apparent by the late 1930s, though their attitude must have hardened during the latter 1920s and 1930s. In 1923, a CSRU monthly delegate meeting entertained a letter from the Roslyns club, which was seeking entry into the CSRU competition. Although it was not specifically minuted that Roslyns was a Muslim club, indeed that would have been understood by the CSRU club representatives, the committee did note that if the club was admitted, then the union's constitution would need to be amended.[48]

Of course, Roslyns' decision to seek inclusion in the CSRU was less about religious harmony than about good rugby. The WPCRFU had entered a period of decline after World War I, and was only revived during the 1930s with the emergence of dominant players such as Dol Freeman and Abdullah Adams, the advent of Rag matches in 1936 and the addition of several new clubs to the competition. But, Roslyns' application does suggest that Muslim clubs were more tolerant in their approach to the relationship between religion and sport as they were prepared to affiliate with the, by then, constitutionally anti-Muslim CSRU. Although Muslims have formed their own organisations throughout their history in Cape Town, Moosa notes that in South Africa, Muslims have largely adopted an accommodating approach, recognising that they must operate within broader societal structures, despite their religious convictions.[49] Yet, despite this conciliatory attitude by Muslim organisations, by the late 1930s the CSRU's position on Muslim players had hardened, which may in part be explained by the increasing public assertion of Islamic identity.

In his presidential address to the CSRU, J.C. Jasson stated on 10 March 1938: 'I am perfectly satisfied that there are Malays [Muslims] playing for some of the clubs, and I recommend that we have a full dressed debate on that question.' In the ensuing discussion, Jasson clearly articulated the Union's religious and even racial position concerning Muslims: 'Are we going to forgo *our birthright* and allow Malays to play in our competition?' (emphasis added). At the same time, another delegate alleged that two clubs, Temperance and Thistles, had fielded Muslim players. The issue was put to a vote, and the constitutional by-law banning Muslims was upheld.[50] In late April the same year, the Progress club informed the CSRU that Thistles had fielded a Muslim player by the name of T. Coosuim, who had been registered to play as a 'Mr Ferreira', in a game against them on 16 April. At the next committee meeting on 5 May 1938, Coosuim/Ferreira was brought in for questioning. President Jasson asked his name, to which the player replied that his name was Gustav Ferreira. He then stated that he was born a Christian and that none of his family was Muslim. A committee member alleged that he had seen Ferreira wearing a fez, the round red hat commonly worn by Muslim men in and around Cape Town, and another member confirmed that he too had seen Ferreira and his brother wearing fezzes. Jasson sensed that Ferreira was being evasive, but gave him the opportunity to produce a baptismal certificate and allowed him to play temporarily.[51] The matter came up again at the CSRU committee meeting two weeks later, where a baptismal certificate for Gustav Ferreira was tabled, which stated that he was born on 19 January 1906. The matter was then adjourned,[52] only to be reopened in July after some members expressed their dissatisfaction with the outcome of the investigation. A letter signed before witnesses from a man named G. Ferreira from Kalk Bay, south of Cape Town, was presented to the committee. The letter claimed that he was the only Mr G. Ferreira in Kalk Bay and that he had been approached by a Mr R. Almachien for his baptismal certificate so that Toya Coosuim could play football using his name. Ferreira stated that he refused to allow this but that his baptismal certificate had been obtained from his Catholic Church. After allegations of intimidation, the meeting decided to appoint a committee of inquiry consisting of the President, the Chairman and a representative each from Thistles and Progress to investigate the matter.[53] The case proceeded immediately and President Jasson submitted the committee's report on 4 August 1938. He stated that after a visit to Kalk Bay, the committee was convinced that the evidence from Progress was correct but that to prove it conclusively they would have to go to court and pay ten guineas court costs. The motion to exclude Coosuim/Ferreira was moved and passed by eight votes to one (the Thistles delegate) with one abstention. Thistles were then penalised all the points they had won whilst Coosuim was playing on their team.[54] The CSRU's Rule 22 banning Muslim players was thus preserved.

Although some Muslims began to play for CSRU clubs after 1960, as late as 1968 CSRU officials argued at a Special General Meeting that Muslims, in particular G.N. Khan and Abdullah Abass, were trying to take over the relatively new governing body for non-racial rugby, the South African Rugby Union.[55] Not long before these allegations were voiced, the strains between Muslim and Christian Coloureds had been so intense that the *Cape Herald*, the leading newspaper for blacks in Cape Town, urged an end to 'ill-feeling between Muslim and Christian'.[56] Within the rugby community, it was commonly thought that the CSRU were overtly racist and that they discriminated against the WPCRFU generally and Muslims more specifically.[57] Whilst tensions were clear, these religious differences did not preclude officials from each union interacting with one another, either at work, socially or under the auspices of rugby administration, where it was common for representatives to meet to plan inter-provincial matches. There were, however, moments of friction where religious differences were palpable.

The perceptions of hostility and discrimination towards Muslims on the part of CSRU officials were reinforced in a pre-match meeting and dinner between CSRU and WPCRFU officials in the late 1950s. The banquet had already been laid when WPCRFU officials entered. To their horror, they discovered a centrepiece comprising a pig's head with an apple stuffed in its mouth. This was regarded immediately as a deliberate insult to Muslims, reinforcing the general perception about the views of CSRU leaders, and the incident filtered down to the WPCRFU players, who embraced it as motivation for one of the bloodiest matches ever staged between the two unions. Indeed, the CSRU team at one point left the field and had to be coaxed back out to finish the match. As then WPCRFU official, Meneer Effendi, describes:

> That match turned out to be a massacre because our players climbed into the City and Suburban players; they had to now pay for that insult. The match was stopped [and] Cities walked off the field. Officials had to go downstairs and persuade them to take the field again ... after half an hour they took the field, boom it was the same thing again until the match now ended. What a bloodbath it was. Well at the end of the day we won; we won the game by quite a big margin.[58]

This may have been an additional motivation in subsequent years as the WPCRFU team defeated the CSRU team every year with the exception of 1967 in the national Rhodes Cup tournament in Johannesburg.[59] Though there was significant mixing between Christian and Muslim players in clubs and associations by the 1960s, largely due to the new polarisation between non-racial and establishment sport, administrators in the CSRU and WPCRFU continued to clash, based on the WPCRFU's perception that CSRU officials remained anti-Muslim.

By the end of the 1960s many of the religious differences that had plagued Coloured rugby faded as more immediate issues, such as the re-zoning of District Six as a whites-only area in 1966 and the subsequent removal of residents over the next five years, dramatically disrupted the Cape Town Coloured community. One of the major protest movements against the proclamation involved a wide range of religious leaders from across the spectrum and racial divide that sought to bring moral pressure to bear on the government. This included collaboration between the Moslem Judicial Council and the Catholic Church for a common prayer period. On 27 February 1966, Muslim prayer services were held across South Africa, with over 3,000 attending at the Muir Street Mosque in District Six. Brutal state repression followed as local Coloured political leaders, many of whom were teachers at Trafalgar High School and other District schools, were arrested, imprisoned and tortured.[60] With Christian and Muslim allied in efforts to save the District, tensions slowly began to ease as a common enemy emerged, the apartheid state. Soon protest faded and the community faced the reality of the forced relocation of tens of thousands of people from the heart of Cape Town to the outer-lying Cape Flats. By 1975 only one-third of District Six's residents remained. As a result, many rugby clubs simply disbanded as players were scattered far and wide whilst others awaited the inevitable arrival of the bulldozers. In addition to the plight of the community in the face of the application of apartheid policies, the increasing solidarity of Coloured and African sportspeople in opposition to exclusion from white sporting organisations and the growing militancy of opposition in the mid-1970s meant that the struggle against apartheid became a more and more pressing and unifying issue. Whilst an element of conservatism remained within the Coloured population in Cape Town that led to the Western Cape staying under National Party rule in the 1990s, it is clear that religion played less of a factor in sport after the mid-1970s than it had in the preceding years.

Conclusion

Whilst religious differences between Muslim and nominally Christian communities within the Coloured population in Cape Town were apparent, members of both faiths shared many common cultural practices, including sporting activities such as rugby. Yet, soon after the foundation of Coloured rugby teams in the Western Cape, two separate unions emerged. The distinctions between the Muslim-dominated WPCRFU and the Muslim-exclusionary CSRU resulted from the myriad ways in which religion, culture and community articulated themselves in the Coloured communities of Cape Town during the early twentieth century. Whilst the WPCRFU and other Muslim-dominated organisations helped to preserve local but also religious identity within the Muslim-majority areas of Cape Town, the enforcement of Group Areas Act provisions and the removal of residents from District Six in the latter 1960s and early 1970s ushered in the demise of clubs, groups and many of the popular cultural practices of urban Cape Town. The Bo-Kaap remained a Muslim area within the city, and the dislocation of rugby club members meant that many teams disbanded. The final dismantling of Coloured rugby structures in 1992 and the resulting annexation by the existing white unions was decried by many who felt that an avenue of community identity had disappeared. The loss of autonomous rugby was a particular concern for members of the Muslim community, who had regarded rugby not simply as a means of ensuring community identity, but also as a proving ground for a hardy Muslim masculinity and an antidote to youthful vice and crime. Indeed, in the late 1990s, it was old WPCRFU officials who began to call for a return to rugby within the Coloured community as the amalgamation of rugby competitions had further eroded Coloured rugby with fewer clubs playing in the new 'unified' sporting structures of the New South Africa. Whilst Muslim clubs were not exclusive terrain and were certainly not evangelistic, they did provide an opportunity for Muslims to recreate with others of their faith in an environment that was Islam-friendly. Indeed, a key difference between this case study and others in this collection is that the sporting arena was not necessarily used as a place to proselytise. Instead, in the case of the WPCRFU, cultural and religious restrictions on the playing of rugby were respected and, in fact, accommodated, whilst the CSRU implemented and, until the 1960s, retained a ban on Muslims joining their affiliated clubs. So whilst religion was not necessarily the most overt feature of the rivalries between the various Coloured rugby unions, its influence was certainly clear and long-lasting.

Notes

1   For example, see D.R. Black and J. Nauright, *Rugby and the South African Nation*, Manchester, Manchester University Press, 1998; D. Booth, *The Race Game*, London, Frank Cass, 1998; A. Grundlingh, A. Odendaal and B. Spies, *Beyond the Tryline*, Johannesburg, Raven, 1995; J. Nauright, *Sport, Cultures and Identities in South Africa*, London, Leicester University Press, 1997.

2   'Coloured' was the term used to describe a wide range of the population of South Africa and refers to people who are not fully African or European including original slaves brought in from south Asia, Malaysia and Indonesia and mixed-race people but excluding descendents of people brought to Natal from India in the latter part of the nineteenth century to work as indentured labourers. Many 'Coloured' South Africans have adopted the term, however, and refer to themselves as the 'we, the so-called Coloureds'.

3   A. Odendaal, 'The thing that is not round: the untold story of black rugby in South Africa', in A. Grundlingh, A. Odendaal and B. Spies, *Beyond the Tryline*, Johannesburg, Raven, 1995, p. 33.

4 J. Nauright, *Sport, Cultures and Identities in South Africa*, London, Leicester University Press, 1997, p. 47.

5 A. Odendaal, 'South Africa's Black Victorians', in J.A. Mangan (ed.), *Pleasure, Profit, Proselytism: British Culture and Sport at Home and Abroad*, London, Frank Cass, 1988, p. 198.

6 N. Ngcelwane, *Sable Kahle District Six: An African Woman's Perspective*, Cape Town, Kwela Books, 1998, pp. 134–5 lists African families in District Six, and elsewhere the book discusses African families in the Bo-Kaap.

7 E. Moosa, 'Islam in South Africa', in M. Prozesky and J. de Gruchy (eds), *Living Faiths in South Africa*, London, Hurst & Company, 1995, p. 130; A. Tayob, *Islam in South Africa: Mosques, Imams, and Sermons*, Gainesville, University of Florida Press, 1999, pp. 21–2.

8 A. Tayob, 'Southern Africa', in D. Westerlund and I. Svanberg (eds), *Islam Outside the Arab World*, Richmond, Curzon Press, 1999, p. 112.

9 Ibid., p. 25. There is considerable debate about the location and timing of the first established mosque in Cape Town.

10 A. Tayob, *Islam in South Africa: Mosques, Imams, and Sermons*, Gainesville, University of Florida Press, 1999, p. 28.

11 E. Moosa, 'Islam in South Africa', in M. Prozesky and J. de Gruchy (eds), *Living Faiths in South Africa*, London, Hurst & Company, 1995, pp. 130, 132–3.

12 There is little written specifically about religion in these communities. The most notable exception is Y. da Costa and A. Davids, *Pages From Cape Muslim History*, Cape Town, Shuter & Shooter, 1994, which documents the role of various imams and religious leaders in the promotion and preservation of Islam in the Bo-Kaap and in other mosques in the region. The book says very little about wider culture and its relationship to religion.

13 A. Tayob, 'Southern Africa', in D. Westerlund and I. Svanberg (eds), *Islam Outside the Arab World*, Richmond, Curzon Press, 1999, p. 112, pp. 111–124; A. Tayob, *Islam in South Africa: Mosques, Imams, and Sermons*, Gainesville, University of Florida Press, 1999.

14 E. Moosa, 'Islam in South Africa', in M. Prozesky and J. de Gruchy (eds), *Living Faiths in South Africa*, London, Hurst & Company, 1995, p. 134.

15 D. Pinnock, *The Brotherhoods: Street Gangs and State Control in Cape Town*, Cape Town, David Phillip, 1984.

16 Ibid., pp. 21–3.

17 One of these suburbs, Mowbray, was the subject of a detailed study: J. Western, *Outcast Cape Town*, Minneapolis, University of Minnesota Press, 1980. Many of Mowbray's residents were removed in the 1970s when the apartheid government classified the area for whites only.

18 Rajab Benjamin and former Montrose players, interviewed by John Nauright, Cape Town, 26 December 1994.

19 The Rhodes Cup, similar to the Currie Cup in white rugby, was played between provincial teams at national level and awarded to the best province. Due to financial and travel difficulties, the Rhodes Cup was decided in a national tournament, held when possible, but not every year.

20 The first records of Muslims playing officially in the CSRU, date from 1961. Minute Books of the Perseverance Rugby Football Club, 1961. Thanks to Mark Wilson for providing access to Perseverance Club records.

21 City and Suburban Rugby Union (CSRU) Minute Books, Monthly Delegate Meeting, 28 September 1923.

22 Winston Kloppers, interviewed by John Nauright, Cape Town, 12 August 2001.

23 See D.R. Black and J. Nauright, *Rugby and the South African Nation*, Manchester, Manchester University Press, 1998, p. 56.

24 G. Jonker, 'What is other about other religions: the Islamic communities in Berlin between integration and segregation', *Cultural Dynamics*, vol. 12, no. 3, 2000, p. 318.

25 J. Maingard, 'Imag(in)ing the South African nation: representations of identity in the Rugby World Cup 1995', *Theatre Journal*, vol. 49, no.1, 1997, p. 18.

26 Magamoed 'Meneer' Effendi, interviewed by John Nauright, Cape Town, 14 December 1994; Gassan Emeran, interviewed by John Nauright, Bo-Kaap, Cape Town, 10 January 1995.

27 D. Pinnock, *The Brotherhoods: Street Gangs and State Control in Cape Town*, Cape Town, David Phillip, 1984, p. 28.

28 Ibid., p. 26.

29 'Skollies' referred to street youths who committed petty crimes. It is derived from a Dutch word meaning 'scavenger'.

30 Cited in D. Pinnock, *The Brotherhoods: Street Gangs and State Control in Cape Town*, Cape Town, David Phillip, 1984, p. 26.

31 N. Ngcelwane, *Sahle Kahle District Six: An African Woman's Perspective*, Cape Town, Kwela Books, 1998, p. 44.

32 Magamoed 'Meneer' Effendi, interviewed by John Nauright, Cape Town, 14 December 1994.

33 Rajab Benjamin and former Montrose players, interviewed by John Nauright, Cape Town, 26 December 1994.

34 R. Rive, *Buckingham Palace District, Six*, London, Heinemann, 1986, pp. 24–5.

35 T.J.L. Chandler, 'The structuring of manliness and the development of rugby football at the public schools and Oxbridge, 1830–1880', in J. Nauright and T.J.L. Chandler (eds), *Making Men: Rugby and Masculine Identity*, London, Frank Cass, 1996, pp. 13–31.

36 For several examples, see contributions in T.J.L. Chandler and J. Nauright (eds), *Making the Rugby World: Race, Gender, Commerce*, London, Frank Cass, 1999.

37 B. Nasson, 'Oral history and the reconstruction of District Six', in S. Jeppie and C. Soudien (eds), *The Struggle for District Six: Past and Present*, Cape Town, Buchu Books, 1990, p. 54.

38 E. Moosa, 'Islam in South Africa', in M. Prozesky and J. de Gruchy (eds), *Living Faiths in South Africa*, London, Hurst & Company, 1995, p. 142.

39 Magamoed 'Meneer' Effendi, interviewed by John Nauright, Cape Town, 14 December 1994; Gassan Emeran, interviewed by John Nauright, Bo-Kaap, Cape Town, 10 January 1995.

40 Gassan Emeran, interviewed by John Nauright, Bo-Kaap, Cape Town, 10 January 1995.

41 Magamoed 'Meneer' Effendi, interviewed by John Nauright, Cape Town, 14 December 1994.

42 Rajab Benjamin and former Montrose players, interviewed by John Nauright, Cape Town, 26 December 1994.

43 Paul Dobson, former head of the Western Province Disciplinary Committee discussed problems created by Coloured clubs playing with white ones in amalgamated competitions during the 1993 and 1994 seasons. Paul Dobson, interviewed by John Nauright, Cape Town, December 1994.

44 Rajab Benjamin and former Montrose players, interviewed by John Nauright, Cape Town, 26 December 1994.

45 Ibid.

46 Ibid.

47 Ibid.; Gassan Emeran, interviewed by John Nauright, Bo-Kaap, Cape Town, 10 January 1995; Winston Kloppers, interviewed by John Nauright, Cape Town, 12 August 2001.

48 CSRU Minute Books, Monthly Delegate Meeting, 28 September 1923.

49 E. Moosa, 'Islam in South Africa', in M. Prozesky and J. de Gruchy (eds), *Living Faiths in South Africa*, London, Hurst & Company, 1995.

50 CSRU Minute Books, Annual General Meeting, 10 March 1938.

51 CSRU Minute Books, Committee Meeting, 5 May 1938.

52 CSRU Minute Books, Adjourned Committee Meeting, 19 May 1938.
53 CSRU Minute Books, Committee Meeting, 21 July 1938.
54 CSRU Minute Books, Committee Meeting, 4 August 1938.
55 CSRU Minute Books, Special General Meeting, 3 March 1968.
56 *Cape Herald*, 14 October 1967.
57 John Nauright, personal communication with former WPCRFU player, 16 November 2001.
58 Magamoed 'Meneer' Effendi, interviewed by John Nauright, Cape Town, 14 December 1994.
59 Ibid.
60 C. Soudien, 'District Six: from protest to protest', in S. Jeppie and C. Soudien (eds), *The Struggle for District Six: Past and Present*, Cape Town, Buchu Books, 1990, pp. 148–50.

8 Appeasing the gods
Shinto, sumo and 'true' Japanese spirit

Richard Light and Louise Kinnaird

Introduction

On the penultimate day of the 2001 spring *bashyo* (tournament) *yokozuna* Takanohana steps up onto the *dohyou* (the raised clay area in which bouts are contested), performs a perfunctory bow and moves to his corner with his back to his opponent to perform *shiko*. From a wide deep stance the *rikishi* raises his extended leg up to meet his outstretched hand, then thumps his foot down on the *dohyou*. With hands placed on his knees he sinks his hips below knee level before repeating the leg raising on the other side. He then moves closer to his corner where he squats down to take a mouthful of water and spits it out whilst holding a sheet of paper above his mouth. After wiping his mouth, he crumples the paper, discards it and grabs a handful of salt as the referee introduces the two *rikishi*. They rise and turn toward each other, toss the salt in the ring and move forward to the centre of the *dohyou*. There they repeat *shiko* before, again, returning to their corners as attendants carrying the banners of the bout's sponsors circle inside the *dohyou*. Both *rikishi* return to the centre to squat on their heels and make eye contact with each other. Following a brief pause and maintaining eye contact, they bend forward, fists loosely clenched and lightly touching the ground, in preparation for engagement (*tachiai*). At the last moment Takanohana withdraws, sits back on his heels with hands on his hips to fix his opponent, Musoyama, with a disdainful look. Musoyama then does the same. The crowd responds as both *rikishi* stand and exchange a further, momentary glare before returning to their respective corners. They take another handful of salt, throw it in the ring, slap their *mawashi* (belt) heavily and return to the centre of the *dohyou*. This procedure is repeated four times and each time the crowd responds with growing enthusiasm as tension and anticipation mount. Finally the two huge men clash violently at the *tachiai* and struggle to gain an advantageous grip on the opponent's *mawashi*. Takanohana seems to establish a better grip on his opponent's *mawashi* but Musoyama drives him backwards and quickly tosses him to the floor with the technique known as *yorikiri*. The huge crowd erupts in wild applause and showers the *dohyou* with the cushions they have been sitting on as a sign of appreciation.

Six and a half minutes passed from the moment Takanohana stepped onto the *dohyou* to the beginning of the bout. The physical contest was over in five seconds. The unvaried ritual performed by *rikishi* is an indispensable and essential part of a sumo performance. The highly ritualised nature of sumo is saturated with cultural and religious subtexts that mark it as a uniquely Japanese practice. Its links with the national religion, Shinto, as well as with a mythological past have been central to both sumo's popularity and its development as a symbol of what both Japanese and non-Japanese see as 'authentic' Japanese culture. Such ritualised practices, particularly those relying on historical legitimation, are particularly relevant at times of rapid social upheaval, when pressures from beyond the national borders threaten to disrupt national unity.

There has been considerable attention paid to the ritualised nature of sport by social scientists who have recognised the similarity between the practice of modern sport and pre-modern religious practices.[1] This has led to a body of work that conceives of sport as a secular religion or a secular ritual that functions much as pre-modern religious ceremony and ritual did. Within this body of work on 'sport as religion', researchers have identified the roles that sport can play in the development of regional, national, cultural and religious identity.[2] As Emile Durkheim's work shows, ritual operates to define in-group and out-of-group membership.[3] Although much has been written on the role that sport can play in achieving social integration,[4] sport, with its highly ritualised practices, may also be a useful tool to ensure that distinctions *between* various communities can be preserved.

Sumo is a highly complex cultural ritual that embodies specific and significant cultural and social meanings. The traditions and ceremonies that characterise contemporary sumo mark it as a uniquely Japanese cultural practice and act to confirm and reinforce a sense of distinct Japanese cultural identity. The constructed history that weds sumo with ancient court practice and Shinto is reinforced by the ritualised nature of its performance. A historical examination of sumo's development into its contemporary form reveals a changing yet important relationship with Japan's indigenous religion, illustrating that sumo's affiliation with Shinto ritual has been central to the development of its cultural and social significance.

Along with Western sports and restructured forms of martial arts known as *budo* introduced in the late nineteenth century, sumo has contributed significantly to the development of a homogenous culture and a sense of national identity in Japan. Its success has been largely the result of its ability to offer a means of defining a distinct Japanese cultural identity, particularly during times of cultural instability. Sumo's links with the national religion and its deliberate political appropriation over the past two centuries have served to promote what most Japanese regard as the unique features of their culture. As such, sumo has played a significant part in political efforts to maintain social cohesion and encourage a sense of national identity during times of profound social, economic and political change during the eighteenth and nineteenth centuries. This chapter examines the means by which sumo's status as a symbol of national culture was strengthened by its adoption of Shinto ritual, and how during times of acute social, cultural and political flux, cultural practices, such as sumo, have served to sustain Japanese identity.

Official accounts of sumo history lay claim to an unbroken 1,500 year history,[5] yet most of the purported ancient traditions were only introduced during the late eighteenth and early nineteenth centuries. They formed part of a deliberate strategy employed by promoters who sought to convince authorities that sumo originated in ancient Shinto and court tradition. To achieve these aims, early sporting entrepreneurs invented a 'respectable' history for a sport that had been little more than a popular form of street-fighting. The expedient association between sumo and Shinto meant the sport could operate as a non-threatening activity that could contribute to a growing sense of Japanese identity, without jeopardising the status of eighteenth and nineteenth century dynastic leaders. This rehistoricisation successfully obfuscated the ways in which, prior to the late eighteenth century, sumo had evolved along two mutually exclusive lines. One form of sumo was first practised as a native religious ritual deeply embedded in ancient agrarian religious tradition. The other form had its origins in brutal fight-to-the-death tests of strength staged for the entertainment of the common classes. Eighteenth-century promoters successfully linked sumo, as a commoner's test of strength, to the history of sumo as a religious ritual and activity of the court. For a culture perceived as being under threat from external forces, the significance of cultural activities such as sumo meant that the population could share in a strengthened sense of cultural homogeneity. The continued success of these measures is evidenced in sumo's current popularity and role as a marker of Japanese national culture and identity.

The process of selecting appropriate elements of a history is not an uncommon practice and has been identified by Eric Hobsbawm and Terence Ranger in a political context, by Lynn Spillman in a nationalist context, and more recently by a range of authors within a sporting context.[6] As Hobsbawm notes within Western societies, old and venerated traditions are often not only recent in origin but are also sometimes invented.[7] Such invented traditions include ritualistic and symbolic practices that are used to inculcate particular values and behaviours by uniting current practice with a 'suitable past'.[8] As such, according to Raymond Williams, traditions are radically selective and operate as powerful political tools.[9] What is remembered, marginalised or even forgotten can validate current actions and power arrangements by relating contemporary practice to a suitable past. Sporting traditions can prove to be powerful links to a suitable past. Within Japan, promoters of sumo during the late eighteenth century adopted selected practices from ancient court sumo and, drawing on religious ritual, invented some completely new traditions designed to embed sumo within Shinto as a religion of rising influence. These modifications, and the fabrication of links with ancient practice, gave the sport the 'suitable historic past' it had lacked and ensured that sumo was acceptable to the political leaders of the time.[10] The status that contemporary sumo enjoys in Japan as well as the cultural meanings attached to it are thus the direct result of the 'Shintoisation' of sumo over two centuries earlier. Whilst the ritualised practice of contemporary Sumo is deemed representative of an 'immemorial' Japanese past, most sumo rituals reveal more about the political ambitions of rulers during the Tokugawa era (1600–1867) than about any ancient culture.

Shinto as a religious and cultural practice

Shinto is the main indigenous religion of Japan, yet it is an elusive practice. It has long formed a central part of Japanese cultural life, yet was not conceived as separate from secular life until the sixth century AD following the introduction of Buddhism. To distinguish it from the imported religion, the term 'Shinto' was created from the Chinese characters read as *shin*, meaning 'god-like nature or being', and the character read as *to*, meaning 'way or teaching'.[11] On its own, the first character is pronounced *kami* in Japanese, which means god, deity or spirit. Thus, Shinto is usually translated as 'the way of the *kami*'. *Kami* are closely associated with nature; special mountains and lakes have their own *kami*, and particular communities have patron *kami* – 'clan gods' for whom they perform special ceremonies for protection.[12] Prior to the development of Buddhism beginning in the sixth century, early agrarian community groups lived in close relationship with the *kami*, and their daily life centred on agricultural ceremonies for fertility and prosperity, nature worship for harmony in the universe, and ancestor worship also for harmony and protection. Unlike most religions, Shinto does not have an elaborate system of doctrines nor philosophical teachings, and only began to develop as an organised religion in response to the introduction of Buddhism.

Rituals and ceremonies focussed on the individual and aimed at purifying the body, mind and soul are central to Shinto. Indeed, the essence of Shinto concerns the relationship between good and evil as represented by pollution and purity: 'Evil is pollution and filthiness, whether physical or spiritual, whereas goodness and purity are essentially one.'[13] Humans are considered to be born pure, with impurities or evil being acquired during life. Such impurities and evil are removed through ritual purification known as *harai* or *harae*. Ian Buruma suggests that: 'Purification exists in religious ceremonies everywhere, but in few cultures is it taken as seriously and as much a part of daily life as in Japan.'[14] Purity and purification rituals are central to the practice of Shinto and many have been incorporated into the contemporary practice of sumo.

Sumo and Shinto ritual

Koike Tamio argues that: 'Shinto is Japan's indigenous religion, and sumo is steeped in Shinto orthodoxy.'[15] Shinto elements can be found in most areas of sumo, from the physical setting to the numerous rituals of a sumo performance. Evidence of sumo's association with Shinto goes beyond the sphere of the factual world, as stories of *kami* fighting for the lands of Japan feature in the world of myth. Prior to becoming a professional sport in the Tokugawa period, sumo was originally performed as *kanjin-zumo* on the grounds of a shrine or temple. The present *dohyou*, is still considered sacred, in honour of the days when tournaments were held on the sacred grounds of shrines and temples. The roof over the *dohyou*, called *yakata*, originally represented the sky to emphasise the sacred nature of the *dohyou*, which signified the earth.[16] Since 1931, the style of the *yakata* has been modelled on the *Geku*, the Outer Shrine of the Grand Shrine of Ise, strengthening the Shinto connection. Until 1952, the *yakata* was supported by four pillars, each of which was wrapped in a different colour. Three decades after sumo moved indoors, the pillars were finally removed, as they obstructed viewing, and the *yakata* has since been suspended over the *dohyou*. In representation of the coloured pillars, huge silk tassels now hang from each corner of the *yakata* or *tsuriyane* (hanging roof) as it is also called.[17]

Currently, Grand Sumo Tournaments are held six times a year. On the day before the commencement of each of these fifteen-day tournaments, the *dohyou-matsuri*, a ring-blessing ceremony, is performed by sumo officials called *gyoji*. Gyoji are the colourfully dressed referees on the *dohyou* who judge each sumo bout. Their elaborate costumes are based on ceremonial court robes (*hitatare*) of the Heian period (794–1185),[18] and their black hats are copies of the hats worn by Shinto priests as depicted in Heian art.[19] *Gyoji* have a semi-priestly status as they perform Shinto purification rituals and oversee other Shinto elements of sumo. As more Shinto rituals were introduced into sumo, the *gyoji* were required to obtain a license, legitimising their participation in Shinto rites. The *dohyou-matsuri* is the main Shinto purification ceremony performed by the *gyoji*. Dressed in the white robes of a Shinto priest, the *gyoji* purify and bless the *dohyou* in a solemn ceremony during which salt, *konbu* (kelp), *surume* (dried squid) and chestnuts are buried in the centre of the *dohyou*.[20] A small *sakaki* tree is blessed and presented to an official waiting outside the *dohyou*. Observing officials and invited guests drink *sake* as it is offered to each of them in turn. The remaining *sake* is poured over the straw boundary of the *dohyou*, at the four points of the compass, as an offering to the gods. The purpose of the *dohyou-matsuri* is to appease the *kami* and ask for their protection of the *rikishi* participating in the upcoming tournament.

The *dohyou-iri* is a brief ceremony in which *rikishi*, wearing elaborate *kesho-mawashi* (ceremonial aprons), are introduced to the audience at the start of each day of a tournament. The *kesho-mawashi* originates from the days when *rikishi* were employed by *daimyo* and would wear the crest of their employer for all to see. Today the expensive *kesho-mawashi* are gifts from sponsors or fan clubs. When their name is called, the participants ascend the *dohyou*, walk around the edge and face the audience. As the last of their group is announced, they turn and face inwards, clap their hands, raise one hand, slightly lift the *kesho-mawashi*, raise both hands, then continue walking around the *dohyou* as they leave the same way they entered.[21] The clapping ritual is an important Shinto element, and replicates the clapping in Shinto shrines that is designed to attract the attention of the gods.[22] The individual *rikishi* also perform purification ceremonies prior to each bout. After two *rikishi* have been called to the *dohyou*, they spend several minutes performing *shikiri* before the actual clash.[23]

In addition to the rituals adopted directly from Shinto customs, many of the remaining ceremonial features of contemporary sumo derive from *sechie-zumo* (court ceremony sumo) of the imperial capitals from 710 AD.[24] Forms of sumo performed as court rituals represented adaptations of sumo as quasi-religious practice for the court and were also deeply rooted in Shinto. As imperial institutions draw strength from Shinto traditions, rituals of the imperial court are thus also essentially religious in nature. *Sechie-zumo* was probably introduced early in the eighth century when Chinese culture was most actively sought by the Japanese imperial court. It is modelled on Chinese wrestling festivals that were held for the Chinese emperor on important ceremonial days at the imperial court.[25] The current practice of *yumitori-shiki*, a bow-twirling ceremony, dates back to the days of *sechie-zumo*. To mark the conclusion of each day of a tournament, a *rikishi* enters the *dohyou* and performs the *yumitori-shiki*. It is said to originate from the *sechie-zumo* of the Heian period, when the winner was presented with an archer's bow. In 1575, Oda Nobunaga, the military leader of Japan, gave one of his bows to the winner of a sumo tournament, who, in accepting the bow, danced to show his appreciation of the gift. Later, at the end of the special Shogunal viewing of a sumo tournament in 1791, the winning *yokozuna* also performed a dance with a bow, confirming this ritual as an important Sumo tradition.[26] In order to understand the socially constructed nature of these ritualised practices, it is necessary to trace the historical development of sumo.

The history and development of sumo

Sumo has a long history in Japan but it is not an unbroken, linear history as the Japan Sumo Association contends. Over the past 2000 years sumo has been practised in a variety of different forms. Many of these forms, such as those performed as agrarian or court ritual, were deeply tied into Shinto beliefs and functioned as forms of religious or quasi-religious practice. Other forms that developed as tests of strength for entertainment amongst the dominated classes or as martial techniques had little connection with Shinto. Sumo features prominently in contemporary accounts of the mythologised origins of Japan. According to the *Kojiki* (Records of Ancient Matters, 712 AD), a sumo bout between two gods, Takemi-Kazuchi and Takemi-Nakata, was staged to determine control of the Japanese islands, and the fate of the imperial line depended on this test of strength. Hikoyama Kozo retells the story adding that Takemi-Kazuchi was from a 'race of divine lineage' whilst Takemi-Nakata was from a 'common race'.[27] The contest ended with Takemi-Nakata begging for his life to be spared in return for giving the islands to his victor. As Takemi-Kazuchi was sent to fight for the lands by Amaterasu, his victory enabled the sun goddess to produce an imperial line that is claimed to be unbroken to the present.[28] Evidence, such as *haniwa* (clay figures excavated from burial mounds) that resemble two *rikishi* in a sumo bout, suggests that sumo was a common element of agricultural rituals throughout the Yayoi and Kofun periods (200 BC–552 AD).[29] During this era, people relied on agriculture for their survival and believed the success of their harvest was dependent on the gods. In addition, sumo formed a religious, agrarian ritual. Sumo bouts were arranged as a means of determining the will of the gods, and it was generally believed that the victor and his supporters would be rewarded with a good harvest.

In addition to the sumo that developed from religious origins, there was also a common form of sumo, *kusa-zumo* (grass sumo), which was a typical element in tests of strength between village strongmen. Sukune's famous first sumo bout is recorded as having taken place on the seventh day of the seventh month, a date historically associated with religious and agricultural festivals. During the time of Emperor Shomu (724–49 AD), *shinji-zumo* (god-service sumo) was part of the annual *tanabata* festival (a celebration of the one night in the year when two mythical star-lovers can meet), which is still held on the seventh day of the seventh month.[30] During the Heian period, a form of sumo was practised as an independent court ceremony called *sechie-zumo*. It was an elaborate annual event, taking place deep inside the imperial palace. The emperor was regarded as the representative of the gods and *sechie-zumo* was used to determine the will of the gods. This ceremony was not a public event and was restricted to a small audience of the emperor and his senior courtiers.[31] With such strong Shinto and imperial ties, sumo was transformed from an agrarian ritual to a religious and political rite through which prayers for nationwide prosperity were offered.

As imperial power was replaced by military power in twelfth-century Japan, the practice of sumo ceased as a court activity.[32] Military leaders incorporated *buke-zumo* (warrior sumo) as a necessary skill for all samurai, alongside archery and swordsmanship. *Buke-zumo* included wrestling techniques that are found in the contemporary practice of judo and jiujitsu. In addition to its function as a military skill for samurai, sumo also emerged as a form of entertainment in the Kamakura period (1185–1333). A tournament performed as part of a Shinto shrine's festival was officially viewed by the leader of the Kamakura military government, Minamoto Yoritomo in 1189. During the Muromachi period (1336–1573), *kanjin-zumo* (religious fund-raising sumo) developed as a means of raising funds for religious purposes. Shrines collected donations from spectators attracted by the sumo performance and these were shared with the wrestlers. Groups of masterless samurai wrestlers (*ronin*) wandered the country seeking *kanjin-zumo* for their own survival.[33] During this period *kanjin-zumo* increasingly developed as a form of entertainment that provided funds for shrines and as a means of financial support for masterless samurai. This type of sumo for entertainment experienced significant growth after 1543 when the Portuguese introduced advanced western military technology thus decreasing the need for hand-to-hand combat.[34]

The Tokugawa period (1600–1867)

The Tokugawa period is, historically, the most significant period in the development of sumo into the form recognised today. Over the period of more than two centuries of comparative peace and order, sumo was modified and rationalised, and ultimately it flourished. Sumo's emergence over this period as both a professional sport and a cultural icon was the explicit result of its association with Shinto. As part of this process the rites and rituals that characterise contemporary sumo were introduced or invented to validate the activity as a quasi-religious practice.

Through victory in the battle of Sekigahara at the start of the seventeenth century, Tokugawa Ieyasu, the first of the Tokugawa leaders, established military control over all of Japan's feudal domains. Assuming the position of Shogun,[35] he then set out to establish absolute political control over what had previously been a disparate group of warring feudal domains or fiefdoms amongst which there had been little sense of Japan as a nation. The Tokugawa policy of *sakoku*, national seclusion, was introduced in 1641 and was central to establishing, and maintaining, the political and social control that was to endure for over two and a half centuries. The Shogunate was initially concerned with *daimyo* (feudal lords) joining forces to launch attacks on the Shogun. In addition to maintaining internal control, Tokugawa Ieyasu faced external threats from Western military powers, indigenous Buddhist uprisings and the growing influence of Christianity.

The emergence and growing popularity of Buddhism threatened the authority of a divinely ordained emperor, and a succession of leaders sought to contain Buddhist uprisings. In 1574, Oda Nobunaga launched an extermination campaign in which 20,000 sect members were burned alive. After him, Toyotomo Hideoyoshi adopted the tactic of incorporation by seeking to establish religious control through the provision of financial support for establishment Buddhism and its indigenous form. By the seventeenth century, the first Tokugawa leader, Tokugawa Ieyasu, established further control over Buddhist institutions by regulating their teaching and other religious activities.[36] Despite continuing pockets of resistance, he had largely reined in rebellious indigenous Buddhism by the early seventeenth century but also had to deal with a growing population of Japanese Christians. By 1614 there were as many as 1 million Christians in Japan, including some feudal lords.[37] At a time of increasing concern with Western colonial expansion and influence in Japan, Christianity presented a significant threat to the Tokugawa rulers' aims of establishing and maintaining universal political control. Portuguese Jesuit priests were regarded by authorities as possible forerunners of Portuguese and Spanish colonisation. The Shogun was also concerned that foreigners in Japan, as well as Japanese Christians, might offer ambitious *daimyo* a means of receiving Western military support to challenge Tokugawa rule. Karel Van Wolferen[38] argues that, more importantly, the Christian belief in an alien lord, positioned above both the Shogun and the emperor, presented a serious challenge to the moral and political authority of the Tokugawa government. During the first few decades of the seventeenth century, missionaries were expelled and Christians who did not recant were tortured, killed or sent into exile.[39] In 1637 rebellious Christians were joined by disaffected *ronin* (masterless samurai) in a 'Christian' rebellion on the Shimabara peninsula in Kyushu. Almost 40,000 Christians and samurai occupied a castle and held out for four months before being overrun by the Shogunate's army. From 1641, with the exception of a handful of Dutch traders, who had convinced the Shogunate they did not worship the same God as the Portuguese or Spanish, contact with the West was forbidden.[40]

A large part of the logic behind the national isolation policy lay in the Shogun's desire to establish a sense of national unity. The notion of a distinctly Japanese 'spirit' and a sense of Japanese national identity began to emerge from the seventeenth century with growing interest in Japan's own ancient literature from the mid-seventeenth century. In response to the increasing threat of ideological influence from Dutch traders in the late seventeenth century, the Shogunate sought to extend its control over religion and education. The need to encourage common culture and a common sense of being Japanese comprised one of the most pressing concerns of the Tokugawa Shogunate, and unity of religion was considered to be one of the more important means of achieving this end. Foreigners were expelled and Christianity was 'ruthlessly eradicated'.[41] Following the repression of rebellious Buddhist sects, Buddhism was promoted as the national religion of Japan, and every family was required to belong to a Buddhist Temple for taxation purposes. Buddhist priests were also officials of the Tokugawa government, and Buddhism fell under strict Tokugawa control.[42]

In addition to elevating Buddhism to the status of official national religion the Shogunate actively promoted Confucianism as the preferred school of thought amongst the ruling classes. Imported from China over a thousand years prior to the Tokugawa period, Confucianism's emphasis on order made it appealing to a government wanting to establish social control. Revived in a modified form, Neo-Confucianism suited the Tokugawa Shogunate's goals of maintaining social order and peace. It emphasised the value of law and respect for social order.[43] During a period of economic and cultural prosperity, the Shogunate decreed that the Shushi[44] school of Neo-Confucian ideology would be adopted as the orthodox teaching of the State. To ensure widespread influence of Shushi morality, the Tokugawa government banned the teaching of non-Shushi Neo-Confucianism in 1790. Gradually, Neo-Confucianists moved away from Buddhism to the extent that they openly opposed it.[45] The Tokugawa government's directive to maintain national unity and follow Shushi teachings led to renewed interest in the study of Japanese classic literature. The highly structured, imported religion continued to be favoured by the ruling classes, and, at the same time, Shinto existed in harmony with Buddhism. It posed no threat to political rule and, deeply embedded in social and cultural practice, remained an important part of the everyday life of most Japanese.[46] Compared to Buddhism, Shinto was unstructured and lacking in formal doctrine. It did not have a set of scriptures to match the volumes available in Chinese Buddhism, and the scholar Kada Azumamaro (1669–1736) received Tokugawa support for renewed study of Japan's own ancient literature. Works such as the *Kojiki*, *Nihon Shoki* and *Manyoshu*[47] became the focus of many years of intensive study, reviving stories of the mythological origin of Japan. The educated classes began to question the wholesale adoption of Chinese thought and ideology. This renewed interest in Japan's own ancient literature formed part of a growing nationalist sentiment in which the search for native Japanese culture and views of the world saw increased interest amongst the ruling classes in the native religion of Shinto. It also encouraged a line of nationalistic thought that saw the Emperor as the rightful head of 'the land of the gods',[48] and rejected all things foreign. This movement was called *kokugaku* or 'National Learning'.

The emergence of professional sumo

The battles leading up to Tokugawa Ieyasu's final victory at Sekigahara at the beginning of the seventeenth century created large numbers of unemployed samurai. In times of unparalleled peace, such *ronin* could not easily find re-employment. Strict rules that forbade movement across classes meant that samurai could not take employment in any of the three lower classes and were restricted to professions defined as befitting the samurai class. Sumo, however, was a practice that was not assigned to any particular class and thus presented a means through which samurai could support themselves. This led to the development of *tsuji-zumo* (street corner sumo), where they fought for money from spectators in the *ukiyo*, the fast growing entertainment quarters of the city, whilst other samurai performed *kanjin-zumo* (fund-raising sumo for religious purposes) at Shinto shrines and temples. Both of these forms provided income for displaced samurai. *Tsuji-zumo* increasingly became a fight to the death between the upper-class samurai and lower-class commoner, and despite its religious links, *kanjin-zumo* was equally violent.[49] For a government concerned with establishing social control, the growing violence and bloodshed was seen as a threat to civil order and in 1648 sumo was officially banned by the Tokugawa regime. The bans, however, did not apply to private sumo performances for *daimyo*, and some of them retained numerous wrestler-samurai for private entertainment. In this regard, the bans may be read as the Tokugawa's attempt to keep sumo as an exclusive entertainment for the upper class where there was no concern with it inciting civil unrest. They declared that the practice of sumo was 'inappropriate to commoners and must henceforth come to an end'.[50] Despite such bans, samurai continued to make a living out of sumo. Again, owing to escalating violence during bouts, further bans were implemented in 1661. This time, with prohibition applying to all types of sumo, *daimyo* refrained from hiring wrestler-samurai for the next thirty years. Whilst other entertainments of the *ukiyo* flourished, sumo was strictly curbed, though its practice never completely ceased.[51]

The sumo that is practised today finds its roots in the late seventeenth century. Changing social and economic conditions from the late seventeenth century provided fertile ground for a renewed interest in native Japanese cultural traditions and ancient literature. The search for authentic Japanese culture throughout this period led to a growth in nationalist sentiment and a gradual rejection of 'foreign' practices and ideas. Within this context, Shinto's popularity increased amongst the ruling classes as it was thought to be an expression of 'true Japanese spirit'. During this period sumo promoters endeavoured to strengthen and explicate the links between sumo and Shinto. When the bans were eventually lifted in 1684, sumo was increasingly linked to Shinto, gradually adopting and modifying Shinto's ritualistic and philosophical basis. By the mid-eighteenth century, sumo closely resembled the form that is still practised today. Although sumo had a long history as a cultural practice of the common people, it was not until it was recast as a uniquely Japanese cultural form, which drew upon indigenous religious principles, that it was promoted as a culturally significant practice for all Japanese.

In attending to the Shogunates's concern with excessive violence, sumo promoters set out to reduce it to an acceptable level, which resulted in a gradual rationalisation whereby practice of sumo was increasingly regulated and controlled. Adopting Shinto rituals was central to promoters' efforts to have bans lifted, and in 1684, after a number of rejections, Ikazuchi Gondaiyu, a *ronin*, obtained permission to stage an eight-day *kanjin-zumo* performance. With each rejected application, Gondaiyu had refined his approach, adding details of regulations designed to curtail the violence of earlier sumo performances.[52] This included the introduction of a restricted fighting area, called the *dohyou*, and a defined set of *kimarite*, or sumo techniques. As *kanjin-zumo* developed official rules that were sanctioned by the authorities, it was excluded from the bans that continued into the mid-eighteenth century.[53] The restructured practice of *kanjin-zumo* marked the beginning of the professional sumo practised today. As sumo underwent further regulation and organisation during the Genroku era (1688–1704), *daimyo* again began hiring wrestlers, including non-samurai wrestlers, called *rikishi* (strong samurai). Despite Tokugawa policies against inter-class movement, the non-samurai members were elevated to the status of samurai. The Shinto rituals introduced in *kanjin-zumo* also provided *daimyo* with the opportunity to display their wealth and social positions through the provision of the elaborate *kesho-mawashi* (ornamental aprons) worn by their *rikishi* during the introduction ceremony.[54]

During the eighteenth century sumo underwent further restructuring and in 1761 was officially called *kanjin-ozumo*. The 'o' added the meaning 'grand' to the title. Every March and October 'grand sumo' was performed in large areas within Shinto shrine or temple grounds, where temporary multi-level viewing stands were constructed as the numbers of spectators swelled.[55] By the mid-eighteenth century, sumo began to appear much as it does today. Regular tournaments were organised by elders called *toshiyori*; a ranking system evolved, creating the *banzuke* (ranking sheet) and rituals such as the *dohyou-iri* (ring-entering ceremony); and *shiko* (raising and stamping feet) became an established part of sumo. The *toshiyori* system had also emerged, whereby retired *rikishi* became *toshiyori*, who not only organised tournaments, but also set up *heya*, or stables, to train new *rikishi*. Indeed, most of the *heya* currently operating in Tokyo were established between 1751 and 1781.[56] Thus, by the late eighteenth century, many of the contemporary trappings of sumo were in place, but it was in preparation for an event in 1791 that the highly ritualistic performance of contemporary sumo was confirmed.

In 1791 a special sumo performance was organised for the young Shogun, Tokugawa Ienari.[57] This event saw the commoners' sumo of the *ukiyo* transformed into a form of entertainment deemed worthy of the highest classes of Tokugawa society. Sumo benefited considerably from such an open show of patronage from the Tokugawa government and Yoshida Oikaze is widely credited with this achievement. Much ruling class interest in sumo arose from its links with Shinto at a time of growing nationalist sentiment. Interest in ancient Japanese cultural ways increased sumo's appeal to the aristocratic elite as they could appreciate its religious and historic rituals. At the same time commoners could continue to enjoy the atmosphere of aggressive physical competition. Yoshida sought to legitimate sumo as a cultural practice suitable for the ruling classes by connecting its practice at the time to eighth-century court sumo and strengthening the links between sumo and Shinto. It was not until the rise in nationalist sentiment and the accompanying development of Shinto as the state religion that sumo was accepted by the ruling classes and the Tokugawa government. A return to pure Japanese ways and a rejection of anything that was non-Japanese saw sumo develop as a uniquely Japanese cultural practice imbued with 'true Japanese spirit'.

Post Tokugawa development

Following the end of over two centuries of self-imposed isolation, the Meiji Revolution (1868–1912) heralded the dismantling of the feudal system in

1871 and the wholesale adoption of Western institutional models as Japan rushed to close the gap between itself and Western industrialised nations. In a quest for modernisation, under government slogans such as 'civilisation and enlightenment', Japan eagerly sought to adopt all things Western,[58] as it swiftly established itself as a modern, industrial and military power. This was initiated by a realisation of its exposure to Western colonial intentions in the mid-nineteenth century, as evidenced in 1854 when American Admiral Perry forced the opening of ports at Shimoda and Hakodate to American trade.

Initial fascination with the West saw widespread adoption of the British and American 'games ideology' and a range of Western team games were introduced into the mass education system. Baseball was introduced in 1872, quickly followed by soccer. Within this context, many Japanese cultural practices, such as sumo, lost favour. They were seen to be unwelcome reminders of Japan's lagging development. With its distinctly feudal rituals and customs, and competitors wearing nothing more than a *mawashi*, sumo was denounced as 'uncivilised'. It was viewed as unsuitable for a modern nation and a hindrance to rapid social and economic development. As a result, sumo's popularity dwindled during the first decade of the Meiji era, its decline further exacerbated by the inability of *daimyo* to financially support sumo wrestlers as they had for most of the Tokugawa era. The dissolution of the feudal domains had effectively wiped out their authority and hereditary incomes.[59]

During the initial widespread adoption of Western institutional models from 1870 to 1880, those promoting the adoption of wholly Western, liberal ideals and practices assumed dominance over conservative forces advocating the preservation of traditional Japanese and Chinese values and practices. From 1880, however, a conservative reaction to what was perceived as the threat of Western excesses to social cohesion and cultural identity gained growing support. This period of emerging nationalism and expanding national confidence and military power heralded significant reforms in the organisation of sumo. Structural changes, combined with the re-establishment of its ties with the imperial line, provided sumo with the impetus to regain much of its lost popularity.

At a time when Japan was under the pressing influence of Western culture, Emperor Meiji asked to view a sumo tournament. The tournament was held in the presence of the emperor on 10 March 1884. By now, sumo was valued as the embodiment of Japanese 'spirit' and as a powerful symbol of Japan's cultural heritage, and as such, provided an ideal means of restoring feelings of Japanese national pride. Indeed, the tournament was promoted with the aim of reviving 'true' Japanese culture before it was totally discarded in the name of 'modernisation'.[60] Importantly, the tournament also reinforced sumo's links with Shinto and re-established its ties with the imperial line of Japan. The popularity of sumo continued to grow to such a level that in 1909 a permanent location for tournaments, the *kokugikan* (national stadium), was built in Ryogoku, Tokyo.[61] The *kokugikan* further established sumo as a prestigious form of entertainment, assuring its future as a recognised Japanese cultural practice.

Military success in China and the defeat of the Russian fleet in 1905 fuelled an increase in nationalism and sparked the rise of militarism that ultimately led Japan into the Pacific War. Under such conditions native Japanese sporting practices such as sumo and the restructured forms of martial arts, such as kendo and judo, experienced an explosion in popularity. This was particularly apparent during the 1930s at a time in which, in the lead up to the Pacific War, the government promoted a belief that, despite America's military might, victory would be achieved through the superiority of *Yamato damashi* (Japanese spirit).[62] The militarist government discouraged foreign sports in favour of Japanese martial arts, increasingly regarded as the epitome of 'Japanese fighting spirit'. The introduction of live radio broadcasts in 1925 provided sumo with a further boost in popularity.[63]

Japan's rising militarism and nationalism in the 1930s prompted the active discouragement of foreign culture, including sport, as a reaction to Western imperialism, and the concomitant rise in the popularity of sumo and Japanese martial arts. As the Japanese army appropriated the *kokugikan*, the May and November tournaments of 1944 were held outdoors on a temporary *dohyou* in a baseball stadium. These tournaments attracted seventy thousand spectators, the largest crowds ever to watch sumo. By contrast, the June 1945 tournament was held in front of a restricted audience of sumo officials and a few wounded soldiers. Through association with pre-war militarism, any cultural practices aimed at fostering spiritual strength were frowned upon by the Supreme Commander for Allied Powers (SCAP). Teaching military subjects in schools and wearing military uniforms was banned. The practice of martial arts, such as kendo, karate and judo, that 'encouraged martial spirit'[64] or any physical training that promoted spiritual education (*seishin kyoiku*) was forbidden.[65] Sumo, however, was excluded from these bans. Whilst SCAP saw martial arts such as karate and kendo as practices explicitly aimed at fostering *seishin kyoiku*, sumo was regarded as less threatening.

Permission was granted by SCAP for the Sumo Association to continue tournaments immediately after the war. The November 1945 tournament was staged in front of a capacity crowd each day. This revival was shortlived, however, as in December 1945, the allied forces took control of the *kokugikan*, turning part of it into a skating rink for American soldiers. In November 1946, special permission was again approved from SCAP to hold a final tournament at the *Ryogoku kokugikan*. From mid-1947 tournaments were held in the grounds of Meiji Shrine.[66] Finally in 1954 a new *kokugikan* was completed across the river in Kuramae, which was later replaced by the present structure in 1985.

Contemporary sumo and globalisation

Processes of globalisation have stimulated increasing flows of culture in which cultural objects and practices are continually transposed and re-contextualised.[67] Under such conditions, administrators in sumo are faced with the dilemma of promoting sumo as a global sporting commodity without losing its powerful symbolism as a unique Japanese cultural practice. Prior to World War II, sumo exhibition tours visited Japanese colonies, such as Korea, and made several trips to Hawaii. The first recorded trip outside Asia was in 1907 when *yokozuna* Hitachiyama and three other *rikishi* toured Europe and the USA.[68] During the post-war period, professional sumo tours continued their frequent visits to Hawaii, and also visited Moscow, Beijing, Shanghai, Mexico City, New York, Paris, Sao Paulo, London, Madrid, Dusseldorf, Hong Kong, San Jose, Honolulu, Vienna,[69] Melbourne and Sydney. International exhibitions of Japan's national sport are viewed as another method of not only generating income for the ongoing promotion of sumo but also maintaining the cultural meaning that is attached to, and conveyed through, its ritualised practice. At the same time, the Japan Sumo Association jealously guards its traditional links with Shinto, thereby highlighting what most Japanese view as the unique features of their culture. Although the Japan Sumo Association welcomes and actively promotes international interest in their national sport, they have been less accepting of foreign participants who are regarded as a potential threat to sumo's cultural integrity and status.

All sumo wrestlers are required to have a Japanese name and to demonstrate that they have adopted a traditional Japanese way of life. The long and demanding climb to the top of the sumo world involves not only physical conditioning and technical development but also the embodiment of a conservative 'traditional' form of culture associated with the concept of a unique Japanese 'spirit'. The extended, demanding and often cruel regimes of training that sumo wrestlers must endure, and the strict control exercised by the Japan Sumo Association, ensure that only foreign wrestlers who are sufficiently 'Japanese' compete at the top levels. In 1972, Hawaiian Jesse Kuhaulua, under his sumo name of Takamiyama, became the first non-Japanese to win a sumo tournament. Reactions to his win were summarised in banner headlines such as 'National Sport in Danger!'. The Sumo Association responded by introducing a rule that disallowed non-Japanese from remaining in the sumo world after retirement. Undeterrred, Kuhaulua gained Japanese citizenship then opened his own sumo stable, Azumazeki-*beya*, in 1986.[70] Takamiyama retired from the *dohyou* in 1984, and attention turned to another Hawaiian, Salevaa Atisanoe, who was quickly moving up the ranks under his sumo name of Konishiki. Konishiki broke the record for the fastest rise to the salaried ranks, and by early 1992 was rumoured to be about to become the first non-Japanese to be promoted to the highest rank of *yokozuna*.[71] Reports of racism and debates over whether or not a non-Japanese should be allowed the coveted *yokozuna* rank abounded in both

Japan and the USA, and the situation even threatened Japan–US trade agreements.[72] Unfortunately, Konishiki's performances weakened and he was moved out of *yokozuna* contention before the debates were properly resolved.

Although the Japan Sumo Association did not make an official rule restricting the *yokozuna* rank to Japanese citizens, they did emphasise that non-Japanese *rikishi* need to demonstrate they are 'Japanised' in order to be considered for *yokozuna* status. In another defensive move, the Japan Sumo Association placed a temporary ban on any more foreigners from entering sumo whilst they considered the situation. It has been suggested they may formulate policies to limit each stable to two foreign *rikishi*.[73] When confronted with the same situation of a foreign *yokozuna* candidate twelve months later, none of the previous year's sensationalism followed. In January 1993, Hawaiian Chad Rowan, wrestling as Akebono, was named the first non-Japanese *yokozuna*.[74]

Conclusion

Hobsbawm argues that the invention of tradition in nineteenth-century Europe arose in response to profound and rapid social change that required new ways of maintaining social cohesion and control.[75] Similarly, invented sumo tradition has operated at an official, political level and an unofficial, 'social' level in rapidly changing social, political and economic conditions to express and confirm social cohesion, identity and the structure of social relations.[76] Since the eighteenth century Shinto rituals have been incorporated into sumo in order to legitimate the activity as a prestigious cultural practice and as an expression and confirmation of a distinct Japanese culture. Through the introduction of Shinto ceremonies, sumo was provided a 'suitable' historic past that validated it as a noble, quasi-religious tradition. This also marked sumo as a cultural practice that was distinctly Japanese and the embodiment of what has, over the past three centuries, come to be regarded as 'true Japanese spirit'. At this time Shinto was increasingly recognised as the authentic religion of the Japanese race, and was, in addition, a religion with growing political influence. Sumo's history as a native Japanese practice and the links established with Shinto from the eighteenth century have assisted its development as a means of expressing and confirming Japanese culture in the face of a range of external threats over the past two centuries. Sumo's growth as a cultural icon is tied into the emergence of the notion of a distinctly Japanese 'spirit' and the consequent historical ebb and flow of nationalist sentiment over the past three centuries.

The deliberately constructed relationship with Shinto in the eighteenth century guaranteed that sumo would become well-established in a climate of emerging nationalist sentiment and a search for an essential and distinctive cultural identity. The subsequent threat of Western colonial ambitions and the excesses of Western liberalism in the nineteenth century created further waves of nationalism in which the search for 'true' Japanese culture and cultural practices confirmed the standing of sumo as a symbol of Japanese culture and 'spirit'. Sumo and the martial arts, such as judo, were again promoted during the 1930s to highlight the strength of Japanese 'spirit' by a militarist government as Japan headed toward war. Shinto's links with right-wing political forces in Japan and its association with the Pacific War continue to present problems for Japan's reconciliation with its Asian neighbours. Visits to the *Yasukuni* Shrine, a Shinto shrine, by politicians to honour war-dead, including war-criminals, always provoke bitter protests from Asian neighbours. Once one of the most prominent shrines of State Shinto, it is also a source of internal friction in Japan as many Japanese feel that it symbolises a dangerous link with a militarist past.[77]

More recently it has been the forces and influence of globalisation that present a threat to the notion of a unique and homogenous Japanese culture. With the collapsing of cultural boundaries and the flow of global culture that accompanies it, globalisation presents another threat to the idea of pure and distinctive Japanese culture. Trans-national movements in culture increasingly challenge the notion of a universal culture that is simply produced, disseminated and maintained.[78] Under these conditions it is likely that the role of sumo in defining a distinctly Japanese cultural identity will be tested. Indeed, the influence of global sport on the role of sport in reproducing dominant and distinct Japanese culture[79] is evident in the popularity of 'J League' soccer in Japan. Sumo, martial arts such as judo and kendo, and conservative team sports such as baseball and rugby continue to reproduce and reinforce a 'traditional', hegemonic form of Japanese culture. However, since 1993 this dominant model of Japanese sport has been challenged by the rise of professional 'J League' soccer. Whilst 'J League' soccer does display some distinctly Japanese characteristics, its practice and the meanings attached to it are strongly shaped by the values embedded in 'the world game' as a global commodity. Under such conditions, global forces will likely challenge the role that sumo plays in the reproduction of a cultural hegemony[80] and the maintenance of a distinctive cultural identity constructed around the notion of mythological origins of the Japanese 'race'.

Notes

1 See for example, R. Light, 'From the profane to the sacred: pre-game ritual in Japanese high school rugby', *International Review for the Sociology of Sport*, vol. 35, no. 4, 2000, pp. 451–63.

2 See for example, A. Guttmann, *From Ritual to Record: The Nature of Modern Sports*, New York, Columbia University Press, 1978; J. Lever, *Soccer Madness*, Chicago, University of Chicago Press, 1983.

3 E. Durkheim, *The Elementary Forms of the Religious Life*, Cambridge, Cambridge University Press, 1976 [1912].

4 See for example, J. Lever, *Soccer Madness*, Chicago, University of Chicago Press, 1983; G. Jarvie, 'Sport, nationalism and cultural identity', in L. Allison (ed.), *The Changing Politics of Sport*, Manchester, Manchester University Press, pp. 58–83.

5 Cited in Nihon Sumo Kyokai, *The Power and the Glory: Australian Grand Sumo Tournaments* (Tournament programme), Sydney, 1997, p. 4.

6 T. Magdalinski, 'Organized remembering: the construction of sporting traditions in the GDR', *European Review of Sports History*, vol. 1, 1998, pp. 144–63; S. Pope, 'Amateurism and American sports culture: the invention of an athletic tradition in the United States, 1870–1900', *International Journal of the History of Sport*, vol. 13, no. 3, 1996, pp. 290–309.

7 E. Hobsbawm, 'Introduction: inventing traditions', in E. Hobsbawm and T. Ranger (eds), *The Invention of Tradition*, Cambridge, Cambridge University Press, 1983, p. 1.

8 Ibid.

9 R. Williams, *Marxism and Literature*, Oxford, Oxford University Press, 1977.

10 To reinforce sumo's invented history and further distance it from its common background, additional Shinto elements were introduced in the early twentieth century. The decorative kimono and black Shinto hat were introduced in 1909. The kimono resembles *hitatare* ceremonial court robes of the eighth century. The hat is based on the traditional costume of Shinto priests in the Heian period (794–1185). In 1931 the style of the *yakata*, the roof over the *dohyou*, was changed as a further measure to reinforce sumo's connection to Shinto. Originally the *yakata* was based on the style of a typical farmhouse roof, but in 1931, it was remodelled on the roof of the Geku, the Outer Shrine of the Grand Shrine of Ise.

11 J. Kitagawa, *On Understanding Japanese Religion*, Princeton, Princeton University Press, 1987, p. 139.

12 R. Ellwood and R. Pilgrim (eds), *Japanese Religion, A Cultural Perspective*, New Jersey, Prentice-Hall, 1985, p. 146.

13 Tamaru Noriyoshi and D. Reid (eds), *Religion in Japanese Culture*, Tokyo, Kodansha, 1996, p. 16.

14 I. Buruma, *A Japanese Mirror: Heroes and Villains of Japanese Culture*, London, Jonathon Cape, 1984, p. 9.

15 Koike Tamio, 'The dawning of a new age of sumo', *Japan Quarterly*, April–June 1993, p. 196.

16 D. Simmons, '*Shihon-Bashira*: then and now', *Sumo World*, July 1995, p. 14.

17 D. Simmons, '*Yakata*: then and now', *Sumo World*, September 1995, p. 14.

18 A. Adams, 'Sumo referees' role is not all pageantry', *The Japan Times*, 7 November 1993.

19 A. Guttmann, *Games and Empires: Modern Sports and Cultural Imperialism*, New York, Columbia University Press, 1994, p. 163.

20 A. Adams and C. Newton, *Sumo*, London, Hamlyn Publishing Group, 1989, p. 7; C. Newton, *Dynamic Sumo*, Tokyo, Kodansha, 1994, p. 18.

21 J. Kuhaulua, *Takamiyama – The World of Sumo*, Tokyo, Kodansha International, 1973, p. 115.

22 It is also argued that the lifting of the *kesho-mawashi* is symbolic of an ancient Shinto myth involving Amaterasu, the sun goddess and ancestress of the imperial line. Amaterasu hid in a cave to escape the violence of her brother, causing darkness throughout the land. Ame-no-uzume, another female deity, performed a dance in front of the cave, which was cheered by other *kami*. The cheering lured Amaterasu out of hiding restoring sunlight to the world. During the dance, Ame-no-uzume 'became divinely possessed, exposed her breasts, and pushed her skirt-band down to her genitals'. D. Philippi, *Kojiki*, Tokyo, University of Tokyo Press, 1989, pp. 140–1. This type of performance was used in religious rites to ward off evil spirits as well as to entertain and invigorate the *kami*. The lifting of the *kesho-mawashi* during the *dohyou-iri* is said to be a 'ritualised version of a more robust gesture usually made to drive out devils'. L.K Choy, *Japan: Between Myth and Reality*, Singapore, World Scientific, 1995, p. 53.

23 The *shikiri* ritual involves lifting each leg high and stamping it down on the *dohyou*, clapping hands with arms held outstretched and palms upward, rinsing the mouth and throwing salt. Each element of the *shikiri* holds special meaning. The leg-stamping, or

shiko, is to stamp out any bad spirits from the *dohyou*. The mouth is rinsed with *chikara-mizu* (strength water), and is spat out behind *chikara-gami* (strength paper). This is to purify the mind and body and has the same function as visitors rinsing their mouths at Shinto shrines. Clapping by the *rikishi* on the *dohyou* is to get the attention of the gods and to show the body and spirit is purified. Salt is a common element of Shinto purification ceremonies and is thrown to purify the ring and protect the *rikishi*.

24 H. Bolitho, 'Sumo and popular culture: the Tokugawa period', in G. McCormack and Y. Sugimoto (eds), *The Japanese Trajectory: Modernization and Beyond*, Melbourne, Cambridge University Press, 1988, p. 19.

25 P.L. Cuyler, *Sumo – From Rite to Sport*, Tokyo, John Weatherhill, 1985, p. 21; H. Bolitho, 'Sumo and popular culture: the Tokugawa period', in G. McCormack and Y. Sugimoto (eds), *The Japanese Trajectory: Modernization and Beyond*, Melbourne, Cambridge University Press, 1988, p. 19.

26 P.L. Cuyler, *Sumo – From Rite to Sport*, Tokyo, John Weatherhill, 1985, pp. 186–7; J. Kuhaulua, *Takamiyama – The World of Sumo*, Tokyo, Kodansha International, 1973, p. 118.

27 Hikoyama Kozo, *Sumo, Japanese Wrestling*, volume 34, Tokyo, Japan Tourist Bureau, c. 1940, p. 12.

28 M. Anzu, *Shinto to Nihonjin (Shinto and the Japanese)*, Tokyo, Jinjashimpou-sha, 1986, p. 16.

29 J. Kuhaulua, *Takamiyama – The World of Sumo*, Tokyo, Kodansha International, 1973, p. 25.

30 P.L. Cuyler, *Sumo – From Rite to Sport*, Tokyo, John Weatherhill, 1985, pp. 23–5.

31 Wakamori Taro, *Sumo no Rekishi to Minzoku (The History and People of Sumo)*, Tokyo, Kobundo, 1982, p. 13.

32 J. Kuhaulua, *Takamiyama – The World of Sumo*, Tokyo, Kodansha International, 1973, p. 36.

33 Wakamori Taro, *Sumo no Rekishi to Minzoku (The History and People of Sumo)*, Tokyo, Kobundo, 1982, pp. 18–19.

34 P.L. Cuyler, *Sumo – From Rite to Sport*, Tokyo, John Weatherhill, 1985, p. 51.

35 The Shogun was the head of the military government of Japan.

36 H. Ooms, *Tokugawa Ideology – Early Constructs, 1570–1680*, London, Princeton University Press, 1985, pp. 171–3.

37 G.B. Sansom, *The Western World and Japan*, London, Knopf, 1962, p. 173.

38 K. Van Wolferen, *The Enigma of Japanese Power*, Tokyo, Tuttle, 1993, p. 368.

39 Over 3000 Christians were executed or died under torture between 1597 and 1660. See G.B. Sansom, *The Western World and Japan*, London, Knopf, 1962, p. 173.

40 K. Van Wolferen, *The Enigma of Japanese Power*, Tokyo, Tuttle, 1993, p. 368.

41 Ibid., p. 369.

42 H.B. Earhart, *Japanese Religion: Unity and Diversity*, third edition, Belmont, Wadsworth Publishing, 1982, p. 136.

43 Tsunoda Ryusaku, W.T. de Bary and D. Keene, *Sources of Japanese Tradition*, volume 2, New York, Columbia University Press, 1964, p. 324.

44 'Shushi' is the Japanese version of the name of the Chinese philosopher, Chu Hsi. See H.B. Earhart, *Japanese Religion: Unity and Diversity*, third edition, Belmont, Wadsworth Publishing, 1982, p. 137; Anesaki Masaharu, *History of Japanese Religion*, London, Kegan Paul International, 1995, p. 224.

45 H.B. Earhart, *Japanese Religion: Unity and Diversity*, third edition, Belmont, Wadsworth Publishing, 1982, pp. 139, 142.

46 Ibid., p. 143; Tsunoda Ryusaku, W.T. de Bary and D. Keene, *Sources of Japanese Tradition*, volume 2, New York, Columbia University Press, 1964, p. 1.

47 *Kojiki*, Records of Ancient Matters, 712 AD; *Nihon Shoki/Nihongi*, Chronicles of Japan, 720 AD; *Manyoshu*, anthology of poetry completed in the eighth century AD.

48 Anesaki Masaharu, *History of Japanese Religion*, London, Kegan Paul International, 1995, p. 309.
49 P.L. Cuyler, *Sumo – From Rite to Sport*, Tokyo, John Weatherhill, 1985, pp. 57–9.
50 H. Bolitho, 'Sumo and popular culture: the Tokugawa period', in G. McCormack and Y. Sugimoto (eds), *The Japanese Trajectory: Modernization and Beyond*, Melbourne, Cambridge University Press, 1988, p. 23.
51 P.L. Cuyler, *Sumo – From Rite to Sport*, Tokyo, John Weatherhill, 1985, p. 61.
52 Ibid.
53 Ibid., p. 63.
54 Ibid., p. 67.
55 Wakamori Taro, *Sumo no Rekishi to Minzoku (The History and People of Sumo)*, Tokyo, Kobundo, 1982, p. 27.
56 P.L. Cuyler, *Sumo – From Rite to Sport*, Tokyo, John Weatherhill, 1985, p. 72; Wakamori Taro, *Sumo no Rekishi to Minzoku (The History and People of Sumo)*, Tokyo, Kobundo, 1982, p. 28.
57 H. Bolitho, 'Sumo and popular culture: the Tokugawa period', in G. McCormack and Y. Sugimoto (eds), *The Japanese Trajectory: Modernization and Beyond*, Melbourne, Cambridge University Press, 1988, p. 26.
58 W.G. Beasley, *The Meiji Restoration*, Stanford, Stanford University Press, 1972, pp. 352–4.
59 J. Kuhaulua, *Takamiyama – The World of Sumo*, Tokyo, Kodansha International, 1973, p. 36.
60 Hikoyama Kozo, *Sumo, Japanese Wrestling*, volume 34, Tokyo, Japan Tourist Bureau, c. 1940, p. 15.
61 C. Newton, *Dynamic Sumo*, Tokyo, Kodansha, 1994, p. 56.
62 Takie, Sugiyama Lebra, *Japanese Patterns of Behavior*, Honolulu, University of Hawaii Press, 1976.
63 Wakamori Taro, *Sumo no Rekishi to Minzoku (The History and People of Sumo)*, Tokyo, Kobundo, 1982, p. 54.
64 Ibid., p. 219.
65 Ibid., p. 290.
66 P.L. Cuyler, *Sumo – From Rite to Sport*, Tokyo, John Weatherhill, 1985, pp. 116–17.
67 D. Palumbo-Liu, 'Introduction', in D. Palumbo-Lui and H.U. Gumbrecht (eds), *Streams of Cultural Capital*, Stanford, Stanford University Press, 1997, pp. 1–22.
68 L. Sharnoff, 'Foreigners making their mark in sumo', *Japan Quarterly*, vol. 37, 1990, pp. 164–70.
69 A. Adams, 'Paris, Vienna Koen Announced', *Sumo World*, July 1995, p. 8.
70 J. Kuhaulua, *Takamiyama – The World of Sumo*, Tokyo, Kodansha International, 1973, pp. 169–71.
71 Konishiki Yasokichi, 'An American sumo wrestler speaks out', *Japan Echo*, vol. 15, no. 2, 1988, pp. 61–2.
72 See R. Delfs, 'Weighty problem. Wrestler's remarks spark new US–Japan row', *The Far Eastern Economic Review*, 21 May 1992, p. 18; Koike Tamio, 'The dawning of a new age of sumo', *Japan Quarterly*, April–June 1993, pp. 194–6; *Nihon Keizai Shimbun*, 20 April 1992, p. 1; P. Sandoz, *Sumo Showdown, The Hawaiian Challenge*, Tokyo, Tuttle, 1992, p. 21; D. Sanger, 'Big American wins big, and sumo is akimbo', *New York Times*, 23 March 1992, pp. 1, 9; 'Sumo star charges racism in Japan', *New York Times*, 22 April 1992, p. 3; 'American sumo star denies accusing the Japanese of racism', *New York Times*, 24 April 1992, p. 11; 'U.S. sumo star, faltering, is counted out for crown', *New York Times*, 18 May 1992, p. 6; L. Sharnoff, 'Foreigners making their mark in sumo', *Japan Quarterly*, vol. 37, 1990, pp. 168–9.
73 'Lean times for sumo', *The Economist*, 19 December 1992, p. 88.
74 Itoh Yoshiaki, 'Yokozuna Chad blazes enormous trail', *The Nikkei Weekly*, 1 February 1993, p. 22.

75 E. Hobsbawm, 'Mass-producing traditions: Europe, 1870–1914', in E. Hobsbawm and T. Ranger (eds), *The Invention of Tradition*, Cambridge, Cambridge University Press, 1983, p. 263.
76 Ibid.
77 K. Van Wolferen, *The Enigma of Japanese Power*, Tokyo, Tuttle, 1993, p. 421.
78 D. Palumbo-Lui and H.U. Gumbrecht (eds), *Streams of Cultural Capital*, Stanford, Stanford University Press, 1997.
79 See R. Light, 'A centenary of rugby and masculinity in Japanese schools: continuity and change', *Sporting Traditions*, vol. 16, no. 2, 2000, pp. 87–104.
80 A. Gramsci, *Selections from Prison Notebooks*, London, Lawrence & Wishart, 1971.

9 What makes a man?

Religion, sport and negotiating masculine identity in the Promise Keepers

George D. Randels Jr and Becky Beal

The Promise Keepers is a Protestant Christian evangelical group that began in the USA in 1990. It is a men's religious and social movement organised to address the changing structure of the family and men's role in both its breakdown and renaissance. Although this group does not engage in sport or directly promote sport as an important part of its movement, it has used sport symbolically to communicate the ideologies of the organisation. Sport venues become religious settings, sport rituals are converted into religious ones, sport heroes are revered as saints and moral exemplars, and sport metaphors are means for communicating key truths and desirable character traits. Importantly, Promise Keepers founder Bill McCartney, in his role as former Colorado University football coach, imbues much of the group's philosophy with a kind of contemporary muscular Christianity, confirming that success in sport may define aspects of masculine spirituality.

Nevertheless, the Promise Keepers does not simply appropriate sport into Christianity, nor does it unambiguously support traditional models of manliness in its quest for a Christ-like masculinity. It is not simply an updated version of muscular Christianity regardless of some apparent over-laps with that movement. Instead, the Promise Keepers utilises diverse, and sometimes contradictory, rhetoric and practice in its ministry, drawing on elements of popular culture, whilst clearly demarcating the boundaries between the contemporary secular world and the Christianity it espouses. So whilst the Promise Keepers relies on sport for its model of manliness, it just as importantly promotes male intimacy at the same time that it remains vehemently anti-gay.[1] The rhetoric of sport and the location of Promise Keeper meetings in sports stadia provide the movement with geographic and linguistic security, such that the basic precepts of heterosexual masculinity are not confused, even when emotional displays are encouraged. The contrast between 'feminine' emotion and hegemonic masculinity is an important point to consider, particularly as the cultural and symbolic signif-icance of mainstream sport resides in its perpetuation of a patriarchal hegemony. Of course we recognise that patriarchy is promulgated not just in athletics, but in other fields, such as politics and business, that rely on the cultivation of similar masculine traits.[2] The gender logic within the Promise

Keepers generally conforms to the traditional Christian understanding of a masculine/feminine hierarchy, which is derived from conventional interpretations of biblical passages, such as the stories of Creation and Fall in Genesis as well as household and worship rules from Pauline epistles, such as Ephesians 5:22–33 and I Timothy 2:8–15.[3] Yet, other expressions of manliness and gender roles, primarily 'servant-leadership' but also 'mutual submission', are also present within this movement and find support within Christianity.

This chapter analyses tensions between sport, masculinity and religiosity in the Promise Keepers' rhetoric and practice, as well as its implications for the development of Christian identity within the USA. Before such a discussion, it is important to review the rise of the Promise Keepers as well as the movement's social context, before providing a theological analysis of the tensions within Promise Keeper identity as it relates to the larger society generally and sport more specifically. As such, we explore the Promise Keepers' application of sport rhetoric as well as the contradictions that arise through the use of sport to maintain identity whilst simultaneously attempting to develop new roles for men.

Promise Keepers and a crisis in masculinity

During times of social upheaval, established social roles fluctuate and may provoke confusion or crises in personal identity, a situation that is particularly evident when considering changing gender roles. Over the past century, the variation in social, economic and political circumstances has led to what some researchers have termed crises in masculinity. John Nauright, for example, has considered British physical deterioration debates of the early twentieth century, whilst others, such as Varda Burstyn, have looked to the rise of feminism and its perceived threat to male power, as evidence of this condition.[4] What these discussions have in common is that organised sport was recognised as a means of ameliorating the situation, which, they argue, developed partly in response to industrialisation. During that time, men followed economic production out of the household, and, as such, suitable male role models for young boys disappeared.[5] Whilst the late nineteenth century may reveal interesting tensions within masculinity, many scholars have identified a more recent, and thus more relevant, gender crisis.[6] They claim that the privileges once bestowed upon the dominant white male social group have come under heavy criticism from various civil rights movements, including, and perhaps especially, the feminist movement. White, heterosexual men have been identified as causing and/or benefiting from the discrimination against, and exploitation of, minority groups. In addition, some argue that men have been psychologically damaged through their estrangement from a domestic environment dominated almost exclusively by women.[7] Underpinning this discourse is a fiscal reality that is signified by the loss of real earning power for a generation of working-class men. This economic shift has left many without financial support, negating their role as provider, as well as without a traditional source of masculine identity.

These events have prompted many men to feel less like a beneficiary of an oppressive system, and more like a victim of one, and they have struggled to recover their position. There have been several denunciatory responses, often referred to as the 'backlash' of the 1980s, as evidenced in Reagan politics and the popularity of reactionary talk-show host Rush Limbaugh. More recently, the grunge music scene has provided a site where white middle- and working-class men can present themselves as not privileged.[8] The cultural scrutiny of the 'invisible' normative standard of whiteness and masculinity has increased men's awareness of the nature of their social iden- tity, offering them important opportunities to redefine their roles. Whilst the responses to this apparent crisis in masculine identity have varied greatly, a number of dedicated men's movements have tried to help men redefine their roles in a changing society.[9]

One such organisation, designed to assist middle-class men in reconciling themselves to their changing position, is the Promise Keepers. The organisa- tion's leadership discusses with some urgency the need to evangelise men *primarily* because it regards American society to be in the process of signifi- cant transitions, and, as founder Bill McCartney notes, men bear the primary responsibility for the nation's social problems. McCartney recognises that part of these changes is the fluidity of masculinity in the late twentieth century: 'We live in a society that is, almost daily it seems, redefining manhood',[10] a sentiment that has attracted a largely white, middle-class following.[11] He further claims that the 'absence of responsible men from the home is now widely regarded as the most important cause of America's social decline' and invites men to 'walk in Christian masculinity'.[12] Similarly, the jacket cover of *Seven Promises of a Promise Keeper* states explic- itly: 'Our nation is suffering from a severe shortage of integrity. It needs men willing to stand strong in the midst of moral chaos.'[13] Rather than emphasising their concerns about the status of masculinity within contem- porary American society, the language subtlety refocuses attention on a broader, and less gender-specific, social crisis. Re-framed in this way, Promise Keepers delivers a positive model that envisions men as potentially the most valuable contributors to society, who are regarded as crucial to resolving this social dilemma. McCartney frequently argues that 'From a Christian perspective, men have a unique, God-given responsibility for the spiritual health of their families', effectively linking masculinity with Christian duty and social responsibility as a means of solving society's ills.[14]

Belonging to the Promise Keepers may be analogous to belonging to the feminist movement. There is no formal declaration nor are dues paid. The leadership of both movements sets and circulates an agenda, and provides opportunities for people to gather and discuss those concerns. A Promise Keeper is one who identifies with the organisation's agenda, which emphasises the need for men to be committed to God, their families, and other men within their local communities. The large stadium events serve as an initial means of getting men interested in carrying on efforts in their local communities, indeed much of the Promise Keepers' work occurs in small groups called 'accountability groups', which are usually associated with a particular local church. The focus of these all-male groups is to help members practise godly masculinity as expressed through the Promise Keepers' central tenets, the seven promises.[15] In addition, the organisation provides a range of print and electronic literature to support the on-going education of men.

The Promise Keepers endeavours to enable men to 'become fully Christlike *and* fully masculine',[16] yet this proffered model is not necessarily cohesive. Whilst the leadership contends that it is working towards defining Christ-like masculinity, the methods they employ appear counterproductive. Much of the current literature on the Promise Keepers describes its complex, and often contradictory, approach to gender,[17] though some have justified the heterogeneous masculinities, arguing that diverse interpretations are necessary to attract a wide variety of men in order to sustain the movement. William H. Lockhart claims that the Promise Keepers employs a pragmatic strategy in its literature, utilising various gender ideologies to communicate its methods to assist men to become more committed to their relationships with their family and God.[18] Mary Stewart Van Leeuwen suggests that pragmatism may be a partial explanation for the ambiguity in the Promise Keeper masculinity, but maintains there are probably unexamined assumptions about the deliberate use of language as well as some intentionally sexist claims within their rhetoric.[19] In addition, it is also likely that the Promise Keepers leadership has not carefully considered nor analysed its own basic philosophies. There is a wide range of authorial voices in the movement's literature, which suggests a plethora of ideologies. Whilst there may have been disagreement amongst various Promise Keepers, it could simply be that there has been no conscious decision on how, or whether, to systematise their beliefs. As such, rather than intentional pragmatism, the contradictions may have resulted from benign neglect. Whatever the reason for the disparate methods and models, a sense of traditional masculinity is clearly present, especially with reference to sport, and whilst alternative models of masculinity are also extant, these are generally presented without explicit reference to sporting metaphors.

Religion and secular culture: situating masculinity and sport

Historically, the Christian tradition has juxtaposed the church and the secular world, although the exact nature of this differentiation has remained controversial. This relationship has been articulated in a number of ways, including literal, metaphorical, material and spiritual interpretations, although probably the most famous explication of the church/world relation is Augustine's Two Cities dichotomy: the heavenly City of God and the earthly City of the Devil.[20] In practice, perhaps the clearest examples of church encountering world, are provided by radical separatist groups, which, in contemporary US culture, would include the old-order Amish Mennonites and the Branch Davidian splinter of the Seventh-Day Adventists. Many evangelical associations also establish cultural and religious boundaries between themselves and mainstream American society, which is often thought to include more liberal, mainstream religious communities, and define themselves 'against the prevailing norms of the dominant culture'.[21] Evangelicals, including the Promise Keepers leadership as well as most of its members, work hard to retain the integrity of these borders, policing the frontier to maintain their Christian values. Of course, evangelicals cannot be regarded as a homogenous group, particularly as tensions exist amongst them, such as concerns about the precise relationship between their community and the dominant culture, as well as the degree to which they need to isolate themselves from mainstream society. For example, Van Leeuwen identifies two broad categories of evangelicals, revivalists and separatists, that take very different approaches. Another tension relevant to this discussion is the proper Christian vision of masculinity, with Lockhart finding four different ideological approaches at work.[22]

Within an evangelical group like the Promise Keepers, then, it is not surprising to find that its rhetoric and practices imply multiple understandings of the relationship between church and world. For this reason, it is important to examine the often contradictory ways that Promise Keepers situates Christianity *vis-à-vis* the broader American community. Only then is it possible to analyse the ways in which the Promise Keepers utilises sport as a mode of communication and a means of promulgating its ideology.

A useful framework for analysing the different conceptions of the church/world binary can be found in the work of American theologian and Christian ethicist H. Richard Niebuhr.[23] In perhaps his most famous work, *Christ and Culture*, Niebuhr establishes a typology of five models that categorise various approaches to the dialectic between church and world, or as he terms it, the relationship between Christ and culture.[24] He adopts the basic anthropological definition of culture as comprising 'language, habits, ideas, beliefs, customs, social organization, inherited artifacts, technical processes, and values'. It is what 'the New Testament writers frequently had in mind when they spoke of "the world"'.[25] Three of Niebuhr's models, Christ Against Culture, The Christ of Culture and Christ the Transformer of Culture, can be used to analyse the ideologies of the Promise Keepers and the differing conceptions of the movement's relationship to the broader community. They provide a framework for understanding the competing visions of masculinity present within the Promise Keepers, and for understanding how sport both meshes and clashes with evangelical Christianity.

Christ Against Culture

In the Christ Against Culture model, Niebuhr suggests that the

> counterpart of loyalty to Christ and the brothers is the rejection of
> cultural society; a clear line of separation is drawn between the brother-
> hood of the children of God and the world. ... That world appears as a
> realm under the power of evil; it is the region of darkness, into which
> the citizens of the kingdom of light must not enter. ... It is a secular
> society, dominated by the 'lust of the flesh, the lust of the eyes and the
> pride of life'.[26]

Whilst this model does not necessarily advocate a complete withdrawal from
society, neither does it preclude it. Rather, it argues for clear boundaries
between church and society. Sociologist Christian Smith claims that
American evangelicalism '*thrives* on distinction, engagement, tension,
conflict, and threat. Without these, evangelicalism would lose its identity
and purpose and grow languid and aimless'.[27] Likewise, the Promise
Keepers is not isolationist, but establishes its identity by employing the
psychosocial rhetoric of separation to distinguish itself from contemporary
social values and practices. Promise Keeper Udo Middelman explains: 'We
live after the Fall. Normality, as it is now, is not what God had in mind. ...
The norms of God are not the same as statistically normal behavior of people
or things.'[28]

The Christ Against Culture model is clearly manifest in the third of the
group's seven promises: 'A Promise Keeper is committed to practicing spiritual, moral, ethical, and sexual purity'.[29] In its focus on purity, the section
'A Man and His Integrity' in *Seven Promises of a Promise Keeper* emphasises the
sinfulness of secular culture. Furthermore, it highlights Christianity's call
for men to live by a different standard, and to strive for a purity they feel is
lacking in the dominant culture. Prominent Promise Keepers author Gary J.
Oliver contends that Americans have a 'moral and ethical crisis sweeping
our nation. ... We are a generation that isn't sure where the line is between
right and wrong. Many don't believe there is a line, or if there is, they don't
care'.[30] He uses a metaphor of a frog that remains in water, even though it is
gradually approaching the boiling point. Recognising the influence that
mass culture has on personal and collective values, Oliver contends that for
'Christian men, it's easier than we think to end up like the frog. Many godly
men ... have yielded to the world's values because they failed to discern the
subtle changes occurring around them. Before they knew it, they were in hot
water.'[31] Likewise, Promise Keeper Jerry Kirk situates the Christian
commitment to sexual purity in stark contrast to secular culture:

> The sad fact is that one is hard pressed to find any encouragement for a
> life of sexual purity in our modern culture. ... Movies, radio 'shock
> jocks', and other media openly and continually encourage infidelity and

promiscuity. ... [A]part from God's Word, your family, and other Christian men, you will receive little encouragement from the culture surrounding you for a pure life.[32]

Besides integrity, understood particularly as sexual purity, Niebuhr's Christ Against Culture model is also relevant in terms of masculine identity. Promise Keeper E. Glenn Wagner argues that pursuing strong relationships with other men – promise number two – contradicts the prevailing myth of 'The Friendless American Male'. Rather than rugged individualism and self-sufficiency, Wagner holds that a biblical mandate exists for male friendships, requiring a break from the barriers of cultural stereotypes. Amongst other things, he calls for a move from the traditional, competitive, macho manliness often associated with sport to a softer masculinity that emphasises caring, emotions and self-disclosure.[33] The Promise Keepers also rejects other prominent aspects of American masculine identity, specifically career and wealth, and it counsels against using 'worldly standards and superficial measuring sticks to determine levels of success and the value of a person ... adopting the world's ideas of what it means to be a winner'.[34] Similarly, in her interviews with members of a Promise Keepers accountability group, Susan Faludi finds that these men seek to replace the focus on occupation and wealth as a marker of male identity and status with an identity centred on Christ.[35]

Christ transforming culture

Despite the strong distinction it makes between contemporary American culture and the Christian life, the Promise Keepers does not fit squarely within the Christ Against Culture model because it is not content to be a separatist group. Clearly it seeks to distinguish between mainstream and Christian perspectives in the areas of integrity and masculinity, but much of the Promise Keepers leadership appears to be at least as concerned with social transformation as it is with individual transformation, the latter being a means to the former. Promise number seven states: 'A Promise Keeper is committed to influencing his world, being obedient to the Great Commandment and the Great Commission.'[36] As such, the Promise Keepers also conforms to Niebuhr's Christ the Transformer of Culture model. Niebuhr understands 'conversionists' to be optimistic about the prospects for changing culture.[37] For them, 'history is the story of God's mighty deeds and of man's responses to them. ... Eternity means ... the presence of God in time ... the divine possibility of a present renewal.'[38] Randy Phillips, President of the Promise Keepers, is indeed a conversionist, suggesting that the USA is 'at the threshold of a spiritual awakening ... when God bestows his grace and power in unusual measures upon a people to extend His kingdom on earth.'[39] He sees the Promise Keepers organisation as central to that new great awakening and believes the seven promises are 'meant to guide us toward the life of Christ and to transform us within so that we might see transformation in our homes, among our friends, in our churches, and ultimately, in our nation'.[40] Others within the movement similarly articulate the need for a national spiritual revival and claim a key role for the Promise Keepers in its instigation.[41]

Importantly, the transformation of culture is linked explicitly to male leadership. Men must lead for the transformation to occur. Promise Keepers authors are essentially agreed that leadership responsibility belongs to men and is a key component of masculinity, though some, such as Oliver, promote mutuality between husband and wife.[42] Most Promise Keepers authors offer biblical proof texts as their primary justification for their position, although some authors also rely on socio-biological arguments.[43] Probably the most frequently cited text on this issue, indeed it is likely the most famous selection from the Promise Keepers literature, is Tony Evans' call for men to take back their roles as leaders from their wives. Evans states that men must not simply ask for power within their relationships; they must assert their right and take it.[44] Although there is accord concerning the primacy of male leadership, the nature of that leadership is not consistent amongst Promise Keepers literature and proponents. Some authors, at least implicitly if not explicitly, support an authoritative style of leadership where the father/husband actively directs the family, whilst most others support servant-leadership, and some use the language of both.[45] These styles differ greatly from one another, and the authoritarian rhetoric creates tension with the servant-leader model. They both contrast starkly with Oliver's vision of mutuality, which is a clearly a minority view, but one that is articulated by a highly esteemed writer. Accountability groups also show variance in leadership style, with both hierarchical and egalitarian structures.[46]

The Christ of Culture

Whether contemporary American culture is portrayed as an insidious force in contrast to Christian values, or as a fallen society that can be redeemed, the Promise Keepers cannot refrain from being part of it. The movement is clearly part of the broader society, and thus mainstream society necessarily influences the religious community:

> Christ claims no man purely as a natural being, but always as one who has become human in a culture; who is not only in culture, but into whom culture has penetrated. Man not only speaks but thinks with the aid of the language of culture ... the forms and attitudes of his mind which allow him to make sense out of the objective world have been given him by culture.[47]

For this reason alone, one might expect overlap with The Christ of Culture model, but other Promise Keepers' rhetoric has stronger ties with particular elements of American culture. Two key areas of overlap are with sport and traditional masculinity.

According to Niebuhr, people who fit this model

> harmonize Christ and culture, not without excision, of course, from New Testament and social custom, of stubbornly discordant features. ... Just as the gulf between the worlds is bridged, so other differences between Christ and culture that seem like chasms to radical Christians and anti-Christians are easily passed over by these men. Sometimes they are ignored, sometimes filled in with convenient material derived from historical excavations or demolitions of old thought structures.[48]

One tension within this model concerns whether past or present culture gets associated with Christ. Niebuhr calls the fundamentalist attack on liberalism as 'itself an expression of a cultural loyalty ... though the culture it seeks to conserve differs from that which its rivals honor'.[49] Niebuhr's examples are support for creationism and alcohol prohibition growing out of allegiance to a prominent historical perspective, but he could have just as easily used traditional masculinity to illustrate the point.

At least one Promise Keepers critic, Brett Webb-Mitchell, apparently would view the group as reflecting The Christ of Culture model. He argues that the Promise Keepers is not really about 'church', but is instead about the individual. Like earlier attempts to Christianise America, the Promise Keepers is 'more American than Christian ... [and] its practices are determined not by God's Kingdom but by America. ... Promise Keepers draws on traditional American ideals of masculinity.'[50] Webb-Mitchell claims that American beliefs embraced by the Promise Keepers include the 1950s-style nuclear family, sports, patriotism, and consumer capitalism. Although Webb-Mitchell fails to recognise the conflicting accounts of masculinity and Promise Keepers traits that oppose dominant American culture, he rightly sees the connections between the Promise Keeper movement and prominent aspects of American society such as sport.

The use of sporting rhetoric

Sport is a key component of the dominant culture in the USA, and the Promise Keepers clearly links its movement with sport, both in terms of its practices and its rhetoric. The organisation's prominence owes much to its founder's notoriety as a former leading college football coach and so, not surprisingly, McCartney commonly uses sport metaphors: 'In my view, every society needs the restraint of the people of God, who act as bulwarks against people's ill-informed and destructive choices, like offensive linemen protecting the quarterback.'[51] He also hosts his own radio show called *4th and Goal – Coaching for Life's Tough Calls*, which maintains a web site that emphasises McCartney's sports background and coaching success.[52]

McCartney is far from the only Promise Keeper to utilise athletic metaphors, and sport is used regularly as a setting for stories depicting male familial relations and proper gender roles. Rev. James Dobson observes:

> The mission of introducing one's children to the Christian faith can be likened to a three-man relay race. First, your father runs his lap around the track, carrying the baton, which represents the gospel of Jesus Christ. At the appropriate moment, he hands the baton to you and you begin your journey around the track. Then, finally, the time will come when you must get the baton safely in the hands of your child. But as any track coach will testify, relay races are won or lost on the transfer of the baton.[53]

Besides the sport metaphors, heroic athletic figures pepper the Promise Keepers' literature. In the first chapter of *What Makes a Man*, Gary Smalley and John Trent establish the image of the Promise Keeper using three examples of men who kept their promises. One of these was baseball star Babe Ruth, who, as legend has it, hit a home run after pointing to the outfield bleachers.[54] Ruth's inclusion in this chapter is ironic given his drinking and womanising, and newspaper columnist Mike Royko includes him in his all-star team of 'The Fellowship of Drinking, Brawling, Wenching, and Gambling Athletes'. Ruth nevertheless remains a revered figure and a role model for men because of his athletic achievements, despite Royko's contention that: 'Religion or good have nothing to do with athletic excellence.'[55] Royko's sentiments are echoed by baseball-player-turned-evangelist Billy Sunday, who likewise rejected the link between morality and success in sport.[56] Nevertheless, the Promise Keepers takes the opposite approach. Besides Ruth, its use of sports heroes includes several associated with its '*Man of his word* New Testament ... [which] features glossy spreads on a range of (literally) muscular Christians – from professional football players Reggie White, Anthony Munoz, and Mike Singletary to Olympic wrestler Dan Russell'.[57]

For Promise Keepers, spirituality, morality and manliness go hand-in-hand with sports and the traits necessary for success within them. Smalley and Trent invoke the oft-cited link between sport and character. They focus especially on the development of behaviours associated with proper masculinity, such as toughness, aggression, physical and mental strength, as well as those associated with a being good worker, such as respect for authority, punctuality and discipline. These ideals are often incorporated into the Promise Keepers' literature that provides advice on good behaviour:

> That day, as I sat for hours listening to Monte, three things stood out in our conversation [commitment, self-control and a clear and significant challenge on which to focus his energy]. Actually, all three of them were steps he had taken to be a success in his sport, and now those same qualities would hold the key to a future full of potential.[58]

In addition, self-confidence is a quality that men are encouraged to have, and again, this trait is promoted through explicit sporting imagery:

> We've now detailed three marks of masculinity: assertiveness, self-control, and independence. The next one is equally important as you look at keeping promises to your wife. Self-confidence is what everyone else in the locker room looks like they have before you hit the field for the big game, or get ready to hit the golf ball off the first tee.[59]

Besides this body of literature, the Promise Keepers' intimate tie to the American fascination with sport is also evidenced in its public gatherings. The theme for the 2001 conferences, 'Turn the Tide: Living Out an Extreme Faith', explicitly links Christianity to the current trend towards extreme sports, such as snowboarding and skateboarding that emphasise self-governance and risk-taking. The conference draws on sport as the vehicle for new relationships: 'Extreme sports are the rage these days, but an extreme faith can change our families, our churches and our communities. We're calling men to an extreme commitment that will change their lives and challenge the culture'. The slogan 'Jesus Christ is an extreme Savior' supports the link between extreme sports and Christianity.[60]

Since its inception, the Promise Keepers has staged its conferences in sports stadia. These meetings look like common sporting events, with participants behaving much like sports fans. As several scholars and journalists have noted, rally attendees revise sporting rituals into religious ones, converting, for example, a well-known cheer into 'We love Jesus, yes, we do. We love Jesus, how 'bout you?' They chant, they hit beach balls back and forth and they do 'the wave' around the stadium. As at any other sporting event, 'fans' are able to purchase 'team' merchandise emblazoned with the Promise Keepers logo. One such T-shirt borrows from baseball, proclaiming Jesus Christ as 'your designated hitter'.[61]

The venue for the rallies is critically important. Social geographers argue that space and place are integrally linked with the creation of meanings. Doreen Massey contends that social locations are gendered: 'And this gendering of space and place both reflects *and has effects back on* the ways in which gender is constructed and understood in the societies in which we live'.[62] This point certainly holds for sport venues. Sport sociologist Bruce Kidd explains the gendering of sport stadia, or what he refers to as 'men's cultural centres'. Sport has been 'a fertile field for the reassertion and legitimation of male power and privilege', not only symbolically, but in the actual social practices involving the stadium, which include those directly involved in sports as well as other economic beneficiaries such as the mass media.[63] Symbolically and practically, these activities primarily benefit men, effectively marginalising women.

The symbolic significance of using stadia for holding events has been consciously acknowledged within the Promise Keepers. According to one organiser: 'We hold conferences in stadiums because the stadium is safe and masculine. It puts guys together in a group. We are all little boys [in a stadium].'[64] This 'safe and masculine' setting affords men more opportunity to display behaviours that are not usually associated with masculinity, especially emotional intimacy and vulnerability. Sport settings are one of the few occasions in the USA for men to openly show emotion and share that physically with other men. John Stoltenberg asked a Promise Keepers fund-raiser why the men at these stadium events felt so comfortable to share their emotions with strangers. The reply reflects the comfort in this type of male, homosocial environment:

> (a sports arena is) one of the few places that men can ever be emotional about anything and be OK without being softies. I think it's also mass validation, a man could not accept a women telling him he needs to be this sort of man. But when men get out here with 50,000 other men, and see the consensus, it gives them the stamp of approval from their peers, and from people they respect in the sense of 'well, he's a man, he knows'. I think God in His sovereign grace put men in an environment where they naturally could relate to each other and be more open to releasing emotion.[65]

Because it is a safe space for men, the stadium venue may enable many Promise Keepers to have a meaningful religious experience that they could never attain in a church. Robert Hicks suggests that the church has failed to provide men with the opportunity for quality religious experiences, primarily because it is a feminine space. Instead, he asserts that sport is a model for positive change, that is, a masculine cultural space led by men:

> How do we reclaim men for the Kingdom of God and get them into the doors of the Church? I wish I knew the answer. But two images come to mind. One is a sterile, cold, formal, flowery image of the church with over half the audience women. The other image is the most recent Flyers hockey game I experienced, and I mean experienced! I looked at the audience, by far more men than women. What were they wearing? Anything! Some were dressed for stock exchange; others for the Philly meat market. How did they behave? Were they passive, quiet, unemotional, refined gentleman? Hardly. They were involved, vocal, upset, yelling, celebrating. I thought to myself, here is a man's world, a place where he can let it all out, be himself, wear anything he desires, and they still let him in. And he actually pays to come. What about the church? No, there a man can't be himself; he has to watch what he says, act appropriately, and wear a neatly pressed and coordinated suit and tie. Then it hit me: We're all dressed the way our mommies wanted us to dress. We're all nice, clean little boys, sitting quietly so we won't get into trouble with our mothers.[66]

These examples demonstrate the need for men to be validated by other men. Although including some 'feminine' characteristics broadens and, perhaps, enhances male roles, male authority is not abandoned, for it is the male voice and social location that sanctions men's behaviour. This overt relationship between religion and sport clearly conforms to Niebuhr's The Christ of Culture framework. It also exists in tension with other elements of Promise Keepers rhetoric and practice that more closely align with the Christ Against Culture and Christ the Transformer of Culture models.

Conclusion

In times when men are renegotiating their identity – times in which men may feel vulnerable – certain symbolic markers of privilege such as sport may help in the transition. These symbols may reassure men of their social and personal worth. Sport clearly provides a comfort zone for many men, and the Promise Keepers thus uses sport symbols and locations to reach a broad audience, to create a 'safe homosocial intimacy'. The use of sport is problematic for the Promise Keepers, however, because of internal tensions within the movement. As Niebuhr's typology illustrates, the Promise Keepers rejects secular culture, desires to transform it, and yet closely adheres to it when utilising sport to impart its message. Despite these tensions, sport plays a key role in the rhetoric and practices of the Promise Keepers, and thus is important in maintaining the group's religious identity. But because of the tension, the Promise Keepers cannot merely be counted as the next generation of muscular Christianity. Its Christ Against Culture rejection of competitive, macho forms of masculinity obviously distinguishes the Promise Keepers from its more muscular ancestors such as the YMCA, Sports Ambassadors and the Fellowship of Christian Athletes. How the Promise Keepers internally negotiates between the muscular and a more sensitive masculinity is crucial to the formation and maintenance of the group's identity. The place of sensitive masculinity is also a source of contention within the organisation, because it shows up both as an anti-cultural element, and as part of the all-male sport culture. The former calls on men to engage in more substantive, more caring and more vulnerable relationships with friends in the smaller accountability groups, and with family, including wives and daughters, whilst the latter focusses strictly on male bonding and authority within the safe space of sport.

Notes

1   M. Garber, 'Two-point conversion', in M. Garber and R.L. Walkowitz (eds), *One Nation Under God? Religion and American Culture*, New York, Routledge, 1999, pp. 280–311.
2   See M. Messner, *Power at Play: Sports and the Problem of Masculinity*, Boston, Beacon Press, 1992; M. Kimmel (ed.), *The Politics of Manhood: Profeminist Men Respond to the Mythopoetic Men's Movement (And The Mythopoetic Leaders Answer)*, Philadelphia, Temple University Press, 1995; J. Nauright and T.J.L. Chandler (eds), *Making Men: Rugby and Masculine Identity*, London, Frank Cass, 1996.

3 There is a wealth of literature on this subject. Primary texts that take this perspective range from the Church Fathers (e.g. Tertullian) to the present day (e.g. the Southern Baptist Convention). For a historical account of modern evangelicals, see M.L. Bendroth, *Fundamentalism and Gender, 1875 to the Present*, New Haven, Yale University Press, 1993.

4 J. Nauright, 'Colonial manhood and imperial race virility: British responses to post-Boer War colonial rugby tours', in J. Nauright and T.J.L. Chandler (eds), *Making Men: Rugby and Masculine Identity*, London, Frank Cass, 1996, pp. 121–40; V. Burstyn, *The Rites of Men: Manhood, Politics, and the Culture of Sport*, Toronto, University of Toronto Press, 1999.

5 See V. Burstyn, *The Rites of Men: Manhood, Politics, and the Culture of Sport*, Toronto, University of Toronto Press, 1999; M. Messner, *Power at Play: Sports and the Problem of Masculinity*, Boston, Beacon Press, 1992; M. Kimmel (ed.), *The Politics of Manhood: Profeminist Men Respond to the Mythopoetic Men's Movement (And The Mythopoetic Leaders Answer)*, Philadelphia, Temple University Press, 1995.

6 See V. Burstyn, *The Rites of Men: Manhood, Politics, and the Culture of Sport*, Toronto, University of Toronto Press, 1999; S. Faludi, *Stiffed: The Betrayal of the American Man*, New York, W. Morrow & Co., 1999; M. Kimmel (ed.), *The Politics of Manhood: Profeminist Men Respond to the Mythopoetic Men's Movement (And The Mythopoetic Leaders Answer)*, Philadelphia, Temple University Press, 1995; D. Savran, *Taking It Like a Man: White Masculinity, Masochism, and Contemporary American Culture*, Princeton, Princeton University Press, 1998; M.S. Van Leeuwen, 'Servanthood or soft patriarchy? A Christian feminist looks at the Promise Keepers movement', *The Journal of Men's Studies*, vol. 5, no. 3, 1997, pp. 233–61.

7 See V. Burstyn, *The Rites of Men: Manhood, Politics, and the Culture of Sport*, Toronto, University of Toronto Press, 1999.

8 Kyle Kusz, 'Extreme sports, white masculinity, and white male backlash politics in late 1990s America', unpublished paper, Department of Kinesiology, University of Illinois, 1999.

9 See M. Messner, *Politics of Masculinities: Men in Movements*, Thousand Oaks, Sage Publications, 1997.

10 B. McCartney, 'Promise Makers', *Policy Review*, vol. 85, 1997. Retrieved 22 May 2001 from the World Wide Web: http://www.policyreview.com/ sept97/promise.html

11 See S. Faludi, *Stiffed: The Betrayal of the American Man*, New York, W. Morrow & Co., 1999, pp. 224–88; B. Webb-Mitchell, 'And a football coach shall lead them: a theological critique of *Seven Promises of a Promise Keeper*', *Soundings*, vol. 80, no. 2–3, 1997, pp. 305–26. Some other research, however, shows more diversity in the accountability groups. See J.P. Bartkowski, 'Breaking walls, raising fences: masculinity, intimacy, and accountability among the Promise Keepers', *Sociology of Religion*, vol. 61, no. 1, 2000, pp. 33–53.

12 Cited in M. Garber, 'Two-point conversion', in M. Garber and R.L. Walkowitz (eds), *One Nation Under God? Religion and American Culture*, New York, Routledge, 1999, p. 300.

13 A. Janssen (ed.), *Seven Promises of a Promise Keeper*, Colorado Springs, Focus on the Family Publishing, 1994.

14 B. McCartney, 'Promise Makers', *Policy Review*, vol. 85, 1997. Retrieved 22 May 2001 from the World Wide Web: http://www.policyreview.com/sept97/ promise.html

15 Lists of the seven promises are widely available, including in A. Janssen (ed.), *Seven Promises of a Promise Keeper*, Colorado Springs, Focus on the Family Publishing, 1994, p. 8:

    1   A Promise Keeper is committed to honoring Jesus Christ through worship, prayer and obedience to God's Word in the power of the Holy Spirit.

    2   A Promise Keeper is committed to pursuing vital relationships with a few other men, understanding that he needs brothers to help him keep his promises.

    3   A Promise Keeper is committed to practicing spiritual, moral, ethical, and sexual purity.

    4   A Promise Keeper is committed to building strong marriages and families through

love, protection and biblical values.

5   A Promise Keeper is committed to supporting the mission of his church by honoring and praying for his pastor, and by actively giving his time and resources.

6   A Promise Keeper is committed to reaching beyond any racial and denominational barriers to demonstrate the power of biblical unity.

7   A Promise Keeper is committed to influencing his world, being obedient to the Great Commandment (see Mark 12:30–1) and the Great Commission (see Matt. 28:19–20).

16   S. Griffith (ed.), *What Makes a Man? Twelve Promises That Can Change Your Life*, Colorado Springs, NavPress, 1992, back cover.

17   See J.P. Bartkowski, 'Breaking walls, raising fences: masculinity, intimacy, and account-ability among the Promise Keepers', *Sociology of Religion*, vol. 61, no. 1, 2000; W.H. Lockhart, ' "We are one life", but not of one gender ideology: Unitya Ambiguity, and the Promise Keepers', *Sociology of Religion*, vol. 61, no. 1, 2000, pp. 73–92; M.S. Van Leeuwen, 'Servanthood or soft patriarchy? A Christian feminist looks at the Promise Keepers movement', *The Journal of Men's Studies*, vol. 5, no. 3, 1997, pp. 233–61.

18   W.H. Lockhart, ' "We are one life", but not of one gender ideology: Unitya Ambiguity, and the Promise Keepers', *Sociology of Religion*, vol. 61, no. 1, 2000, pp. 73–92.

19   M.S. Van Leeuwen, 'Servanthood or soft patriarchy? A Christian feminist looks at the Promise Keepers movement', *The Journal of Men's Studies*, vol. 5, no. 3, 1997, pp. 233–61.

20   Augustine, *City of God*, trans. G.G. Walsh, D.B. Zema, G. Monahan, and D. Honan, ed. V.J. Bourke, New York, Image Books, 1958.

21   R. Balmer, 'Keep the faith and go the distance: Promise Keepers, feminism, and the world of sports', in D.S. Claussen (ed.), *The Promise Keepers: Essays on Masculinity and Christianity*, Jefferson, McFarland & Company, 2000, p. 196. See also C. Smith, *American Evangelicalism: Embattled and Thriving*, Chicago, University of Chicago Press, 1998.

22   M.S. Van Leeuwen, 'Servanthood or soft patriarchy? A Christian feminist looks at the Promise Keepers movement', *The Journal of Men's Studies*, vol. 5, no. 3, 1997, pp. 233–61; W.H. Lockhart, ' "We are one life", but not of one gender ideology: Unitya Ambiguity, and the Promise Keepers', *Sociology of Religion*, vol. 61, no. 1, 2000, p. 74.

23   Niebuhr (1894–1962) was a prominent academic, who taught at Yale University in the middle part of the twentieth century. Although overshadowed outside of the academy by his more famous older brother, Reinhold, Niebuhr was highly esteemed among scholars of religion and remains influential today.

24   H.R. Niebuhr, *Christ and Culture*, New York, Harper & Row, 1975 [1951].

25   Ibid., p. 32.

26   Ibid., pp. 47–8. Niebuhr cites I John 2:16.

27   C. Smith, *American Evangelicalism: Embattled and Thriving*, Chicago, University of Chicago Press, 1998, p. 89 (emphasis in original).

28   U. Middelman, 'Where others fear to tread', in S. Griffith (ed.), *What Makes a Man? Twelve Promises That Can Change Your Life*, Colorado Springs, NavPress, 1992, p. 201.

29   A. Janssen (ed.), *Seven Promises of a Promise Keeper*, Colorado Springs, Focus on the Family Publishing, 1994, p. 8.

30   G.J. Oliver, 'Black-and-white living in a gray world', in A. Janssen (ed.), *Seven Promises of a Promise Keeper*, Colorado Springs, Focus on the Family Publishing, 1994, p. 84.

31   Ibid.

32   J. Kirk, 'God's call to sexual purity', in A. Janssen (ed.), *Seven Promises of a Promise Keeper*, Colorado Springs, Focus on the Family Publishing, 1994, p. 92.

33   E.G. Wagner, 'Strong mentoring relationships', in A. Janssen (ed.), *Seven Promises of a Promise Keeper*, Colorado Springs, Focus on the Family Publishing, 1994, pp. 57–9. See also B. Sanders, 'The truth will set you free', in S. Griffith (ed.), *What Makes a Man? Twelve Promises That Can Change Your Life*, Colorado Springs, NavPress, 1992, pp. 54–5;

J. White, 'Commitment and accountability', in S. Griffith (ed.), *What Makes a Man? Twelve Promises That Can Change Your Life*, Colorado Springs, NavPress, 1992, pp. 143–5.

34 K. Abraham, 'God loves losers, too!', in S. Griffith (ed.), *What Makes a Man? Twelve Promises That Can Change Your Life*, Colorado Springs, NavPress, 1992, p. 56.

35 S. Faludi, *Stiffed: The Betrayal of the American Man*, New York, W. Morrow & Co., 1999, pp. 238–41. See especially the quotations from interviewees Martin Booker and Mike Pettigrew.

36 The Great Commandment is to love God with one's entire heart, soul, mind, and strength (Mark 12:29–30), and the Great Commission is Jesus' charge to evangelise all nations (Matthew 28:19–20).

37 H.R. Niebuhr, *Christ and Culture*, New York, Harper & Row, 1975 [1951], p. 191.

38 Ibid., p. 195.

39 R. Phillips, 'Seize the moment', in A. Janssen (ed.), *Seven Promises of a Promise Keeper*, Colorado Springs, Focus on the Family Publishing, 1994, p. 3.

40 Ibid., p. 9.

41 See W. Boone, 'Why men must pray', in A. Janssen (ed.), *Seven Promises of a Promise Keeper*, Colorado Springs, Focus on the Family Publishing, 1994, pp. 25–31; L. Palau, 'The great commission', in A. Janssen (ed.), *Seven Promises of a Promise Keeper*, Colorado Springs, Focus on the Family Publishing, 1994, pp. 193–202.

42 G.J. Oliver, *Real Men Have Feelings Too*, Chicago, Moody Press, 1993.

43 For the biblical proof-texts, see B. McCartney, 'Promise Makers', *Policy Review*, vol. 85, 1997. Retrieved 22 May 2001 from the World Wide Web: http://www.policyreview. com/sept97/promise.html. For socio-biology arguments, see G. Smalley and J. Trent, 'The promises you make to yourself', in S. Griffith (ed.), *What Makes a Man? Twelve Promises That Can Change Your Life*, Colorado Springs, NavPress, 1992, pp. 40–2.

44 T. Evans, 'Reclaiming your manhood', in A. Janssen (ed.), *Seven Promises of a Promise Keeper*, Colorado Springs, Focus on the Family Publishing, 1994, p. 79.

45 The clearest example of authoritative-style leadership is T. Evans, 'Reclaiming your manhood', in A. Janssen (ed.), *Seven Promises of a Promise Keeper*, Colorado Springs, Focus on the Family Publishing, 1994. Udo Middelman uses the language of servanthood, but may also hold on to authoritarianism when he claims that servants 'have seen the right way and want to limit the painful results of the merely personal ways of others'. U. Middelman, 'Let men be servants', in S. Griffith (ed.), *What Makes a Man? Twelve Promises That Can Change Your Life*, Colorado Springs, NavPress, 1992, p. 197.

46 J.P. Bartkowski, 'Breaking walls, raising fences: masculinity, intimacy, and accountability among the Promise Keepers', *Sociology of Religion*, vol. 61, no. 1, 2000, pp. 39–42.

47 H.R. Niebuhr, *Christ and Culture*, New York, Harper & Row, 1975 [1951], p. 69.

48 Ibid., pp. 83–4.

49 Ibid., p. 102.

50 B. Webb-Mitchell, 'And a football coach shall lead them: a theological critique of *Seven Promises of a Promise Keeper*', *Soundings*, vol. 80, no. 2–3, 1997, pp. 306, 310.

51 B. McCartney, 'Promise Makers', *Policy Review*, vol. 85, 1997. Retrieved 22 May 2001 from the World Wide Web: http://www.policyreview.com/sept97/promise.html

52 *4th and Goal*, Retrieved 25 October 2001 from the World Wide Web: http://www.4thandgoal.org

53 J. Dobson, 'The priority of fathering', in A. Janssen (ed.), *Seven Promises of a Promise Keeper*, Colorado Springs, Focus on the Family Publishing, 1994, p. 124.

54 G. Smalley and J. Trent, 'What are promises?', in S. Griffith (ed.), *What Makes a Man? Twelve Promises That Can Change Your Life*, Colorado Springs, NavPress, 1992, pp.15–16.

55 M. Royko, 'An impious team', *Kingsport Times News*, 22 January 1988, p. 8A, cited in R.J. Higgs, *God in the Stadium: Sports and Religion in America*, Lexington, University of Kentucky Press, 1995, pp. 13–14.

56 Sunday's dichotomy between athletic and moral excellence goes beyond the superfluousness of morality for athletic success. Sunday contends that baseball has a negative impact

on moral character, and that it distracts from the more important work of actually bene-fiting humanity. B. Sunday, 'Why I left professional baseball', *Young Men's Era*, vol. 19, no. 30, 27 July 1893, p. 1, cited in T. Ladd and J.A. Mathisen, *Muscular Christianity: Evangelical Protestants and the Development of American Sport*, Grand Rapids, Baker Books, 1999, p. 80.

57 J.P. Bartkowski, 'Breaking walls, raising fences: masculinity, intimacy, and accountability among the Promise Keepers', *Sociology of Religion*, vol. 61, no. 1, 2000, p. 47.

58 G. Smalley and J. Trent, 'Practicing learned hopefulness', in S. Griffith (ed.), *What Makes a Man? Twelve Promises That Can Change Your Life*, Colorado Springs, NavPress, 1992, p. 226.

59 G. Smalley and J. Trent, 'The promises you make to your wife', in S. Griffith (ed.), *What Makes a Man? Twelve Promises That Can Change Your Life*, Colorado Springs, NavPress, 1992, p. 64.

60 See the Program Overview, Promise Keepers Conferences, *Promise Keepers Official Home Page*. Retrieved 1 July 2001 from the World Wide Web: http://www.promisekeepers.org/conf/conf10.htm.

61 Photograph in D. Minkowitz, 'In the name of the father', *Ms.*, November–December 1995, p. 71.

62 D. Massey, *Space, Place, and Gender*, Minneapolis, University of Minnesota Press, 1994, p. 186 (emphasis in original).

63 B. Kidd, 'The men's cultural centre: sports and the dynamic of women's oppression/men's repression', in M. Messner and D. Sabo (eds), *Sport, Men, and the Gender Order: Critical Feminist Perspectives*, Champaign, Human Kinetics, 1990, p. 32.

64 C.H. Lippy, 'Miles to go: Promise Keepers in historical and cultural context', *Soundings*, vol. 80, no. 2–3, 1997, p. 297, quoting an unnamed speaker in the *United Methodist Review*, 9 August 1996, p. 9.

65 J. Stoltenberg, 'Whose God is it anyway? Male virgins, blood covenants and family values', *On the Issues*, vol. 4, no. 2, 1995, p. 26.

66 R. Hicks, 'Why men feel so out of place at church', in S. Griffith (ed.), *What Makes a Man? Twelve Promises That Can Change Your Life*, Colorado Springs, NavPress, 1992, pp. 155–6.

10 *Muhammad Speaks* and Muhammad Ali

Intersections of the Nation of Islam and sport in the 1960s

Maureen Smith

America, more than any other country, offers our people opportunities to engage in sports and play, which cause delinquency, murder, theft, and other forms of wicked and immoral crimes. This is due to this country's display of filthy temptations in this world of sport and play.[1]

Introduction

With the advent of its first issue, *Muhammad Speaks* established itself as the voice of the Nation of Islam's Messenger, Elijah Muhammad. Dedicated to 'Freedom, Justice, and Equality for the Black Man', the first issue was printed in October 1961 and the newspaper's circulation increased at a rate comparable to the discontent of African Americans in the USA during the freedom struggle of the civil rights movement.[2] Advocating freedom and separation from whites, the newspaper served a critical role in promoting racial pride, as well as ministering the beliefs and teachings of Elijah Muhammad and the Nation of Islam. Some of these teachings explored issues surrounding a range of athletic pursuits, and initially the Nation rejected the 'evils' of professional sport and games. Yet, through the pages of *Muhammad Speaks* it is possible to identify a shift in the Nation of Islam's position on sport, as the organisation's leadership came to recognise the political utility that an association with a prominent Muslim athlete, such as Muhammad Ali, could offer their movement. Once Ali's use to the Nation of Islam was exhausted, the leaders once again resumed their opposition to professional sport.

The Nation of Islam, according to Wallace D. Muhammad, was both a religion and a social movement.[3] It was a Black 'nation' within the USA which 'believed that African-Americans must free themselves physically and psychologically'.[4] The organisation 'commenced' in the 1930s when the Moorish Science Temple broke into a number of separate 'warring factions' and echoed sentiments familiar to those who had followed Marcus Garvey and the Universal Negro Improvement Association. The Nation of Islam was a new Black Islamic movement, which established its own temples, created its own bureaucracy, assigned its own officials, started its own schools and even trained its own paramilitary, the Fruit of Islam. The Honorable Elijah Muhammad had been selected by Master Farad Muhammad (also known as W.D. Fard) to lead the Nation and return the people to the 'old time religion of African Americans'.[5] Elijah Muhammad claimed that African Americans were 'royals of the Original People from the holy city of Mecca' and that the white man was the devil.[6] He taught that God was a Black man and that ancient Black civilisation was the original site of divine culture.[7] Muhammad empowered African Americans through Islam and set forth guidelines and economic and moral codes of behaviour to follow. He ordered that 'Muslims pray five times a day, eat once a day, and abstain from pork, alcohol, tobacco, narcotics, gambling, sports, long vacations from work, and sleeping more than is necessary for health'.[8] In the mainstream American press, the religion was not recognised as a 'legitimate' religion and was regarded variously as a cult or a Black supremacist organisation.

The Muslim teachings were detailed in several Nation of Islam publications, including Muhammad's book, *Message to the Blackman in America*.[9] As part of this message, Muhammad addressed the role of sport in Black culture in the USA. Despite his admonishment of Black athletes and their decision to pursue a professional career in sport, the leader and his newspaper changed their position after one of their disciples rose to the top of his field. When Cassius Clay wrested the Heavyweight Championship of the World title from Sonny Liston, Clay had already been attending meetings of the Nation of Islam. Within days of his victory, Clay announced his conversion to the Muslim religion and his subsequent name change from Cassius Clay, his slave name, to Muhammad Ali, a name bestowed upon him by the religion's leader, Elijah Muhammad.[10] Ali's subsequent career is chronicled in the pages of *Muhammad Speaks*, as Muhammad and the Nation of Islam's stance on sport and professional athletes changed radically.

Whilst organised sport has provided both an avenue for the acculturation of a number of minority groups within American society as well as a means of retaining an independent cultural identity,[11] the Nation of Islam was reluctant to incorporate sport into its philosophy, for, in the 1960s, organised, professional sport represented yet another arena in which African Americans were subjected to segregation and disenfranchisement. Yet with the success of Muhammad Ali, the Nation of Islam, whilst not rejecting their previous position, quietly overlooked the 'evil' aspects of Ali's profession and embraced professional sport as an avenue through which their message could be communicated to a wider audience. This chapter explores the meaning of sport within the Nation of Islam and the role of Muhammad Ali in promoting sport and the Islamic religion during the 1960s. Despite the Nation of Islam's eagerness to embrace Ali and the promotional potential his success inspired, tensions arose as a result of their philosophy of sport, compounded by conflicts between Ali's religious and athletic identities. This chapter examines these pressures and provides insight into the various ways that sport and, in this context, the athletic achievements of Muhammad Ali were used to symbolise Black Islamic identity and retain the religious and political integrity of the Nation of Islam. Beyond this, Ali presented an opportunity to further the cause of the Nation, promising a healthy increase in recruits as well as a larger market for its message, as promulgated in *Muhammad Speaks*. As such, Ali's sporting achievements served important political purposes for the movement, contributing both to their on-going domestic struggle for civil rights as well as to the establishment of links with Islamic communities abroad. When Ali no longer served an explicit political purpose, or had perhaps simply become too popular within mainstream white America, he was denounced by the Nation, as was organised sport once again. Within a matter of five years, the political, religious and sporting landscape was drastically altered. The country experienced a shift in philosophies and race relations, and the Nation of Islam reached a zenith in their popularity with the help of a 'loudmouthed' fighter.

The Nation of Islam and their philosophy of sport

The first reference to sport in *Muhammad Speaks* appeared in the December 1961 issue, with an advertisement for Joe Louis Milk and a picture of boxer Archie Moore at a Baltimore luncheon. Published monthly until July 1962, and then semi-monthly from August 1962, each issue contained at least one article or picture of professional male athletes in America, always in the last pages of the publication. From the beginning of 1963, *Muhammad Speaks* was published weekly. The reportage of sport in the newspaper was generally non-controversial and focussed on providing 'facts', such as 'Baseball's Top NL Negroes',[12] or a profile of heavyweight champion Sonny Liston.[13] By early 1962, the paper started publishing articles with a more critical edge, which focussed on African-American participation in professional sport, beginning with a three-part series on the absence of Black quarterbacks in the National Football League[14] and an article entitled 'Recreation vs. wreck-reation: expert defines role of physical culture in big city ghetto'.[15] In the 15 October 1962 issue, Elijah Muhammad contributed a column that warned against the evils of sport and play, which formed the basis of an essay that was later published in his book, *Message to the Blackman in America*. Despite mentioning Muhammad Ali in the book a number of times and praising him for his religious conversion, Muhammad dedicated a chapter to what he perceived to be the destructive role of sport in America, focussing specifically on how it affected the Black man.[16] In his column, Muhammad proclaimed the evils of sport and linked the practice of Christianity to the growing popularity of sport and the damage the games caused:

> Hundreds of millions of dollars change hands for the benefit of a few to the hurt of millions, and suffering from the lack of good education, with

their last few pennies they help the already helped to try winning with these gambling 'scientists' who have prepared a game of chance that the poor suckers have only one chance out of nine hundred to win. Therefore, the world of sports is causing tremendous evils.[17]

Beyond gambling, Muhammad attributed to Christianity:

the destruction of homes and families, the disgrace, the shame, the filling up of jails ... with the victims of sports and play, the loss of friendship, the loss of beautiful wives and husbands, the loss of sons and daughters to these penal institutions.[18]

He also believed that 'the poor so-called Negroes are the worst victims in this world of sport and play because they are trying to learn the white man's games of civilization'.[19] He stated that 'sport and play (games of chance) take away the remembrance of Allah (God) and the doing of good',[20] and concluded his column with an invitation for new members. His public disdain for sport would be revisited, yet was often overlooked in the following years when Cassius Clay announced his conversion to Islam, his name change and his membership in the Nation of Islam.

Converting to Islam: the 'birth' of Muhammad Ali

In his autobiography, Malcolm X recounts his first introduction to Muhammad Ali, when the boxer was still known as Cassius Clay. Clay, with his brother Rudolph, attended a rally at a Detroit Mosque in 1962. He introduced himself to Malcolm X in a manner that indicated the militant Muslim should recognise the young fighter. Malcolm X recalled that: 'Up to that moment, though, I had never even heard of him. Ours were two entirely different worlds. In fact, Elijah Muhammad instructed us Muslims against all forms of sports.'[21]

Malcolm X later accompanied Clay to Miami for his title fight against Sonny Liston. At this time, Malcolm X was under suspension in the Nation of Islam for comments he had made regarding the assassination of President Kennedy, and his presence at Clay's training camp further displeased Elijah Muhammad. Malcolm X had 'emerged as the major voice of the Nation of Islam' and was preaching a similar doctrine of race separation, freedom and fight for justice as a younger Elijah Muhammad had in the 1930s.[22] Recalling the pre-fight chances of a Clay upset, Malcolm X said: 'They felt that Cassius hadn't a prayer of a chance to win. They felt the Nation would be embarrassed through my linking the Muslim image with him.'[23] Indeed, the Nation of Islam neglected to even send a representative of *Muhammad Speaks* to the fight, proof positive, according to Malcolm X, that the Nation did not expect Clay to win: 'Even though Cassius was a Muslim brother, the Muslim newspaper didn't consider his fight worth covering.'[24] Malcolm X claimed that despite this apparent lack of faith on the part of the Nation of Islam, he knew that Clay would emerge victorious: 'I flew back to Miami feeling it was Allah's intent for me to help Cassius prove Islam's superiority before the world – through proving that mind can win over brawn.'[25] Malcolm X appealed to Clay's religious commitment, suggesting his role was part of the larger struggle between Muslims and Christians. Malcolm X saw the fight as 'the truth', and referred to it as a 'modern crusade', with the 'Cross and the Crescent fighting in the prize ring – for the first time'.[26] He asked Clay, 'Do you think Allah has brought all this intending for you to leave the ring anything but the champion?'[27]

The first mention of Clay as champion came in the 13 March 1964 issue of *Muhammad Speaks*, though this article was actually about a message of thanks that Clay sent through his brother to a rally held at Savior's Day in Chicago. Elijah Muhammad responded:

> I'm so glad that Cassius Clay admits he is a Muslim. He was able, by confessing that Allah was the God and by following Muhammad, to whip a much tougher man. ... Clay had confidence in Allah, and in me as his only Messenger. This assured his victory and left him unscarred.[28]

It was also at this Savior's Day meeting that Muhammad predicted his newest member 'would develop into a major world figure'.[29]

After his victory, Ali began appearing in the paper on a weekly basis, sometimes in relation to his boxing, but more often as a spokesperson for the group. His activities in this strategic role included traveling internationally as a representative of the Nation of Islam; entering the ring as a convert; speaking with Black leaders throughout the USA and internationally; and acting as a disciple of Elijah Muhammad. In each of the hundreds of articles about his boxing over the course of six years, Ali attributed his success to Elijah Muhammad, to his membership in the Nation of Islam and to Allah. Ali's first cover was on 10 April 1964 with a bold print headline that read 'Walk the Way of Free Men!' The caption underneath the picture of Ali with Elijah Muhammad read 'The Honorable Elijah Muhammad through his teachings of the Nation of Islam, has made him strong both morally and spiritually, says new Heavyweight Boxing Champion Muhammad Ali.'[30]

Two weeks later, in another cover story, Elijah Muhammad penned an article 'They Hate the Champ', which signalled the beginning of a campaign to promote Ali as a Muslim and a Black man, who did not need white America for his success, and who was, in fact, a source of discontent for that society.[31] As a result of this crusade, Ali became, as David Wiggins suggests, 'the movement's most important symbol of black masculinity, a man of heroic stature who came to represent the struggle for civil rights'.[32] Moreover, Muhammad 'used the controversy surrounding Ali to his own advantage, branding criticism of the heavyweight champion as religious persecution and hatred of Muslims'.[33] Wiggins credits Muhammad with recognising the symbolic potential of Ali as a Muslim heavyweight champion. His subsequent orchestration of 'a public relations campaign ... transformed Ali into the movement's leading example of black pride'.[34] Wiggins also notes that around the time of Ali's entrance into the Nation of Islam, Malcolm X had been suspended, later to be expelled, from the organisation, providing the perfect opportunity for a young, charismatic leader to continue disseminating the message. Elijah Muhammad used Ali as an 'example of righteousness for blacks who had been instilled with a false sense of racial inferiority by white Christian Americans'.[35]

The representation of Ali as a target of discrimination continued for the next five years, with much of it fuelling the Nation of Islam's cause. His public persona was carefully shaped by the newspaper and was in sharp contrast to the images that white writers were presenting. *Muhammad Speaks* documented Ali's donations, his work with children and with his community, his black pride, and his politics regarding race and religion. And only three years after dismissing sport as 'evil', *Muhammad Speaks* was espousing the 'clean, healthy and purposeful living' that the Nation believed sport could offer its youth. Under a picture of Ali playing outside with children, the caption explained:

> World's Heavyweight Champion playfully spars with group of children on one of the afternoons which the Champ devoted entirely to the entertainment and inspiration of Negro youths. ... No boxer in modern times has concerned himself with the plight of Negro youth. Muhammad's appearance evokes an instant identity and response from Negro youth across the nation as the young Muslim champion ... sets an example of clean, healthy and purposeful living.[36]

Ali visited public schools at the request of 'Negro teachers' who 'felt the need to present a real-live black hero to their children to offset the daily "white heroes" they see and hear on television and radio'.[37] At the same time, white mainstream newspapers persisted in referring to Ali as Cassius Clay and discredited him based on his religion, his call for the separation of the races, his pre-fight predictions of knockouts, and on what was deemed his boastful and bragging manner.

In addition to his domestic activities, Ali also provided the Nation of Islam with much-needed links to international Islamic communities and Black nationalist causes. The rise of Black nationalism in the 1960s, and the contributing role of the Nation of Islam, occurred against the backdrop of the Vietnam War and the independence struggles of colonised African nations. At that time, 'nationalist leaders perceived the African-American struggle in world solidarity as a struggle against colonialism, racism, and capitalist expansionism'.[38] Thus, the theme of pan-Africanism and the religious ties between the two continents were evident. In May

1964, Ali toured several African nations, a trip that was significant for several reasons and certainly not without symbolism. As a representative of Elijah Muhammad, Ali was welcomed as a 'prodigal son' and even commented that he had not been 'home' in over 400 years. Seeing the advancement of the countries he visited, Ali mentioned that he had been exposed to phony allegations by the USA concerning the civilisation of African nations.

Ali's international successes and extensive travels only increased his popularity both in the USA and worldwide, a fact that did not go unnoticed by the Nation of Islam. The movement established an international fan club and on occasion printed letters of support for Ali in their pages, from as far away as Pakistan, Ireland, Ghana and Sweden.[39] According to *Muhammad Speaks*, Ali had the strongest international backing of any previous champion.[40] As a result of his tours and subsequent international bouts, the Nation of Islam proclaimed Ali as the first true world champion, giving the title new meaning. Moreover, they could claim him as the first Muslim world champion. Though Ali was exiled from the American boxing ring, it was apparent that the rest of the world welcomed the 'world champion' with open arms. On the American homefront, however, the champion was encountering contempt outside the ring for both his religious beliefs and the application of those beliefs when he refused to enter the draft for the Vietnam War.

Ali rejects the white establishment

The uproar about Ali's draft status and his subsequent comments dominated the Black press, and articles outlined the support of Black leaders and international figures.[41] Whilst Ali had the support of Black leaders, including Reverend Dr Martin Luther King Jr, support from the boxing community was absent. I.F. Stone wrote: 'Cassius Clay's reaction to becoming eligible for the draft was characteristically candid. ... We suspect he voiced the sentiment of most Negroes. But boxing groups found the remark "unpatriotic" and "disgusting".'[42] Ali commented frequently on the contradictions of a black American fighting for the freedom of another country when he was not free in his own, asking 'Why should they ask me and other so-called Negroes to put on a uniform and go 10,000 miles from home and drop bombs and bullets on brown people in Viet Nam whilst so-called Negro people in Louisville are treated like dogs and denied simple human rights.'[43] On another occasion, Ali clarified his stance, stating: 'If I thought my joining the war and possible dying would bring peace, freedom, justice and equality to the 22 million black men in America, they would not have to draft me. I would join!'[44] Letters, articles and editorial cartoons criticised the draft, the war and the issue of black soldiers dying on the front line. The discrimination Ali faced from the white press and public, as well as from other black Americans, confirmed the perception of

Ali as a Black Muslim victim of white Christian persecution, a construct that was repeated for a number of athletes throughout the lifetime of *Muhammad Speaks.*

Whilst other articles relating to sport appeared in the newspaper, they all served the central purpose of promoting Black athletes who had rejected the white establishment and who supported Black Muslims, or at least Islamic ideals. On several occasions the newspaper published articles that focused on other Black athletes who were sympathetic to the goals of the Nation of Islam, even if they were not members themselves, including Bill Russell and Jim Brown.[45] Black athletes were often photographed with Ali, confirming the Nation's expectations that Ali could wield his influence over other Black athletes. Under one image of Ali dressed in a suit and tie, the caption noted that one of his missions was to help design 'a new image for Black athletes in America'.[46] When he defended his heavyweight title against Floyd Patterson, who was regarded as representative of Christianity and assimilation, Ali promised Patterson a copy of Muhammad's *Message to the Blackman in America* after the fight. In addition, a gentlemen's agreement was made whereby, should he lose, Patterson consented to spending forty-eight hours with Ali, to experience his lifestyle and religion and to 'get a better understanding of the followers of the Honorable Elijah Muhammad'.[47]

Ali's successful impact on other Black athletes is evidenced by the increased activism of Black college athletes in 1968, including the New York Athletic Club boycott, and the proposed Olympic boycott. Much of this was due to Ali's refusal to fight in Vietnam, a subject that dominated both the Islamic and mainstream press. Ali met with prominent Black athletes, including Jim Brown, Bill Russell and Lew Alcindor, to discuss his decision to refuse military induction. Alcindor would later boycott the Olympic basketball team and attribute part of his raised consciousness to Ali.[48] During the months preceding the 1968 Olympics, a number of articles appeared that addressed the proposed boycott by Black athletes, as well as the inclusion of South Africa in the Games. Moreover, the Olympic Project for Human Rights, in a December 1967 meeting, presented a list of demands to avoid an Olympic boycott. The first demand was the 'restoration of Muhammad Ali's title and right to box in this country'.[49] After the Olympic victory dais protest by Tommie Smith and John Carlos, articles appeared in support of their action, as did advertisements for medallions commemorating the victory dais protest.[50] *Muhammad Speaks* continued to address the increased activism of athletes, as tennis player Arthur Ashe joined the likes of Russell and Brown as Black athletes who merited attention and praise for their activism.[51] As more Black athletes entered the intercollegiate and professional ranks, the dialogue concerning issues related to discrimination in sports intensified. Much of the debate centered on the economic dependency both college and professional Black athletes exhibited.

The dollars and sense of the Nation of Islam's association with Ali

One of the main concerns about Black participation in organised, professional sport was their exploitation. Whilst Black athletes were representing an increasingly large proportion of all athletes, the numbers of African Americans involved in the administration and ownership of sporting corporations were low. As such, the opportunities for career advancement within the industry available to Black athletes once their playing days were over were limited. Moreover, despite the large salaries of some, the majority of Black college athletes were economically dependent on coaches for scholarships and their education, whilst professional Black athletes were also bound to their teams by restrictive contracts.[52] The Nation of Islam took proactive steps in this regard, orchestrating the selection of Herbert Muhammad as Ali's manager, as well as assisting in the founding of Main Bout, Inc., 'the first and only Negro-led' boxing promotions company, owned and operated by Ali and company.[53] The formation of such a company was consistent with recent events, such as Ali's draft status, the creation of Jim Brown's economic union and the increased awareness of Black athletes being exploited by white owners and managers. It also promoted the Nation of Islam's call for economic self-reliance. An article in *Muhammad Speaks* emphasised that the Nation of Islam was not affiliated with the promotions company, but that two Muslims, Herbert Muhammad, Elijah Muhammad's third son, and John Ali, were involved. Former champ Joe Louis said 'Muhammad is surrounded by talented and unselfish friends and advisers – and they spare no effort in seeing that he ends up not simply a winner in the ring – but a winner in cash receipts.'[54] In fact, in his fight with Zora Folley, the championship bout cashed in a record gate of $244,471.[55]

The Nation of Islam's orchestration of Ali's professional career ensured that the champion would appear as a responsible and philanthropic member of his community. Despite the fact that his earnings derived from professional sport, his generous donations to the Black community were praised. Herbert Muhammad was Ali's personal and business manager and the newspaper highlighted the influence the Messenger's son had over Ali.[56] Herbert Muhammad helped craft Ali's public image as the Muslim World Heavyweight Champion. He 'projected a series of programmatic developments which would not only enhance his ring reputation, but will assure his historic role in domestic and world affairs'.[57] Ali's service to his community was at the forefront of his public persona, including his work as a minister for the Nation of Islam. The newspaper noted that 'every phase of the champion's activities has touched directly on the welfare of the black community'.[58] The issue of money as the goal of Ali's fight career was disputed by one prominent Black doctor, who argued: 'Everyone knows that if Muhammad was interested in money he could make millions by simply bowing to the practices of so many ex-fighters before him.' He mentioned the fighter's faith in Allah and the example the boxer set. He claimed that money had not changed the fighter, but that 'he has maintained principles, has maintained faith in his religion and his teacher and has become a new example to all the peoples of Africa and Asia. This is not the road to making money – it's the road to history and greatness.'[59] Still, another noted that Ali's joining the Nation of Islam had 'surely been the road to the pot of gold at the end of the rainbow'.[60] Despite the money the champ earned, issue after issue detailed his generous donations of time, effort and money for worthy community causes. The Nation of Islam, reflective of the rise in Black nationalism and the demands for economic self-reliance, touted Ali and his professional career as evidence of the success of such a philosophy. The dialogue concerning Ali's finances would resurface in the coming years.

Conflict over sport within the Nation of Islam

Despite the support Ali received from the leadership of the Nation of Islam, the attention devoted to sport and to athletes still contradicted the basic tenets of the movement. Occasionally, *Muhammad Speaks* addressed the contradiction, which did not go unnoticed by all in the sporting world. In a five-part series for *Sports Illustrated* that traced Ali's career and his participation in the Nation of Islam, Jack Olsen noted the contradiction between the acceptance by Black Muslims of Muhammad Ali and 'their bestowal upon him of the supraholy name, Muhammad Ali', and the Nation's anti-sport philosophy. He wondered how a religion that had regarded sport as a 'filthy temptation' could 'manage to embrace the world's best-known athletic figure'.[61] He asked Ali, whom he referred to as Clay throughout the series, about the discrepancy. Ali's response was that he had already been 'an established pro before he became a member. Boxing was "the onliest way" he had making his "livelihood"'.[62] He also suggested that 'some of our leaders mentioned that it would be bad for the public to say that my religion caused me to be financially hurt and stopped from boxing'.[63] Others saw the Nation's embrace of Ali as financially motivated, noting that when the movement was forced to 'choose between accounts receivable and the Scriptures, they vote for accounts receivable every time'.[64] One of Ali's relatives called the Black Muslim religion 'the most bendable religion in the world' and mused that the religious group had 'thought sports was a mortal sin till Cassius came along. Now they're all running around in jockstraps.'[65] He even expressed surprise that they could hold Ali in such high regard as a Muslim when the athlete clearly broke many of the religion's tenets, such as eating more than once a day, using foul language and earning a living from sport. The value of Ali to the group was clear: 'They're getting a lot of mileage out of him now, but they'll drop him like a hot potato when he's outlived his usefulness to them.'[66]

After Ali's first defence of his title against Sonny Liston ended in the first round, *Muhammad Speaks* addressed the contradiction between philosophy and reality and provided a justification of how Ali could be a Muslim as well as a professional boxer:

> It is a well-known fact that the Honorable Elijah Muhammad does not advocate the pursuit of professional sports for our people – particularly boxing, because it is an especially unnecessary display of brutality and savagery, usually pitting one black person against the other for the entertainment of white audiences.[67]

Still, the newspaper admitted that Elijah Muhammad was 'solidly behind those of our people who are forced through circumstances or necessity to engage in such activities for their livelihood'.[68]

On other occasions, the opposition to sport was patently obvious. After Ali defeated George Chuvalo in 1966, the newspaper printed an article that publicly rebuked Ali's efforts in the ring. Complaining that Chuvalo had fought below the belt and that this illegal behaviour was permitted by the referee, the article urged Muslims to view Ali's reactions as a result of 'his dependence upon his own "natural ability" to overcome a hate-filled and vicious opponent – instead of upon his previous open acknowledgement and dependence upon Allah and His messenger'.[69] Ali responded to Chuvalo's infraction of the rules with a flurry of violent punches, appropriate behaviour in the ring, but deemed both inappropriate and excessive by Elijah Muhammad and *Muhammad Speaks*. They felt that Ali was 'guilty of allowing his opponent to test him for the sport of it; absorbing needless blows to the body simply to "show off" his pugilistic prowess'.[70] They were adamantly opposed to what they interpreted as Ali's lack of faith and stated in unmistakable terms: 'We cannot back one who will not acknowledge the Divine Guidance of Allah and His messenger from which all strength derives which has made such success possible.'[71] Next to this article, Ali himself apologised for his failure to put Allah and the Messenger ahead of all else.[72]

Despite their admonition of sport, the newspaper utilised Ali as a popular figure in American society and as a victim of racial and religious persecution to advertise the religion, to sell more newspapers and to help increase the awareness of the Nation of Islam. In an issue that detailed Ali's return to the USA and his first appearance at a Harlem rally held for Elijah Muhammad, a picture of Ali and Muhammad appeared, with a headline that read: 'How Harlem Hailed the Messenger of Allah'. There is no mention of Ali in the article, and from the picture one might wonder which messenger was being hailed, but the article clarifies any confusion and reaffirms that the day was about Elijah Muhammad.[73] Indeed, it was a common practice to place Ali's picture strategically by articles, regardless of whether they mentioned him or not.

Other promotional items appeared in the newspaper. There was a half page advertisement for an exhibition bout between Ali and Cody Jones, with tickets ranging from a donation price of $1.50 for bleacher seats to $10. Tickets were sold at four locations, conveniently all businesses owned and operated by members of the Nation of Islam, such as Temple No. 2 Cleaners and Shabazz Restaurant.[74] There were package trips to Ali's fights, which included transportation, tickets and dinner. One issue offered a challenge to all readers: whoever sold the most newspaper subscriptions during the month-long contest would earn a free trip to Ali's bout with Floyd Patterson in Las Vegas.[75] In March 1965, a new column appeared for the first time; it would run for the next four years. 'From the Camp of the Champ' detailed the routines and daily activities of the boxer, from personal details about his life, training routines, speaking engagements and philosophies. The newspaper promised readers 'the exclusive news of the world's champion's plans and programs for 1966'.[76] Fan letters and poems soon appeared, establishing another regular feature, 'Poetry Corner', which published poetry written both by Ali's fans and by the fighter himself. Ali's poetry fell into two categories: poems about his fights and poems about his religion.[77] His devotion to his faith, Allah and Elijah Muhammad were clear and remained so for the five years the fighter dominated the pages of *Muhammad Speaks*.

The beginning of the end

Wiggins has analysed the rift that developed between Muhammad Ali and Elijah Muhammad which surfaced in the pages of *Muhammad Speaks*.[78] After Ali indicated to Howard Cosell on ABC Sports that he would return to the ring because he needed to make money, Elijah Muhammad suspended the Champion from the movement and removed his holy name, Muhammad Ali. Muhammad explained that by making such statements, Ali had 'stepped down off the spiritual platform of Islam to go and see if he can make money in the sport world'.[79] Ali's words indicated to the Messenger that the fighter had placed 'his hopes and trust in the enemy of Allah (God) for survival', and also had revealed his love for 'sport and play', which the Holy Qu'ran and the Nation of Islam clearly opposed, and which Muhammad had already warned him about following his victory over George Chuvalo.[80] Ali's indiscretion offered Elijah Muhammad an opportunity to educate his followers on the evils of sport by suggesting that Ali's dependence on white America revealed a lack of faith in Allah. In the Nation's eyes, Ali was to be a Muslim first and a fighter second, but his statement disclosed, at least to Elijah Muhammad, that in fact Ali was and always would be a fighter first and foremost. He accused the Champion of wasting his money and was supported in this claim by two of Ali's business managers, Herbert Muhammad and John Ali. The irony of these accusations was perhaps lost on the Nation of Islam leadership. Whilst Ali assisted the movement in selling both their newspaper and their religion, the Nation of Islam and Elijah Muhammad certainly profited, and at the same time, Ali had been acclaimed for his philanthropic activities, for the donations and services he provided his community. Yet his claim to need the money from his professional career angered Muhammad, who reverted to his former position that espoused the evils of sport. His need for Ali no longer as great, nor as effective, Ali was dismissed as both a fighter and as a Muslim. After Ali's suspension from the Nation of Islam, the newspaper's coverage of sports returned to the patterns of earlier issues, with a brief article in each issue, located towards the back of the paper, which rarely contained anything of substance. Ultimately what led to the dismissal of Ali from the Nation of Islam at the dawn of a new decade was the issue of power: the power of a young, charismatic, popular Black athlete versus the power of an aging leader of a politically charged religious organisation.

Conclusion

Gardell states that 'Besides Malcolm X, none of Elijah Muhammad's disciples gave the nation more visibility than Muhammad Ali.'[81] Jeremiah Shabazz shares this sentiment and comments on the far-reaching power of Muhammad Ali as a member of the Nation of Islam:

> When Elijah Muhammad spoke, his words were confined to whatever city he had spoken in. But Ali was a sports hero, and people wanted to know what he had to say, so his visibility and prominence were of great benefit to the Nation. His voice carried throughout the world, and that was a true blessing for us. There's no doubt, our following increased enormously, maybe a hundred percent, after he joined the Nation.[82]

Muhammad Ali was instrumental in championing the growth of the Nation of Islam and 'had it not been for the Messenger's ability to raise dedicated champions for the cause, the Nation would probably have remained an obscure organization at the margins of the black community'.[83] Instead, Muhammad Ali became an international figure not only as a result of his skills in the boxing ring, but also, and almost as much, for his membership in an organisation that proudly touted him as one of their own on the international stage.

Despite the opposition of Elijah Muhammad to sport and play, and his public rebuking of sport in official publications of the Nation of Islam's weekly newspaper, the leader and his organisation embraced the Heavyweight Champion. Ali's membership and rise in popularity within the movement coincided neatly with the departure of Malcolm X from the Nation. Where Malcolm X challenged the power of Elijah Muhammad with his ideas and philosophy, Muhammad Ali was a suitable replacement whose popularity rested not on his intellectual acumen, but on his athletic prowess. Ironically, Ali's involvement in the world of professional sport was used by Muhammad both to enhance the Nation of Islam and as the justification for his expulsion from the movement. Yet the attention devoted to Ali, their most popular messenger, through the Nation's official organ, *Muhammad Speaks*, enhanced the appeal of the controversial religious movement and simultaneously promoted values contradictory to those of its leader, Elijah Muhammad. By analysing the publications of the Nation of Islam for both their philosophy of sport and their coverage of sport, clear contradictions and paradoxes emerge that illuminate the role that sport can play in the service of religion.

Notes

1   E. Muhammad, *Message to the Blackman in America*, Newport, United Brothers Communications Systems, 1992, p. 246; *Muhammad Speaks*, 15 October 1962, p. 9.

2   *Muhammad Speaks*, October 1961, p. 1. Circulation figures were published for a seven-month period on the front page of the newspaper. January 1962 – 150,000 circulation; February 1962 – 175,000 circulation; March 1962 – 200,000 circulation with 800,000 readers; April 1962 – 225,000 circulation with 900,000 readers; May 1962 – 300,000 circulation with 1.2 million readers; June 1962 – 310,000 circulation with 1.25 million readers; July 1962 – 360,000 circulation with 1.4 million readers. For more on the newspaper, see M. Gardell, *In the Name of Elijah Muhammad: Louis Farrakhan and the Nation of Islam*, Durham, Duke University Press, 1996, p. 64. Gardell states that the newspaper offered 'high-quality coverage of news relevant to the African-American community, both domestic and international'. *Muhammad Speaks* became the 'most widely read paper in black America' with a circulation of over 600,000 a week. Gardell cites John Woodford who claims the circulation was actually 650,000 when Woodford was editor-in-chief. An even higher circulation figure of 850,000 a week was claimed in the mid-1970s (A. Rassoull, 'National Secretary cites accomplishments', *Muhammad Speaks*, 23 August 1974, cited in M. Gardell, *In the Name of Elijah Muhammad: Louis Farrakhan and the Nation of Islam*, Durham, Duke University Press, 1996, p. 360). Gardell concludes that *Muhammad Speaks* was 'simply one of the best contemporary black weeklies in the United States' , p. 64.

3   C.E. Marsh, *From Black Muslims to Muslims: The Transition from Separatism to Islam, 1930–1980*, Metuchen, Scarecrow Press, 1984, p. 51. For more on the history and philosophy of the Nation of Islam, see L.A. Caro, *Malcolm and the Cross: The Nation of Islam, Malcolm X, and Christianity*, New York, New York University Press, 1998; J. George, *Nazis, Communists, Klansmen, and Others on the Fringe: Political Extremism in America*, Buffalo, Prometheus Books, 1992; M.F. Lee, *A Nation of Islam, An American Millenarian Movement*, Lewiston, Edwin Mellen Press, 1988; C.E. Lincoln, *The Black Muslims in America*, Grand Rapids, W.B. Eerdmans, 1994; C.E. Marsh, *From Black Muslims to Muslims: The Resurrection, Transformation, and Change of the Lost-Found Nation of Islam in America, 1930–1995*, Lanham, Scarecrow Press, 1996; A. Rashad, *Islam, Black Nationalism and Slavery: A Detailed History*, Beltsville, Writers' Inc. International, 1995.

4   C.E. Marsh, *From Black Muslims to Muslims: The Transition from Separatism to Islam, 1930–1980*, Metuchen, Scarecrow Press, 1984, p. 57.

5   M. Gardell, *In the Name of Elijah Muhammad: Louis Farrakhan and the Nation of Islam*, Durham, Duke University Press, 1996, p. 52.

6   Ibid., p. 50.

7   Ibid., p. 50.

8   C.E. Marsh, *From Black Muslims to Muslims: The Transition from Separatism to Islam, 1930–1980*, Metuchen, Scarecrow Press, 1984, p. 58.

9   For other publications by Elijah Muhammad that detail the ideology of the Nation of Islam, see *The Supreme Wisdom: Solution to the So-Called NEGROES' Problems*, Newport, National Newport News and Commentator, 1957; *The Supreme Wisdom, Volume Two*,

Newport, United Brothers Communications Systems, n.d.; *Message to the Blackman in America*, Philadephia, Hakim's Publication, 1965; *How to Eat to Live*, Chicago, Muhammad's Temple of Islam No. 2, 1967; *How to Eat to Live, Part Two*, Chicago, Muhammad's Temple of Islam No. 2, 1972; *The Fall of America*, Chicago, Muhammad's Temple of Islam No. 2, 1973; *Our Saviour Has Arrived*, Chicago, Muhammad's Temple of Islam No. 2, 1974; *The Flag of Islam*, Chicago, n.p., 1974.

10 One practice of the Nation of Islam was the bestowing of a new name on the member. The shedding of the old name and subsequent adoption of the new name was symbolic of a 'mental emancipation' from their slavename.

11 See for example, S. Riess, *City Games. The Evolution of American Urban Society and the Rise of Sports*, Urbana, University of Illinois Press, 1989.

12 *Muhammad Speaks*, 4 February 1962, p. 22.

13 *Muhammad Speaks*, 18 February 1962, p. 22.

14 'Why no Negroes in pro ball?', *Muhammad Speaks*, 31 January 1962, p. 22; 'Why no Negroes in pro ball?: Pro owners to blame, says former great Duke Slater', *Muhammad Speaks*, 4 February 1962, p. 22; 'Why no Negroes in pro ball?: "Unwritten code," says Ex-Bear Bobby Watkins', *Muhammad Speaks*, 4 March 1962, p. 23. The newspaper published articles that looked at relevant issues in the sports world on average three times per year. For other articles that were published during this time, see 'Experts say: African athletes may soon dominate world of sports', *Muhammad Speaks*, 24 September 1965, p. 20; 'Karate: why the business of self defense is booming among Negroes', *Muhammad Speaks*, 18 February 1966, pp. 16–17; 'Doctors claim benefits to youngsters outweigh dangers in contact sports', *Muhammad Speaks*, 17 June 1966, p. 18; 'Hints for health: baseball, as an exercise, is great unless overdone', *Muhammad Speaks*, 17 June 1966, p. 17; 'The desperate search for "white hopes" – black pearls in the athletic world', *Muhammad Speaks*, 5 January 1968, pp. 17, 22; 'Survey reveals conspiracy: to block black quarterback spot in professional football', *Muhammad Speaks*, 10 May 1968, p. 29; B. Sharrieff, 'Sport and play is not glorified in the Sudan', *Muhammad Speaks*, 5 July 1968, p. 26; 'Race dominant in athletics – but why?', *Muhammad Speaks*, 7 February 1969, p. 13.

15 *Muhammad Speaks*, 13 May 1962, p. 22.

16 Elijah Muhammad refers to Muhammad Ali on four pages throughout his book. He discusses the name that was bestowed upon Muhammad Ali after he converted to Islam. Noting that no Black man could get international respect if they still used a 'slavename', Muhammad uses Ali as an example: 'The example was evident when I took Muhammad Ali (the World's Heavyweight Champion) out of the white man's name (the name itself made him a servant and slave to the white man). All Africa and Asia then acclaimed him as also being their champion. This shows you that all previous black men of America who were bestowed with the title of the world's heavyweight champion were only exalting the white man of America, Europe and Australia'. E. Muhammad, *Message to the Blackman in America*, Philadephia, Hakim's Publication, 1965, p. 43. Muhammad was a strong believer that when a Black man changed his name, it was an empowering act, but one that frustrated and troubled white America because of their clear lack of control over the Black man: 'Watch how anxious the white man is to hold you and call you by his name. He still would like to call the champion, Cassius Clay, after himself, and he would like to call me Poole, after himself. This is to keep the blind, blind; the deaf, deaf and the dumb, dumb to the knowledge that even the name alone is sufficient to free you of this evil people'. E. Muhammad, *Message to the Blackman in America*, Philadephia, Hakim's Publication, 1965, p. 48. He makes use of Ali's name on two other occasions in the book, pages 47 and 73. Ironically, in his essay about sport, Muhammad makes no mention of the boxer's name nor participation in the very culture he is criticising.

17 *Muhammad Speaks*, 15 October 1962, p. 9. These same words were published later in E. Muhammad, *Message to the Blackman in America*, Philadephia, Hakim's Publication, 1965, pp. 246–7.

18 *Muhammad Speaks*, 15 October 1962, p. 9.

19 Ibid.

20 Ibid.

21 Malcolm X with Alex Haley, *The Autobiography of Malcolm X*, New York, Grove Press, 1964, p. 303.

22 C.E. Marsh, *From Black Muslims to Muslims: The Transition from Separatism to Islam, 1930–1980*, Metuchen, Scarecrow Press, 1984, p. 62. Malcolm X, as the Nation's spokesman, was able to generate a great deal of increased attention for the Nation of Islam, including media attention. He was interviewed in a television documentary, 'The Hate That Hate Produced', which aired nationwide in a five-part series in June and July 1959. Soon after airing, articles about Malcolm X and the Nation of Islam were written in mainstream American publications. See A. Balk and A. Haley, 'Black merchant of hate', *Saturday Evening Post*, 26 January 1963, pp. 68–75; 'Black supremacists', *Time*, 10 August 1959, pp. 24–5; 'Black supremacy cult in U.S., how much of a threat?', *US News*, 9 November 1959, pp. 112–14; C.L. Cooper Jr, 'Aftermath: the angriest Negroes revisited', *Esquire*, June 1961, pp. 164–6; A. Haley, 'Mr. Muhammad speaks', *Reader's Digest*, March 1960, pp. 100–4; 'Muslim message: all white men devils, all Negroes divine', *Newsweek*, 27 August 1962, pp. 26–7; W. Worthy, 'Angriest Negroes: Muslims', *Esquire*, February 1961, pp. 102–5.

23 Malcolm X with Alex Haley, *The Autobiography of Malcolm X*, New York, Grove Press, 1964, p. 306.

24 Ibid.

25 Ibid.

26 Ibid.

27 Ibid., pp. 306–7. Also see D.K. Wiggins, 'Victory for Allah: Muhammad Ali, the Nation of Islam, and American society', in E.J. Gorn (ed.), *Muhammad Ali: The People's Champ*, Urbana, University of Illinois Press, 1995, pp. 88–116. Wiggins recounts the snub of the Clay–Liston fight by *Muhammad Speaks* and indicates that their non-attendance was evidence that they believed Clay had little hope of beating Liston.

28 'Cassius sends greetings to Savior's Day', *Muhammad Speaks*, 13 March 1964, p. 2.

29 C.E. Marsh, *From Black Muslims to Muslims: The Transition from Separatism to Islam, 1930–1980*, Metuchen, Scarecrow Press, 1984, p. 80.

30 'Walk the way of free men!', *Muhammad Speaks*, 10 April 1964, p. 1.

31 *Muhammad Speaks*, 24 April 1964, pp. 1–2.

32 D.K. Wiggins, 'Victory for Allah: Muhammad Ali, the Nation of Islam, and American society', in E.J. Gorn (ed.), *Muhammad Ali: The People's Champ*, Urbana, University of Illinois Press, 1995, p. 89.

33 Ibid., p. 94.

34 Ibid., p. 94.

35 Ibid., p. 95.

36 *Muhammad Speaks*, 19 March 1965, p. 23.

37 'Muslim champ spends day at Chicago school, molds concept of "black heroes"', *Muhammad Speaks*, 18 February 1966, pp. 9, 12. For other articles that detail his service to his community, see 'How days of a boy on borrowed time were extended by heavyweight champ', *Muhammad Speaks*, 22 April 1966, p. 9; 'Champ fights to save children from blighted lives – takes time out to work with children of the poor', *Muhammad Speaks*, 15 July 1966, p. 7; 'Champ Ali urges Blackstone Rangers to practice Messenger's "black unity"', *Muhammad Speaks*, 2 September 1966, p. 8; 'Champ offers closed TV of fight to 6 colleges', *Muhammad Speaks*, 28 October 1966, p. 9; 'Spiritual example displayed by champion overshadows strength, physical prowess', *Muhammad Speaks*, 25 November 1966; 'Muhammad Ali becomes single biggest black contributor to UNCF charities', *Muhammad Speaks*, 3 March 1967, p. 20; 'Bout proceeds to go to starving: World Champion offers to fight for Mississippi children', *Muhammad Speaks*, 21 July 1967, p. 7; 'Muhammad Ali chosen to head black Watts Summer Festival in California', 8 August 1967, p. 4.

38 C.E. Marsh, *From Black Muslims to Muslims: The Transition from Separatism to Islam, 1930–1980*, Metuchen, Scarecrow Press, 1984, p. 76.
39 Ali's International Fan Club is advertised for the first time in *Muhammad Speaks*, 23 April 1965, p. 4. For articles that emphasise the Nation of Islam's claim that Ali was the true world champion, see 'Thunderous welcome: the Champ in Cairo', *Muhammad Speaks*, 3 June 1966, pp. 3–6; 'Champ reports: visit to Egypt', *Muhammad Speaks*, 10 June 1966, p. 5; 'Described the Messenger and America – the Champ's report, Middle East News', *Muhammad Speaks*, 17 June 1966, p. 7; 'The first true "World Champion", – Champ would like title fight in every nation', *Muhammad Speaks*, 22 July 1966, p. 9; J.H. Jackson, 'In Chicago or China, he's the only World Champion – impact of Muhammad Ali on world scene', *Muhammad Speaks*, 10 November 1967, pp. 9, 24; J.H. Jackson, 'Part II: world impact of Champ', *Muhammad Speaks*, 17 November 1967, pp. 7–8.
40 For other articles that reported on Ali's trip to Africa, see 'Before leaving for Africa – a Champ's day in Boston', *Muhammad Speaks*, 22 May 1964, p. 8; C.P. Howard Sr, 'How Africa greets the Champ!', *Muhammad Speaks*, 5 June 1964, pp. 1, 3, 9; C.P. Howard Sr, 'Africa opens arms for return of "prodigal son"', *Muhammad Speaks*, 5 June 1964, pp. 2, 5; C.P. Howard Sr, 'On tour with Ali: Egypt thanks Messenger!', *Muhammad Speaks*, 3 July 1964, p. 4; 'A stronger, wiser Champion – world leaders asked Ali: "How is Mr. Muhammad?"', *Muhammad Speaks*, 17 July 1964, p. 2.
41 Articles written by Black leaders in support of Ali's refusal to enter the draft appeared in the weekly. These leaders included Floyd McKissick, of CORE (Congress of Racial Equality), Stokely Carmichael, of SNCC (Student Non-Violent Coordinating Committee), activist Dick Gregory, Congressman Adam Clayton Powell, Whitney Young (Director of the National Urban League), and A. Philip Randolph (American Federation of Labor – Congress of Industrial Organizations).
42 I.F. Stone's Weekly quoted in 'Famed publisher believes Champ's view reflected opinions of most Negroes', *Muhammad Speaks*, 8 April 1966, p. 5.
43 'Champion takes greatest struggle – freedom, justice, equality!', *Muhammad Speaks*, 28 April 1967, p. 9.
44 'World wide protest rips Champ's unjust draft call', *Muhammad Speaks*, 7 April 1967, p. 9.
45 For articles about Bill Russell, see *Muhammad Speaks*, 14 August 1964, p. 21; 'Book reviews: Bill Russell's autobiog tells his views on life', *Muhammad Speaks*, 15 April 1966, p. 17; 'Russell's rise reflects awesome quality, quantity of black athletes', *Muhammad Speaks*, 29 April 1966, p. 26. For articles about Jim Brown, see *Muhammad Speaks*, 9 October 1964, pp. 4, 22; B.O. Fain, 'Believes what Brown said was true', *Muhammad Speaks*, 8 November 1964, p. 8; 'Portrait of the athlete who says: to hell with integration, just don't segregate me', *Muhammad Speaks*, 26 November 1965, pp. 23, 26; 'Brown of Cleveland: portrait of the pride, power of the black athlete', *Muhammad Speaks*, 3 December 1965, p. 24; *Muhammad Speaks*, 4 February 1966, p. 9. Brief articles also appeared about John Mackey, Curt Flood and Pele: 'Black athlete making way in business', *Muhammad Speaks*, 26 March 1965, p. 22; *Muhammad Speaks*, 23 August 1966, p. 22; 'Black athletes alter Brazil: why they prefer Pele to the Pope', *Muhammad Speaks*, 15 April 1966, pp. 24, 27; T. Bey, 'World's greatest soccer player greets Muslim Champ', *Muhammad Speaks*, 23 September 1966, p. 22.
46 *Muhammad Speaks*, 2 April 1965, p. 6.
47 'Champ goes into training for title fight with Floyd Nov. 22 in Las Vegas', *Muhammad Speaks*, 1 October 1965, p. 9. For another article about the agreement between the two fighters, see 'Muhammad promises Floyd free copy of Messenger's book after the fight', *Muhammad Speaks*, 29 October 1965, p. 9. It is not clear in the weekly if Patterson upheld his end of the wager, to spend the day with Ali, after his loss. Ali offered a similar invitation to Joe Frazier, see 'Joe Frazier welcome to attend any Muslim mosque of Islam: Muhammad Ali', *Muhammad Speaks*, 15 March 1968, p. 31.
48 For one article that addresses the meeting of Ali and other black athletes, see 'Black athletes backed the champ!', *Muhammad Speaks*, 16 June 1967, p. 7.

49 Harry Edwards, *The Revolt of the Black Athlete*, New York, Free Press, 1970, p. 58.

50 For articles leading up to the 1968 Olympic Games that addressed the issue of protest, see 'Jackie Robinson speaks out for Olympic boycott', *Muhammad Speaks*, 15 December 1967, p. 10; '38 Nations may boycott Olympics: Alcindor heads black absentees in U.S.', *Muhammad Speaks*, 8 March 1968, p. 17; S. Bossette, 'Part II: The black athlete becomes a giant', *Muhammad Speaks*, 5 April 1968, pp. 11, 26, 30; 'Sprinters say they were robbed of races due to positions in boycott', *Muhammad Speaks*, 21 June 1968, p. 26; 'Why athletes keep secret boycott plans', *Muhammad Speaks*, 2 August 1968, p. 27; 'Why black athletes should fight for black humanity', *Muhammad Speaks*, 8 August 1968, pp. 7, 8, 31. For articles written after the Olympics, see 'A salute to Tommie Smith, John Carlos & Co.', 1 November 1968, p. 13; L. Kashif, 'Return of the black Olympic heroes', *Muhammad Speaks*, 8 November 1968, pp. 13, 14, 28; 'Organization of Afro-Asians salute stand taken by black athletes', *Muhammad Speaks*, 22 November 1968, p. 35; 'L.A. Councilman says Smith and Carlos saved Olympics', *Muhammad Speaks*, 13 December 1968, p. 36; 'Smith, Carlos tell youth to take up golf, swimming', *Muhammad Speaks*, 13 December 1968, p. 36; 'Black firm memorializes heroes Smith, Carlos', *Muhammad Speaks*, 10 January 1969, p. 13; 'Trenton Mayor's assistant rips Olympic ouster of Tommy Smith and John Carlos', *Muhammad Speaks*, 10 January 1969, p. 18.

51 For articles about Arthur Ashe, see 'World tennis champion Arthur Ashe declares his militancy, determination to struggle for his people', *Muhammad Speaks*, 27 September 1968, p. 16; 'Arthur Ashe may shun pro ranks for work with blacks', 3 January 1969, p. 34; 'Ashe hopes to unite black athletes in new grouping', *Muhammad Speaks*, 28 February 1969, p. 35. For other articles that appeared in *Muhammad Speaks* that addressed Black athletes and their increased discontent with white sport, see 'Why superstar Robinson sees baseball as "dead end" for black players', *Muhammad Speaks*, 29 March 1968, p. 30; 'Did Jackie Robinson's new stand make him "enemy" of old line whites?', *Muhammad Speaks*, 10 January 1969, p. 28; D. Casimere, 'The black art of Earl the Pearl', *Muhammad Speaks*, 14 February 1969, p. 35; A. Duckett, 'Robinson adds Rustin to roster of "toms"', *Muhammad Speaks*, 16 May 1969, p. 30; J. Woodford, 'The money conspiracy against the black athlete', *Muhammad Speaks*, 6 June 1969, p. 35; D. Casimere, 'Harry Edwards: revolt of the black athletes', *Muhammad Speaks*, 5 September 1969, pp. 33–4; D. Casimere, 'Harry Edwards: black student revolt, part II', *Muhammad Speaks*, 12 September 1969, pp. 27, 30; 'White sportswriter relays racist plan to limit number of black athletes in colleges', *Muhammad Speaks*, 5 January 1969, p. 24; 'Black college athlete official hits NCAA drive to silence young athletes', *Muhammad Speaks*, 31 January 1969, p. 32.

52 See Jack Olsen's *Sports Illustrated* series on the Black athlete. 'The black athlete – a shameful story', 1 July 1968, pp. 15–27; 'Pride and prejudice', 8 July 1968, pp. 18–31; 'In an alien world', 15 July 1968, pp. 28–43; 'In the back of the bus', 22 July 1968, pp. 28–41; 'The anguish of a team divided', 29 July 1968, pp. 20–35.

53 'Joe Louis joins heavyweight boxing champion: happy I'm in his corner, says Joe', *Muhammad Speaks*, 21 January 1966, p. 9.

54 Ibid., p. 9. For other articles that mention Main Bout, Inc. see 'Muhammad set to sign for 3rd defense of crown', *Muhammad Speaks*, 4 February 1966, p. 9; 'World tour on agenda of Champ Muhammad', *Muhammad Speaks*, 11 February 1966, p. 9; 'Muhammad, Main Bout, Inc., moving on to victory', *Muhammad Speaks*, 18 February 1966, p. 9.

55 'Champ seeking new world to conquer after Folley', *Muhammad Speaks*, 31 March 1967, p. 9.

56 'Muhammad's 5 title fights closes most spectacular year in ring history', *Muhammad Speaks*, 30 December 1966, p. 7. This article is one example of the power Herbert Muhammad was given with Ali's career, saying that the fighter's affairs would be 'under the scrutiny of Herbert Muhammad'.

57 'Champ geared for crucial Astrodome test with deadly-puncher Williams', *Muhammad Speaks*, 11 November 1966, p. 8.

58 'Champion and new manager take time out to offer thanks to worldwide fans', *Muhammad Speaks*, 18 November 1966, p. 9. For more on Ali as a minister, see 'World champion moves step closer to fulltime task as Muhammad's Minister', *Muhammad Speaks*, 3 March 1967, p. 7; 'Muhammad–Terrell fight set world record', *Muhammad Speaks*, 16 December 1966, p. 7: 'It is the task I am best suited for and it is as a minister that I look forward, in the near future, to assume my duties in comradeship with my brothers and sisters for the remainder of my life.'

59 'Critics pay homage to the Champ: Muhammad has praise for Chuvalo', *Muhammad Speaks*, 8 April 1966, pp. 5–6.

60 C.P. Howard Sr, 'On tour with Ali: Egypt thanks Messenger!', *Muhammad Speaks*, 3 July 1964, p. 4.

61 J. Olsen, 'Part 4: a case of conscience: learning Elijah's lesson in hate', *Sports Illustrated*, 2 May 1966, p. 52. To read the complete five-part 1966 *Sports Illustrated* series, see: 'A case of conscience', 11 April 1966, pp. 36–8, 43–4, 46, 51–3; 'Part 2: a case of conscience: growing up scared in Louisville', 18 April 1966, pp. 95–103; 'Part 3: a case of conscience: hysteria is a sometimes thing', 25 April 1966, pp. 48–50, 53–4, 56, 61–2, 64, 67; 'Part 5: a case of conscience: all alone with the future', 9 May 1966, pp. 36, 39–40, 42, 45–46, 48, 53.

62 J. Olsen, 'Part 4: a case of conscience: learning Elijah's lesson in hate', *Sports Illustrated*, 2 May 1966, p. 52.

63 Ibid.

64 Ibid.

65 Ibid., pp. 52–3.

66 Ibid., p. 52.

67 'The world salutes a real champ, Muhammad Ali', *Muhammad Speaks*, 4 June 1965, p. 8.

68 Ibid., p. 8.

69 'Muslim view: Muhammad-Chuvalo fight', *Muhammad Speaks*, 15 April 1966, p. 5.

70 Ibid.

71 Ibid.

72 M. Ali, 'Muhammad Ali: Allah and His Messenger the true source of my strength, power', *Muhammad Speaks*, 15 April 1966, p. 5.

73 'How Harlem hailed the Messenger of Allah', *Muhammad Speaks*, 17 July 1964, p. 3.

74 *Muhammad Speaks*, 26 February 1965, p. 4.

75 *Muhammad Speaks*, 27 October 1965, p. 9.

76 'Muhammad Ali's triumphs in '65 Great, but 1966 portends even greater', *Muhammad Speaks*, 7 January 1966, p. 9.

77 'From the camp of the Champ', *Muhammad Speaks*, 25 March 1965, p. 9. The newspaper covers Ali's fights during the 1960s, including Ali and his opponents: Ali vs. Sonny Liston (25 February 1964 and 25 May 1965); Ali vs. Floyd Patterson (22 November 1965); Ali vs. George Chuvalo (29 March 1966); Ali vs. Henry Cooper (21 May 1966); Ali vs. Brian London (6 August 1966); Ali vs. Karl Mildenberger (10 September 1966); Ali vs. Cleveland Williams (14 November 1966); Ali vs. Ernie Terrell (7 February 1967); Ali vs. Zora Folley (22 March 1967).

78 D.K. Wiggins, 'Victory for Allah: Muhammad Ali, the Nation of Islam, and American society', in E.J. Gorn (ed.), *Muhammad Ali: The People's Champ*, Urbana, University of Illinois Press, 1995, pp. 102–3. See also E. Muhammad, 'We tell the world we're not with Muhammad Ali', *Muhammad Speaks*, 4 April 1969, p. 3; 'Clarification of actions taken by Messenger Muhammad against Muhammad Ali's actions', *Muhammad Speaks*, 11 April 1969, pp. 2–3; John Ali, *Muhammad Speaks*, 11 April 1969, p. 3; Herbert Muhammad, *Muhammad Speaks*, 11 April 1969, p. 3.

79 E. Muhammad, 'We tell the world we're not with Muhammad Ali', *Muhammad Speaks*, 4 April 1969, p. 3.

80 Ibid., p. 3; E. Muhammad, 'Clarification of actions taken by Messenger Muhammad', *Muhammad Speaks*, 11 April 1969, pp. 2–3; John Ali, *Muhammad Speaks*, 11 April 1969,

p. 3; Herbert Muhammad, *Muhammad Speaks*, 11 April 1969, p. 3. Also, see D.K. Wiggins, 'Victory for Allah: Muhammad Ali, the Nation of Islam, and American society', in E.J. Gorn (ed.), *Muhammad Ali: The People's Champ*, Urbana, University of Illinois Press, 1995, pp. 102–3.

81 M. Gardell, *In the Name of Elijah Muhammad: Louis Farrakhan and the Nation of Islam*, Durham, Duke University Press, 1996, p. 67.

82 Ibid., p. 68.

83 Ibid., p. 64

11 Epilogue

Tara Magdalinski and
Timothy J.L. Chandler

Whilst it remains popular to call sport a religion, we maintain that focussing on mere structural similarities provides little insight into the complexities of the relationship between the two. Rather, as the title of our book attests, we argue that by looking at sport in the service of another institution, we may learn how cultural practices communicate and reinforce a range of ideologies. In this collection, we have been particularly interested in exploring the mechanisms by which religious communities replicate themselves whilst undergoing cultural transformation. Each of the chapters has illuminated facets of this process, drawing on a range of religious, national and sporting contexts to provide an initial foray into the role of sport as a specific religious instrument.

Despite our interests in the role of sport as an ideological tool, throughout the process of compiling this volume we kept returning to the basic equation of sport *as a religion*. Indeed, a number of authors have made compelling arguments for sport to be regarded as something of a religion, with most focussing on the ways that sport, for many fans, is complicit in 'shaping their world and sustaining their ways of engaging it'.[1] Joyce Carol Oates suggests that: 'The decline of religion as a source of significant meaning in modern industrialized societies has been extravagantly compensated by the rise of popular culture in general, of which the billion-dollar sports mania is the most visible manifestation.'[2] By examining the changing relationship between religion and Western society in a post-industrial age, we might be able to find some way of regarding the functions of sport and religion as synchronous. In pre-industrial agrarian communities, where the distinction between work and leisure was less defined than in industrial societies, perhaps religion functioned as something of an escape from the drudgery of the 'real' world. Karl Marx argued convincingly that religion was an opiate for the masses, a means by which the daily toils and struggles could be subsumed under the promise of greatness and riches in the afterlife. It is common parlance to speak of sport in modern times in a similar way. Just like the Romans with their circuses, perhaps the modern sports arena provides an escape from the pressures and demands of daily existence. Sport can take spectators to a world where a different hierarchy reigns; fans speak of 'losing themselves' in the mass fervour expressed at a sporting event. We do not deny that sport can be regarded as a 'religious-like' experience, that spectators do feel true devotion to their teams and, yet, even the most die-hard fan does not pray to their favourite athletes as they would a god; it is more likely that they would pray to their god, on behalf of their team! So no matter which way we looked at it, we were reminded of our basic concern; to determine not whether sport is a civic,[3] folk[4] or popular religion,[5] but rather how one institution is incorporated into the evangelising mission of the other.

If we view the relationship in this way, then it is readily apparent that sport and religious engagement both represent shared cultural practices, ones that may even transcend and alter perceptions of 'real life'. Yet despite even the most ritualistic nature of fandom, sport still simply does not address the basic questions that religious communities try to answer. Indeed, in many ways, as Joan Chandler argues, sport cannot offer, nor does it even profess to offer, answers to some of life's most enduring questions: Who are we? Where are we going? Why are we here? Nowhere was this more clear that in the events of 11 September 2001.

In the aftermath of the terrorist attacks on the USA, all major league sport, and much college, semi-professional and high-school sport throughout the country, was cancelled. Despite Frank Deford's contention that sport provides a 'precious and comforting assembly',[6] and that sport might have offered Americans solace in the time of national grief, many administrators, athletes and fans were satisfied that the decision to abandon organised sport was appropriate. In a time of national tragedy: 'Sports didn't turn out to be the crutch the country needed.'[7]

Nearly four decades earlier, following the assassination of US President John F. Kennedy, all major league sports cancelled their matches between the time of the shooting and his funeral except for the National Football League, which continued with its schedule. In defending his position, NFL Commissioner Pete Rozelle commented at the time that: 'It has been traditional in sports for athletes to perform in times of great personal tragedy.'[8] According to James Mathisen, the American public 'responded positively' to Rozelle's decision, which was 'justified on the basis of sport's integrative presence during a time of intense national crisis and mourning'.[9] For Mathisen, this provides some evidence of sport's role as a folk religion in America. For this reason, many were convinced that sport should have remained in place following the 11 September attacks, even though Rozelle himself in later years revealed that his decision to continue football after Kennedy's assassination had been the single greatest regret of his life.

But in the aftermath of 11 September, despite claims that sport represents a kind of civil religion, organised sport could not comfort the millions traumatised by the attacks. As *Sports Illustrated*'s Richard Hoffer indicated, the cancellation of games after 11 September revealed just how 'inadequate our religion of sports was in this crisis'.[10] Perhaps the very rationality of sport undermined its potential to function as a 'religion', which necessarily requires revelation. Or indeed, perhaps the cancellation of games demonstrated a greater recognition that sport's inherent frivolity was simply inappropriate.

So, for us, sport is clearly not a religion, for when it comes to the crunch, it fulfils few of the functions of religion. Instead, we are satisfied that the approach we have taken with this collection provides a useful way of engaging with cultural institutions that seem at once equivalent and yet enormously incongruent. To this end, the contributions address the role of sport in the construction and preservation of a range of identities, for to simply argue that sport may stand in for organised religion negates the complex and diffuse ways in which sporting practices may be incorporated into larger processes of community maintenance. We contend that these relationships are far more valuable in terms of understanding the roles that sport can occupy. So again, we refer back to the title of the collection and suggest that it encapsulates one aspect of this highly fascinating relationship, and conclude that the significance of these cultural practices is revealed when regarding sport in the *service* of religion, rather than regarding sport *as* a religion in and of itself. As such, we hope that this volume will encourage others both to extend and challenge this 'doctrine'.

Notes

1 J.L. Price, 'An American apotheosis: sport as popular religion', in B.D. Forbes and J.H. Mahan (eds), *Religion and Popular Culture in America*, Berkeley, University of California Press, 2000, p. 202.
2 Cited in ibid.
3 M. Novak, *The Joy of Sports. End Zones, Bases, Baskets, Balls, and the Consecration of the American Spirit*, New York, Basic Books, 1976.
4 J.A. Mathisen, 'From civil religion to folk religion: the case of American sport', in S.J. Hoffman (ed.), *Sport and Religion*, Champaign, Human Kinetics, 1992, pp. 17–33.
5 J.L. Price, 'An American apotheosis: sport as popular religion', in B.D. Forbes and J.H. Mahan (eds), *Religion and Popular Culture in America*, Berkeley, University of California Press, 2000, pp. 201–18.
6 F. Deford, 'Delay of games', *Sports Illustrated*, vol. 95, no. 12, 24 September 2001, p. 63.
7 R. Hoffer, 'Play suspended', *Sports Illustrated*, vol. 95, no. 12, 24 September 2001, p. 30.
8 J.A. Mathisen, 'From civil religion to folk religion: the case of American sport', in S.J. Hoffman (ed.), *Sport and Religion*, Champaign, Human Kinetics, 1992, p. 26.
9 Ibid.
10 R. Hoffer, 'Play suspended', *Sports Illustrated*, vol. 95, no. 12, 24 September 2001, p. 30.

Index